该专著的出版得到了中南大学外国语学院省级重点学科外国语言文学的经费资助，特此鸣谢

流动中的跨境学术移民

跨文化工作场域中的中英学者们

Transnational Academic Mobility

The Experiences of Chinese and British Migrants in Transnational Academic Field

刘田丰◎著

知识产权出版社
全国百佳图书出版单位

图书在版编目（CIP）数据

流动中的跨境学术移民：跨文化工作场域中的中英学者们 = Transnational Academic Mobility: The Experiences of Chinese and British Migrants in Transnational Academic Field：英文/刘田丰著. —北京：知识产权出版社，2017. 11

ISBN 978-7-5130-4929-0

Ⅰ.①流… Ⅱ.①刘… Ⅲ.①文化交流—研究—中国、英国 Ⅳ.①G125

中国版本图书馆 CIP 数据核字（2017）第 109045 号

内容提要

本书主要研究的是在跨国教育的全球化背景下，在中英联合办学的高等教育机构里工作的中英跨国学术移民，以及此类高端移民在异国的日常工作和生活，从而挖掘出这种流动性的移民过程在空间和时间上的社会学意义。本书既描述了宏观关注国际高等教育联合办学的前沿动向，又结合实际阐释了跨国高端移民的日常跨文化交际行为。本书既可为政府工作报告提供调研资料，又可作为跨国高等学术机构的参考文献，同时也可供国际学生、旅居学者或跨文化工作者进行未来职业规划对参考。

责任编辑：许　波　徐家春　　　　**责任出版**：孙婷婷

流动中的跨境学术移民：跨文化工作场域中的中英学者们

LIUDONGZHONG DE KUAJING XUESHU YIMIN：KUAWENHUA GONGZUO CHANGYUZHONG DE ZHONGYING XUEZHEMEN

刘田丰　著

出版发行：	知识产权出版社有限责任公司	网　　址：	http://www.ipph.cn
电　　话：	010-82004826		http://www.laichushu.com
社　　址：	北京市海淀区气象路50号院	邮　　编：	100081
责编电话：	010-82000860 转 8380	责编邮箱：	xbsun@163.com
发行电话：	010-82000860 转 8101	发行传真：	010-82000893/82005070
印　　刷：	虎彩印艺股份有限公司	经　　销：	各大网上书店、新华书店及相关专业书店
开　　本：	720mm×1000mm　1/16	印　　张：	20.5
版　　次：	2017年11月第1版	印　　次：	2017年11月第1次印刷
字　　数：	360千字	定　　价：	66.00元

ISBN 978-7-5130-4929-0

Preface

In the context of transnational higher education, this study examines Chinese and British academic migrants' everyday work-life practices in a Sino-UK university joint venture. The study breaks new ground by teasing out the difficulties, problems, misunderstandings, contradictions, and tensions that occur in an unfamiliar transnational academic field for academic migrants. Correspondingly, it also looks at the career opportunities and international social and academic connections that gradually cultivated in the transnational working environment. The study offers a deeper understanding of transnational academic space by providing empirical insights into transnational academics' moving strategies, their pedagogic creativeness, and how their sense of belonging is intertwined with different places on the 'host' university campus.

The study adopted a variety of qualitative methodological tools (semi-structured interviews, photo interviews and participant observation) to explore the everyday texture of academic migrants' working practices in transnational workplace. The findings suggest the 'unexpected' barriers in the 'new' transitional academic workplace have significance for academic migrants' further professional improvement and transnational mobility. It also reveals how academic migrants are not just passively adapting or integrating into the 'new' transnational professional structure, but also positively challenging and changing its boundaries.

The research sheds light on scholarly debates on transnational academic mobility and the internationalisation of higher education in the Sino-British context. It goes beyond the national boundaries of higher education and places the investigation in a broader frame of social, cultural and spatial analysis in order to generate a deeper understanding of academic migrants' everyday practices. It argues for a transnational and enduring understanding of academic migrants' experience and points out that those experiences are nationally unbounded, yet locally specific. It also takes a step forward in academic mobility studies, by using grounded evidence gathered in transnational academic space to challenge the mono-academic cultural stereotypes bounded within national borders.

Here, I wish to acknowledge the encouragement, help and support from my faculty, supervisor, colleagues, friends and family during the completion of this dissertation and my doctoral studies in this four memorable years in London. Firstly, I would like to give my sincere thanks to Professor Katie Willis and Dr. Katherine Brickell for their expertise, guidance and support for my research through out the challenging Ph. D process. I would like to also give my thanks to the Department of Geography at the Royal Holloway University of London. This is very good Geography Department, not only because it is ranked 2nd in the UK and 1st in England for world-class research, but also because there are many wonderful people I have met during my time here. I would also like to say a special thanks to Rupert Griffiths and Weiqiang Lin, who are my closest friends and colleagues, for their warmth, friendship and academic support in the past few years. Finally, a special thank goes to my parents, they are the best in the world. I am dedicating this work to both of them.

Glossary and List of Acronyms

APR-Annual Performance Review

BRIC-Brazil Russia India China

CAS-Chinese Academy of Science

C-BERT-Cross-Border Education Research Team

CEC-The Co-ordinating European Council

CPC-Communist Party of China

GBP-Great British Pound

GDP-Gross Domestic Product

HEI-Higher Education Institute

HESA-Higher Education Statistics Agency

HSMP-Highly Skilled Migrant Programme

IBC-International Branch Campus

IELTS-International English Language Testing System

MIDA- Migrations pour le Dévelopment en Afrique

MNE-Multinational Enterprise

MOE-Ministry of Education

OECD-Organisation for Economic Co-operation and Development

PGCHE-Postgraduate Certificate in Higher Education

PSW-Post Study Work

QAA-Quality Assurance Agency for Higher Education

QTS-Qualified Teacher Status

REF-Research Excellence Framework

RMB-Chinese Yuan

THE-Times Higher Education

TNE-Transnational Education

TOKTEN-Transfer of Knowledge Through Expatriate Nationals

UNDP-United Nations Development Programme

Contents

Chapter One
Transnational Academic Mobility: Chinese and British Academics in Transnational Academic Space

The origins of this thesis are my childhood experiences of academic life in China and my subsequent experiences of academic life and cultures in France and England. I grew up on the university campus of Xiangtan, Hunan province, China where both of my parents were university lecturers. In China, unlike the UK, it is normal for staff and their families to live and work on the campus, and indeed the campuses are more like towns in their own right, with all amenities readily available. The first twenty-one years of my life were spent in this environment, both as a resident and later also as an undergraduate student.

After my undergraduate studies, I left to study a master's degree in France. This was my first experience of a different country and a different academic environment and challenged my assumptions of both Chinese and Western education systems. When I returned to China to take up a lecturing position at Central South University, these experiences influenced my approach, experience of teaching and the university environment.

In 2011, I returned once more to Europe to study for a Ph. D in

London. These movements back and forth between East and West, as resident, student and academic connected strongly with my formative years. Through these experiences, academic migration, the motives and experiences of academic migrants formed a strong current in my understanding of my place in the world and that of many of my friends and family. Although my intention has always been to return to China to work in academia after completing my Ph. D, the motives for staying or leaving, the differences in teaching styles and the experience of the university environment have formed a large part of my academic life experiences. This thesis represents an academic investigation of the issues with which I have been not only familiar with, but have also grappled with throughout my life.

Introduction: Transnational Encounters Across Space and Time

In the last two decades[1], higher education has become increasingly transnational in character, with international branch campuses and educational programmes springing up in large numbers[2]. This has been in part shaped by a corresponding increase in transnational academic migration, with international links becoming 'increasingly systematic, dense, multiple and transnational' (Kim, 2010: 400). There is a growing body of migration research exploring the transnational mobility of students, but little is known about the transnational mobility of university researchers and academics, and their grounded working experiences in the host countries (Jons, 2009; Fehey and Kenway, 2010). There is evidence that encourages scholars to look more closely at academic migrants and their everyday activities (Larner, 2014). Holloway and Jöns (2012) have called for more research on these highly-skilled migrants from various cultural backgrounds, particularly world-class universities with global branches. In this thesis, I echo their call and address this gap by focusing on

[1] In the last decade of 20th century and the first decade of 21st century, the cross border movement of international students, academics, programmes and institutions stepped into a new level (Warwick, 2014).

[2] There are currently 235 international campuses worldwide (C-BERT, 2015).

Chinese and British academic migrants in a Sino-UK university joint venture, and use the university campus as the main context through which to explore their experiences.

UK and Chinese academic institutions and academic migrants are the focus of this study for a number of reasons. Academic institutions in the UK are of particular interest, because they have managed to maintain a relatively strong position in the recruitment and retention of highly-skilled overseas academics in the face of growing global competition (Walker, 2015). HESA data for 2013—2014 states that 29% of all UK university academics were non-UK academics, a slight rise (or one percentage point) in comparison to the data gathered in 2012. Of these overseas academics, China provides the largest single group of ethnic minority academic staff in the UK (HESA, 2013/2014). Equally, UK universities are also keen to establish international branch campuses. By 2012, UK institutions had established 25 international branch campuses worldwide, and UK was listed in third place of the top five source countries of branch campuses after the US and Australia (Knight, 2015). Increasing numbers of British academics are adopting a 'fly-in and fly-out' (THE, 2014) working style in order to adapt to this 'transnational agenda' and accumulate international experiences.

Although the topic is under-researched, the small body of literature that does exist in relation to academic mobility is largely made up of national-scale studies and political perspectives (e. g. Altbach and Knight, 2007; Robinson and Guan, 2012). In this thesis, I argue for a more grounded perspective, applying critical scrutiny to the social and cultural aspects of academic mobility in individual and situated contexts (Roberston, 2010; Cantwell, 2011; Chen, 2015). Rather than taking national immigration policy trends as a starting point of research, my focus will be on what the everyday working experiences of Chinese and British academic migrants reveal within the context of the global processes of increasing internationalisation. The study breaks new ground by teasing out where the difficulties, problems, misunderstandings, contradictions and tensions might occur in an unfamiliar academic field for transnational academic migrants. Moreover, to ask how these issues influence the three key themes of their work activities overseas, namely their future movement, pedagogic creativeness and how their identity, sense of belonging and social interactions are bounded to the use of place on campus. As 'time and space have shrunk' (Olson and Kroeger, 2001: 16) in transnational higher education, the 'host' academic field is gradually rebuilt by people of different cultures rather than insulated by national or institutional boundaries. The thesis argues for a translocal and enduring understanding of academic migrants' experience and points out that those experiences are nationally unbounded, yet locally specific.

More specifically, I examine the impact of relocation challenges on academics' daily working practices in three aspects: (1) observing migration as a continuous process, and pointing out the differences in immigration polices and administrative systems between China and the UK (Zhuang and Tang, 2012) and how these might positively and negatively impact academic migrants' movement; (2) observing migration as a creative process, and teasing out the differences in pedagogy (De Villiers, 2004; Jiang, *et al.*, 2010; Luxon and Peelo, 2009; Hsieh, 2011) and whether these differences generate new or hybrid forms of pedagogy; and (3) observing migration as a place-connected process, and exploring the spatial configuration of the campus (Cox, *et al.*, 2012) and its effect upon everyday working practices and experiences. These are dealt with in each of the empirical chapters, which will be outlined in more detail shortly.

In the following sections, I give a more detailed description of the context of international education and the theoretical background that is pertinent to my research. These sections are followed by a description of my specific research questions, a summary of the content of the chapters and the contributions of the study.

1 Background of the Study

1.1 International Education

Since the turn of the century ‘transnational education’ (Wilkins and Huisman, 2012) has been a rising phenomenon under the internationalism of higher education, driven by political, economic, social, and technological advances. It can take several forms, including ‘distance education, franchised programmes, collaborative ventures and international branch campuses’, the latter of which accounts for ‘most of the growth in transnational higher education’ (Wilkins and Huisman, 2012: 628) in the first decade of this century. Among 281 international branch campuses worldwide (C-BERT 2015), China is the second largest host country and the UK the third largest of the source countries (Knight, 2015). China and the UK thus form an important part of the international academic backdrop. Together they have already taken the lead in building inter-country academic collaboration to promote transnational education, and correspondingly, academic mobility.

The ‘transnational education’ phenomenon indicates that the higher education systems at the national level cannot remain immune from external forces. Higher education systems are in fact increasingly pursuing an international goal. The governments of these two countries are increasingly aware of the contribution that higher education institutions can make to promoting relations between the UK and China. According to a speech given by the Chinese ambassador Liu Xiaoming at the University of Durham on the 29th May 2012, British universities have begun to strengthen their input to research in China with more than 30 universities setting up Chinese research centers or institutes. For example, the University of Oxford established a Chinese Research Centre, and a Centre for Chinese Studies was established at King’s College London in 2010.

At the same time, UK institutions increasingly recognise the possibility of taking their educational programmes to the students (Waters, 2007). The establishment of international programmes and institutions has grown rapidly in recent years. In 2012, there were 71 Sino-British educational programmes and 5 joint venture universities in China (MOE, 2012). While as of 2015, there are 240 Sino-British joint university programmes, and 12 joint higher educational institutions in these two countries (MOE, 2015)[1]. Thus, as mentioned earlier, an important reason for locating the research in these two countries is their role as representatives of one of the most mature source/host countries of international branch campuses in transnational education.

However, when one looks more closely at these institutions' educational practices, it is hard to put all the branch campuses into a simple category. There are a variety of motivations and organisational structures that lie behind these institutions. This is in contrast to the approach taken by the existing literature, that generally defines the branch campus as 'an educational facility owned, at least in part, by a foreign institution, which operates under the name of the foreign institution, where students receive face—to—face instruction to achieve a qualification bearing the name of the foreign institution' (Wilkins and Huisman, 2012: 628). This is an over-simplification that does not adequately account for the real situation. Some Sino-British universities, for example, are either not owned by a foreign institution or do not award qualifications, such as Xinhua International Institute of Economics. So, without consideration of the complexity

[1] These 13 joint institutions are: Sino-British College, University of Shanghai For Science and Technology; Shanghai International College of Fashion and Innovation, Donghua University; Xi'an Jiaotong-Liverpool University; NUIST Reading Academy; The University of Nottingham-Ningbo; SWJTU-Leeds Joint School; HBU-UCLan School of Media, Communication and Creative Industries; Birmingham Institute of Fashion and Creative Art Industries; Birmingham Institute of Fashion and Creative Art, Wuhan Textile University; Bangor Collage, Central South University of Forestry and Technology; Xinhua International College of Economics; Surrey International Institute, Dongbei University of Finance and Economics; China Medical University- the Queen's University of Belfast Joint College (MOE, 2015).

of the Sino-British branch campuses, it would be problematic to analyse Chinese/British academic migration as if all institutions were the same. This is the underlying reason that I chose to focus on a single institution in this research.

In order to identify this single institution, my initial sampling process drew from the list of the major joint venture licensed universities under the 2014 legislation in China. The rationale for choosing the sample university is based on the consideration that this is one of the pioneering joint-venture institutions in China. It is relatively more experienced with respect to other institutions and could be usefully used as a model for prospective international institutions. Moreover, it has independent campuses and corporate capacity, which helps me to locate the conception of a transnational workplace as a 'multicultural evaluating and bounded entity' in a concrete way.

1.2 International Academic Mobility

The process of educational internationalisation has resulted in the increased mobility of academics across national borders (Dunn and Wallace, 2006; Kim and Locke, 2010; Poole and Ewan, 2010). More specifically, the transnational movement of academics is attributed to both the international expansion of Western universities to other countries and the 'magnetic' nature of 'host' universities that attract international academic migrants (Bennion and Locke, 2010). Recent literatures on knowledge diaspora and returnees tend to focus on the debate of 'brain circulation' rather than earlier discussions framed by 'brain drain' or 'brain gain' of the country. It is argued that the inflow and outflow of these highly-skilled migrants can be considered a powerful vehicle that can stimulate knowledge exchange and global human capital connectivity between countries (Solimano, 2008; Chen, 2015). In choosing Chinese and British academics who work in the milieu of 'transnational education', my research aims to capture the 'everyday' texture of the transitional mobility process. They are the two flows of academic migrants that have not frequently been addressed in current research. This is an area of research, however, that can reveal the complexity of the transnational educational system, and of transnational academic mobility.

At the national level, it can help us to understand the role of the 'receiving' and the 'sending' country, or the so-called 'host' and 'home' country in a transnational educational field. For example, China is the sending country for Chinese academics and the receiving country of British academics and the Chinese academic returnees. By constructing the research in this way, the educational system in these two countries is approached as mutually connected rather than separated by national boundaries. On the individual level, the research also emphasizes that academic mobility is not a fixed one-way process. By focusing on two groups of academics, namely Chinese and British academic migrants, I aim to reveal the inter-relatedness between these two groups of academic migrants' overseas experiences, which are influenced by the same Sino-UK transnational field. In these ways, the relationship between daily working practices and the context of global processes of internationalisation are kept in focus.

The two groups of academic migrants being targeted in this research exhibit two explicit patterns of transnational academic mobility-institutionally-organised and individually-motivated migration. Most British academic migrants in China are concerned with institutional expansion (the building of branch campuses), mainly with business motives, and generally require temporary relocation of the academics with their offshore teaching assignments (some British academics are recruited directly by the 'host' institution). This demands new and sometimes 'unusual' sets of skills from the international academics who are involved in the transnational educational delivery (Gribble and Ziguras, 2003; Eldridge and Cranston, 2009). While, the Chinese academic migrants in the UK (apart from those visiting scholars) are often 'individually motivated', which generally involves the choice of the individual academics to relocate themselves 'permanently' as academic migrants (Pherali, 2014).

This research can help us better understand the complexity of academic mobility and reveal the hidden threads of their offshore experiences. This is approached by investigating the host experiences of British and Chinese academics, which will be valuable to other transnational academics outside of the study group. Moreover, it also contributes to gaps in the current literature, as identified by Ren and Caudle (2014) who suggest there are few China – West comparative studies on (HE) work issues in existing publications. In sum, the cultural geographical analysis I adopt offers a valuable perspective for understanding the issues relating to spatial and cultural experience of international academics in the environment of transnational education.

2 Theoretical Framework

The study centres on the dilemmas and the influences of transnational academic practices linked to the process of academic mobility and university expansion across national borders. The emphasis upon daily lived experience in the research is theoretically anchored in transnationalism around questions of how 'global processes are experienced in localised, everyday, embodied ways' (Hyndman, 2002: 212). Although all transnational activities are conceptualised as 'processes that exist or work across borders' (Warwick, 2014: 93), transnationalism is a loaded word which has different meanings when looking at different groups of transnational migrants. It would be significant to explain how the transnational process of this particular group, namely academic migrants, gradually involved in an identical transnational academic field (Sino-UK transnational academic space) that is possibly different from other groups of highly skilled migrants. So, the empirical resources of this research mainly devote to the conceptual ideal of transnationalism (Guarniso and Smith, 1998) in connection with international higher education and academic mobility.

I use grounded transnationalism and transnationalism from below/above as the oretical anchors from which to support and develop my research structure. To investigate transnationalism from above is to locate the research in the field of transnational higher education, where the academic distinction between nations is weakened 'from above' by the extension of transnational university institutions and the exchange of 'transnational capitals'. While, to guide transnationalism from below in this study is to perceive how migrants' attendant cultural hybridity is influenced by the cultural constructions, social interactions, university space and academic freedom, *etc.* from the local level. This study also aims to ground transnationalism by identifying the everyday practical constraints of academic migration through different localities, academic practices, and specific social relations.

Within this context of transnationalism, Bourdieu's notion of field, habitus and different forms of capital (Bourdieu, 1977) are used as heuristic tools to explore the complexity of academic migrants' daily experience in the 'host' institution. For example, the transnational educational field that is provided by international branch campuses is the field within which academic migrants can learn the 'rules of the game' which results in the accumulation of different types of capital and realising the capital conversion across national boundaries. However, Bourdieu's conceptual ideal of a theory of practice and analytic power of *Homo Academicus* (ibid.) is limited in the social and cultural aspects of a single national backdrop. In order to break the limitation and connect Bourdieu's theory with mobility and transnationalism, some scholars extend it to an additional 'spatial capital' (Soja, 2009) or 'mobility capital' (Leung, 2012), which works simultaneously with other forms of capital. Datta and Brickell (2012: 11) suggest that Bourdieu's notion of habitus, capital and field have tremendous potential in examining 'the translocal field of practice where migrants' (social or cultural) capital are exchanged differently in different spaces, places and scales'. So, in this research, I link Bourdieu's Franco – centric empirical scope into a larger transnational academic field, namely Chinese and British academia, to see how academic migrants' diverse working practices operate 'specifically local and spatially global' (Datta and Brickell, 2012: 2).

In this transnational field, habitus[1] provides a method for simultaneously analysing 'the experience of social agents and... the objective structures which make this experience possible' (Bourdieu, 1988: 782). So, in my study, firstly, I use the notion of habitus as a complex interplay between past and present. The qualitative data from the study shows how professional habitus from the home university can still be embedded in academic migrants on the host campus, generating uncertainty, ambivalence, and anxiety in their offshore experience. Secondly, the concept of habitus is a research tool that can be used to identify factors that contribute to the varied experiences among scholars of different ages, genders, disciplines, academic ranks, and geographical backgrounds, which challenge the ideal of British and Chinese academic migrants as a unitary group of people. Finally, I take habitus not only in the sense of academic migrants' adaptations, reactions, and resistance towards a new educational environment but also of their struggle to make the institution a different place.

I also employ the notion of capital to understand how overseas academic life experiences can be understood as a means of 'transnational capital accumulation' (*i. e.* the accumulation of capital of different sorts transnationally). Migrant academics are found to occupy an ambiguous position. On the one hand, they are 'outsiders' with little familiarity with the nature of the local academic system, while on the other hand, the highly educated profile of migrant academics means that they often possess the kinds of cultural capital valued by

[1] Formally, Bourdieu defines habitus as a property of social agents (whether individuals, groups or institutions) that comprises a 'structured and structuring structure' (Bourdieu, 1996: 170).

the local educational system. My research thus focuses on the accumulation/devaluation of economic, social, cultural and symbolic capital among Chinese and British academic migrants and asks how these capitals can eventually be converted and transformed into forms of capitals which are helpful for their future professional progress (See Figure 1-1).

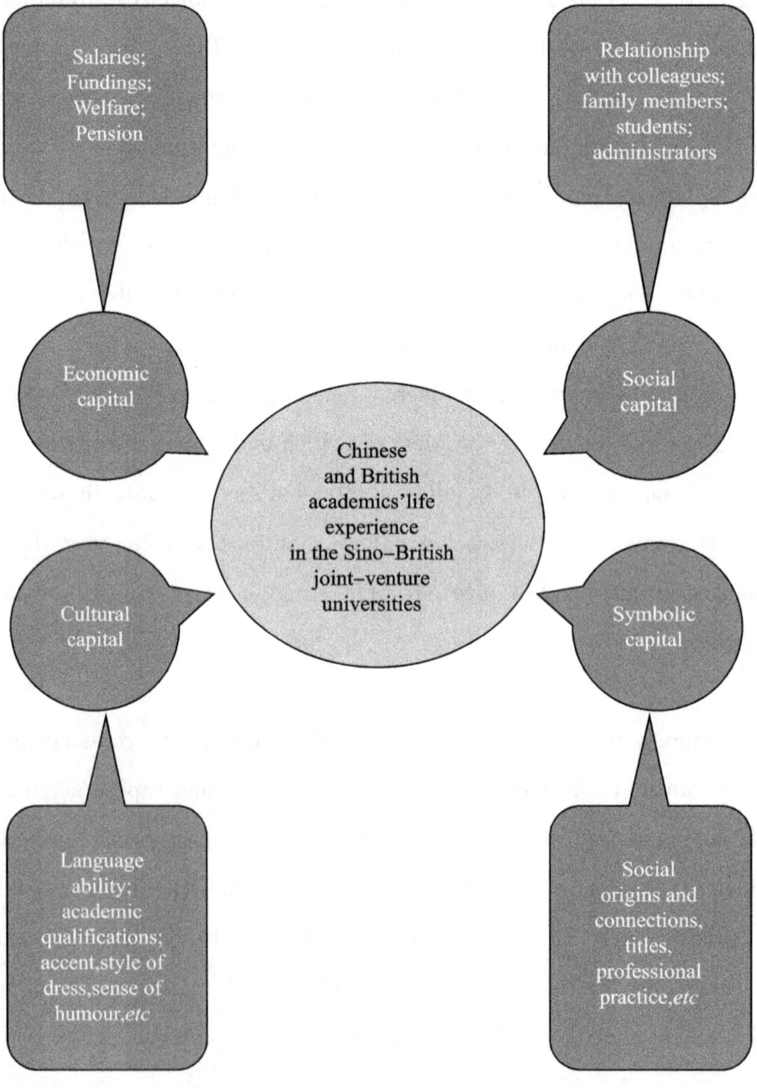

Figure 1-1 Overseas academic life experience as a means of capital accumulation

The whole theoretical framework of the thesis is illustrated in Figure 1-2. The figure reveals that one of the main theoretical approaches of the study is to employ grounded everyday practices as a dynamic source to illustrate and reflect the broader transnationalisation process by using Bourdieu's theory of practice. Focusing on the grounded experiences of transnational academic migrants, the study adds rich grounded resources to the current literature on transnationalism by linking transnational academic mobility with their social, cultural and space interactions and practices on local bases. By organising multi-angled comparative discussions between Chinese and British transnational academic migrants' everyday experiences, the study challenged the stereotyped presumptions of grounded transnational experiences.

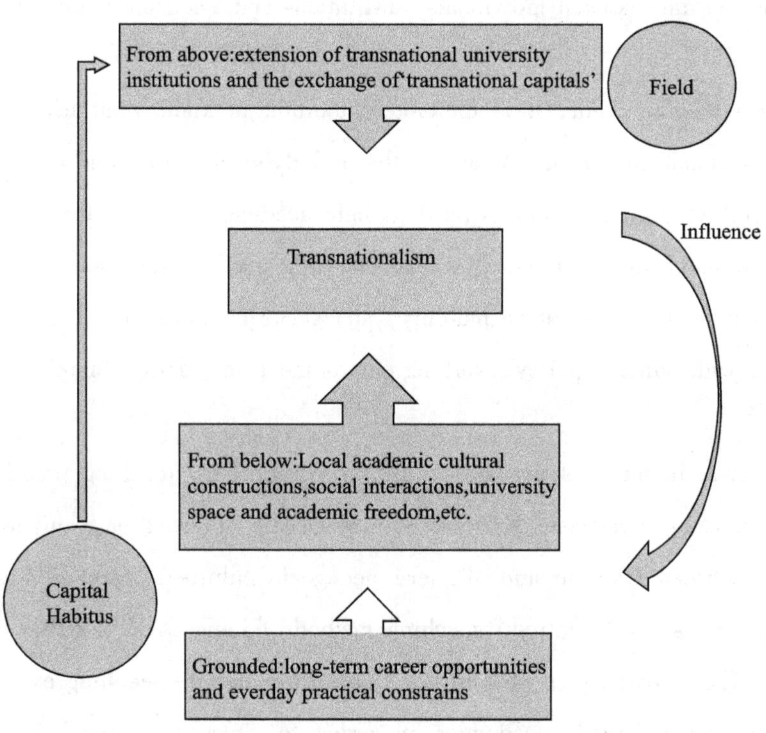

Figure 1-2 Theoretical framework of the thesis

3 Purpose Statement and Research Questions

Intellectual human capital tends to flourish around top-ranked universities and the university itself also becomes more internationalised. It is argued that the cultural context of the 'host' local academic environment poses a real tension to migrants' effective integration into the academic community (Pherali, 2011), and the offshore academic profession in the process of internationalisation faces significant challenges worldwide (Larner, 2014). Against this backdrop, the purpose of the study is to explore the factors that influenced academic migrants' grounded offshore working practices in the context of transnational higher education, in order to identify the challenges, dilemmas and solutions which would contribute to transnational individuals, institutions and academic migration.

As a starting point, it is therefore important to know what triggers Sino-British academic movement. What are the underlying dynamics and outcomes for their mobility? How do overseas postings help academics in their future careers? So, the research first examines how academic migrants' current work experiences affect their decisions of future mobility, and seeks to understand the ways they negotiate with national policy, working environment and family commitments.

Second, in terms of academic working experiences, teaching practice is a crucial area to investigate. Existing studies usually present a relatively clear division between Chinese and Western pedagogic cultures, such as 'teacher-centred' or 'student-centred' teaching methods (Jiang *et al.*, 2010; Hsieh, 2011). The research presented in this thesis examines the teaching experiences of Chinese and British academics in order to draw a nuanced picture of pedagogical issues and break down crude stereotypes. It reveals the complexity of transnational teaching practice, and shows how transnational academics gradually negotiate with diverse teaching and learning habitus, creating the possibility of pedagogical 'innovation'.

The third theme of the study is that through mobility academics engender their own social and cultural connectivity with places and materials in the 'host' university. It points to the work-life practices other than teaching. The study seeks to investigate work, leisure, and living spaces that Chinese and British academic migrants utilise and to find some distinctions or similarities between the ways that these two groups of academics use them, revealing the underlying social, cultural and academic misunderstandings/dilemmas of working in a transnational university space. It mainly focuses on academic migrants' sense of belonging and identity embedded in their place-making process in the 'host' campus spaces, and their social interactions in those places. In other words, this study aims to present an indepth portrait of contemporary Sino-British academic everyday workplace through their connections with local places in the transnational institution.

This research sheds light on the academic debate of transnational academic mobility and transnational higher education guided by the following research questions:

How do Chinese and British academic migrants' current working experiences inform their future migration strategies, trajectories and motivations?

How do Chinese and British academics' transnational teaching experiences influence pedagogy? How far is the distinction between 'Chinese' and 'Western' academic culture played out in pedagogical practice? Do transnational academics create a 'new' style of teaching methods?

How do Chinese and British academic migrants use university space in practice and how does this differ from their experiences at ‘home’? How do Chinese and British academic migrants’ working lives and the physical space of the ‘host’ university mutually constitute each other? To what extent can place and materials in places influence academic migrants’ social relations?

4 Significance of the Project

In this research, I develop an understanding of university internationalisation from the perspective of the grounded daily professional lives of academic migrants. I explore how transnational higher education and national educational ideology shape Chinese and British academic migrants’ everyday working experiences in the institutional space of a transnational university campus. More specifically, I examine the transnational academics’ involvement in the transnational university in three interrelated aspects, namely relocation motivation, teaching practice, and other academic practices, in order to illustrate the impact of the transplantation on the body in relation to time and space.

This research deepens existing understanding of internationalism, transnationalism and highly-skilled migration by further developing the conceptual framework of the relationships between academic migration, transnational education, and place. By examining the grounded experience of transnational education programmes, it contributes to theoretical and empirical perspectives on how globalisation processes are practised and felt in localised everyday working life. To be specific, the main contributions can be gathered as follows:

With respect to geography of education, this research complements the small but growing body of research on transnational academic mobility (see: Fahey and Kenway, 2010; Yang and Welch, 2010; Tremblay, 2014; Scott, 2015). Until now, we still have limited resources to help us understand what is actually entailed in the process of movement for academic migrants, especially their motivation, struggles and possibilities. An understanding of mobility among academics and researchers matters to the whole transnational infrastructure of HE and acts as a counterpoint to research upon international student mobility. By looking at academic migrants' grounded transnational experiences, such as their cultural misunderstandings, social relationships, academic requests and outcomes, *etc.*, rather than policy trends or overall movement, I bring a valuable perspective of the mobile experience of academics to the geography of education literatures.

The research also contributes to and extends literatures on highly-skilled migration. There are considerable literatures on highly-skilled international labour migration (See, for example, Ryan, 2014; Wise, 2015; Windsor, 2015). For example, the transnational migrants who work in the international firms are also working for a global entity as academic migrants in this study; however, their offshore experience is assumed to have some dissimilarities from academics, in terms of practices, social networks, and residence configurations, *etc.* This research reveals findings that add or contrast with work on intra-company transfers (e. g. Beaverstock, 2005), by considering transnational academics as highly skilled transnational migrants. The focus of the study is not to compare the perspectives of these two groups of migrants, but to add a crucial part to the whole picture of highly-skilled migration, which includes diverse groups from different professional fields.

The research thus adds value to the conceptual framework of transnationalism. It is noticeable that the discourses on academic mobility largely 'remain locked under a nationally bounded space, focusing extensively on the logic of human capital and national economic growth and competitiveness' (Chen, 2015: 15). This study tries to challenge this by stretching academic migrants' work life in a transnational university space that is composed of a single professional field across national boundaries. Structured in this way, the edge of discourses on academic mobility is extended: the motivations of mobility are evaluated in a continuous process that points to various future possibilities rather than fixed towards a single country; offshore academic practices, such as teaching, cannot be shoe-horned into one or several stereotyped pedagogies, because academic migrants' academic capital is accumulated across time and space; the working space of academics should not be taken for granted, as it can be regarded as important places that can demonstrate how internationalism of higher education is being negotiated in material ways.

In the context of transnationalism discussed above, this study uses Bourdieu's theory of practice as a conceptual tool for understanding the qualitative nature of academic migrants' everyday work. It draws on his conception of field, habitus and different forms of capital and asks how they can be extended from a Francocentric to a transnational context. The study asks how these concepts can be applied to varied cultural backdrops and how they change throughout time and space. Recent advances in the use of Bourdieu's concepts (such as field, capitals and habitus) may be treated as generalisable. This gives us the possibility of joining the analytic insights given by Bourdieu's theory to a more grounded line of research in academic migration studies.

Methodologically, this study adopts a relatively large and well-structured sample, using qualitative research, and supplements existing research. I will explore the variation of academics' experience arising from discipline, gender, institution, seniority, length of sojourn in the host country, and type of migration etc. The mixed methods adopted in this research, namely semi-structured interviews, photo elicitation, and participant observation, are helpful in tackling the potential ways in which academic migration might be understood.

Last but not least, practically my study also sheds light on transnational university construction and current talent policies in China and the UK. It can be argued that academic mobility can be relatively influenced by national policies on highly-skilled migration; however, the institutional culture and grounded experience are also key elements to conduct academic mobility. It is important to learn academic migrants' difficulties, needs and opinions on particular issues. Therefore, the research provides rich empirical resources for policy-makers and university administrators, which might lead to better cooperation between institutions and nations.

5 Structure of the Thesis

This introduction chapter provides an overview of the study, including research background, theoretical framework, research questions, structure and significance of the study. The second chapter reviews literature on the internationalisation of higher education, transnationalism and Bourdieu's theory of practice. Chapter Three focuses on the methodology of the research, which involves the rationale for choosing methods, research site selection, data collection procedure and my positionality and reflections on the fieldwork process.

The major findings of the research are presented in the subsequent three main empirical chapters: the offshore working challenges and the reasons for 'going back' (Chapter Four); pedagogical challenges and adjustments in transnational teaching practice (Chapter Five); academic migrants' working practice and international university spaces (Chapter Six). All these three chapters discuss Chinese and British academic migrants' offshore experience and form them into three different aspects that cover the main academic practices. Those three themes are closely interconnected with each other, not only because they show the diversity and the 'whole' picture of transnational academic migrants' working life, but also because they extend the existing discourse on academic mobility by adding the element of 'grounded academic experiences' into the discussions.

Chapter Four teases out some of the threads in the complex web of challenges and dilemmas they encounter in their workplace and responses to their migration motivations. This chapter explores Chinese and British academic mobility from a grounded practice approach: building for the future through national policy 'from above' and cultivating/devaluing transnational capital in the workplace 'from below'. It argues that the decision to return for academic migrants is often motivated by occupational or economic reasons that are influenced by newly-updated national immigration policy. However, they do not move solely for better career opportunities, with other reasons, such as academic freedom, bureaucracies of university administration, social attachment, cultural belonging, self-realisation, and family commitment also crucial in their return moves. It further suggests that the act of leaving the 'host' country is closely connected with individual choices that negotiate forces ranging from larger to smaller scales nation-state, university, and family.

Chapter Five reflects on the situation of an increasing number of university academics whose 'workplace' is transnational, and in turn, how this reality affects their pedagogies. Many of the participants in this study previously had transnational experiences, and thus come into contact with a range of pedagogical styles. In this chapter, I systematically consider how geographical location is associated with particular curriculum opportunities and how transnational education can then modify this, creating the possibility for the negotiation and development of different pedagogies. I consider first the influence of past teaching experience on current teaching practice, and investigate the difficulties academics face during offshore teaching if they continue using their 'old' teaching methods. Then, I focus on Chinese and British academic migrants' adjustments in teaching practice, and ask whether they have adopted a host pedagogy or created a 'new' pedagogy which is particularly tailored for their offshore teaching. In the final part, I explore the built environment of the university (classroom), to ask how teaching space can alter the teacher's pedagogy in the 'host' university. I demonstrate through these three sections that teaching practice is inextricably bound up with place, materials, and forms of knowledge that help academic migrants relocate themselves in transnational higher education. It argues that the academic migrants are not just passively integrating to the existing teaching rules and structures in the 'host' university. Instead, they are simultaneously drawing upon their capitals accumulated through transnational teaching, and use them to create a new space for pedagogical possibilities and higher education innovation.

In Chapter Six, I respond to the call to more robustly bond the notion of place with transnational academic migrants' experience, whilst also demonstrating the powerful link between place and story. In order to do this, I question, from a material perspective, how academic migrants' place-making practices shape and are reciprocally shaped by the host places. I also ask how academic migrants' social relations are intertwined with a selection of places on campus, and how they mutually affect each other. I use Bourdieu's notion of habitus and social capital to help consider the question of how everyday working life and place are constitutively entangled in a transnational higher education environment. Through this research and analysis, I identify the main factors that affect Chinese and British academics' everyday working experience through a spatial lens and demonstrate how such a 'spatial lens' adds to existing debates on transnational academic migration.

To conclude, the final chapter, Chapter Seven, revisits the key issues that are discussed in the previous chapters. I demonstrate how the dynamics of transnational academic mobility and grounded transnational working experiences are involved in a continual process that is not only effected by global mechanisms and local forces but also closely attached to individual relationships with various factors, such as capital, habitus and place. It concludes with the implications and limits of the study and the suggestions for future studies.

Chapter Two
Internationalisation and Transnational Academic Mobility

Introduction

Academic mobility has increased noticeably in recent years as a result of international communication, economic and culture integration and the internationalisation of higher education (Yang and Welch, 2010). The simultaneity of interlocking relations between spontaneously mobile individuals, national and supra-national policy frameworks and institutional networks of universities in the global knowledge flows, all contribute to a picture of contemporary patterns of academic mobility that differs from past trends (Kim and Locke, 2010). However, studies of international academic mobility usually focus on students, the international recruitment market and the international trade in higher education and research (see, for instance, Byram and Dervin, 2008), and discussions on transnational academic migrants are still limited. How academic migrants' transitional experience is located in academic mobility studies, and to what extent those experiences contribute to the internationalisation of higher education/transnationalism, are the central questions of this literature review.

The first part of the literature review discusses existing studies that relate to my research in the context of academic mobility: the internationalisation of higher education. It looks broadly at international academic migration in terms of the concepts of 'brain drain' 'brain gain' 'brain circulation', and specifically at international student mobility. The scale then narrows to a discussion of the internationalisation of higher education in China and the UK, and the current flows of Chinese and British academic migrants. This is followed by a section that explains the 'structural driving forces' of academic mobility from a national (for Chinese academics) and an institutional angle (for British academics). It looks first at a comparison of recent national migrant policies towards Chinese academic migrants at the national level of these two countries. Then secondly it considers the British university branch campuses in China, which are regarded as a 'vehicle' to move British academic migrants from the UK to China. Overall, this part of the review concentrates on internationalism of higher education and the conditions favouring and inhibiting academic mobility in national and institutional contexts. This background introduction raises questions about the recent trends and gaps in academic discourse on the topic of the motivations of academic migrants in Chapter Four.

The second part of the review looks specifically at research on transnationalism and transnational academics. After a short review of transnationalism, which forms the basic theoretical framework of the thesis, I introduce the connections between transnationalism and academic mobility. I then go on to explain the distinction between different academic cultures and academic migrants' offshore practices and challenges in the context of transnationalism. Those challenges are related to all three of my empirical chapters. Then, it is followed by an explanation of different pedagogic cultures, which are closely connected to one of the main challenging practices of academic migrants, namely teaching. The pedagogical section points directly to the pedagogical discussion in Chapter Five, which looks closely at the responses to these challenges. This is followed by a discussion of research that addresses academic accumulation, which indicates how academic migrants from different educational fields cope with the current transitional reality.

The third part of the review deals with other conceptual tools of this study, namely the notion of field, capital, habitus, and the notion of place in geography. First, I look at Bourdieu's theory in the context of academic migration. There are three sections here, looking at Bourdieu's concepts of field, capital and habitus respectively. Then, I introduce the concept of place and build up a link between place, habitus and academic migration, which relates to the discussion on university space and academic experience in Chapter Six.

Finally, the conclusion proposes a research agenda for investigating transnational academic mobility in this study. In this chapter, I develop my overall argument for bringing together the existing literature discussed here and my own research.

1 The Process of Internationalisation of Higher Education in Chinese and British National Contexts

The internationalisation of higher education is clearly in the air. A range of publications reveal that expansion of higher education has been acting upon the global stage instead of being rooted in the conventional nation-state (Altbach, 2015; Crisan-Mitra and Borza, 2015; Gopal and Zha, 2015; Hartmann, 2014; Healey and Bordogna, 2014; Kim, 2014; Knight, 2015; Wit, 2014). Talking about the internationalisation of higher education worldwide, there are intensive discussions around the concepts of brain drain, brain gain and brain circulation (see: Séguin et al. 2006; Welch and Zhen, 2008). I will begin my review by introducing this global trend in academic mobility, and more specifically how it is becoming increasingly composed of ‘widespread and multifaceted’ elements (Altbach, 2015). First, internationalisation of higher education is not a one-way process, which just 'exports' education or academics out of the country; 'home' universities are also under a considerable degree of 'international' influence too (Trahar and Hyland, 2011). A 'global market' for academics had therefore been set up, which provoked a 'new' trend in migration policies in different countries. Second, the number of international institutions, the so-called 'international, bi-national, transnational, cosmopolitan, multinational, or global universities' (Knight, 2015: 107), that have been built beyond country borders, continues to rise rapidly. The discourse of 'polycentric world politics' (Rosenau, 1990) reminds us not to underestimate the power of such international bodies, especially their power upon academic mobility (Lepori, *et al.*, 2014). Third, driven by global forces, student mobility, as an important component of international academic mobility, is flowing across national borders. It is recorded that more than 1.6 million students now study outside their home countries (Altbach, 2015). Thus, I will explore the internationalisation of higher education in conceptual, national, institutional and individual aspects.

1.1 Evolution of Concepts in Internationalisation of Higher Education: Brain Drain, Brain Gain, and Brain Circulation

1.1.1 Brain Drain

Traditionally, the migration of educated people from developing countries to developed countries was regarded as a problem of 'brain drain'. It has been argued that the loss of significant numbers from the elite group, through brain drain, represents a major and permanent loss to the country of origin, which invested so much of its limited capital on their education (Welch and Zhen, 2008). The topic of the 'brain drain' was introduced to United Nations debates in the late 1960s. In the 1970s, policy-makers mainly focused on how to discourage the 'brain drain' and on how to compensate the countries that the highly skilled were migrating from. A series of UN documents in the late 1970s identified the return of professionals to their developing home countries as an important strategy for development. The International Organisation for Migration launched a programme to assist educated migrants return to their home countries in Latin America in the 1970s, and initiated a similar programme in Africa in the 1980s.

Although more and more countries have launched similar programmes in order to attract educated migrants to return home, the stratified nature of the global knowledge network (Altbach, 2002) underlines the fact that the flow of intellectuals is still very much from the South to the North (Kapur and McHale, 2005; Ellerman, 2006). As Solimano (2002) argues, such flows deepen the existing global inequality of knowledge creation and application: developed countries compete to attract research talent from developing countries, who then consolidate the already strong knowledge base in the former (Hugo, 2002), at the cost of the latter.

1.1.2 Brain Gain

Every year, governments make sustained efforts to reverse the tide of brain drain. China represents an important example-attempting to turn the tide. China developed programmes to entice highly-skilled scientists and researchers to return, and use their skills in the service of the country. In the early 1990s, President Jiang Zemin (1993—2003) did much to kick-start moves to attract China's highly skilled to return. He recognised that in a more global context and with China's increasing openness, it was no longer possible to prevent its citizens from pursuing advanced studies abroad, and that China had to compete internationally in order to attract them back. Since then, further moves have been instituted to allow greater freedom of movement internationally and to deploy Chinese nationalism, in an effort to entice highly-skilled overseas Chinese to bring their skills back home, even if not permanently (Welch and Zhen, 2008).

For China, deploying the diaspora option is now a priority (Zweig and Fung, 2004; Welch and Zhang, 2005), representing a more nuanced response to promote brain gain. Individual universities, notably the most prominent national institutions that were able to take advantage of their membership of the 211 Programme[1], and the even more selective 985 Programme[2], offered incentives in the form of salary bonuses, research funds and equipment, housing, and assistance with children's schooling, in an effort to induce selected individuals to relocate back to China (Welch and Zhen, 2008). And the newer 111 Programme[3] which is designed to recruit Chinese intellectuals from abroad to work in mainland universities, even on a temporary basis, represents further strategies to deal with brain drain. Such knowledge bridges, built with overseas Chinese intellectuals, many of whom are keen to contribute to the homeland, from abroad, are in part responsible for China's rapidly rising scientific stature:

---

[1] Programme 211 is a project of national key universities and colleges initiated in 1995 by the Ministry of Education of the People's Republic of China, with the intent of raising the research standards of high-level universities and cultivating strategies for socio-economic development. During the first phase of the project, from 1996 to 2000, approximately US $ 2.2 billion was distributed.

[2] Programme 985 is a project first announced by CPC General Secretary and Chinese President Jiang Zemin at the 100th anniversary of Peking University on May 4, 1998 to promote the development and reputation of the Chinese higher education system (and codenamed after the date of the announcement, 5/98 or 98/5, according to the Chinese date format). The project involves both the national and local governments allocating large amounts of funding to certain universities in order to build new research centres, improve facilities, hold international conferences, attract world-renowned faculty and visiting scholars, and help Chinese faculty attend conferences abroad.

[3] 111 Programme: The Ministry of Education issued a regulation on September 11 (2006) to help tackle course innovation in colleges and universities, marking the implementation of 'Plan 111'. The plan aims to upgrade scientific innovation and peer competition of Chinese universities by establishing innovation centres and gathering groups of first-class minds from around the world. It will bring in about 1000 overseas talents from the top 100 universities and research institutes worldwide. These experts will team up with domestic research infrastructures alongside the creation of 100 subject innovation centres to be set up in universities. At least 10 overseas talents should be employed in each innovation centre. In each of these teams, at least one should be an overseas academic master while the foreign representatives can only emanate from the top 100 universities and research institutes. Generally, the academic masters should not be older than 70, with the exception of Nobel Prize winners, with other representatives under 50. Each academic master should work at least a month within China with other members of the visiting teams working there for three months.

'China takes the prize for its astonishing increased output over the last few decades. In the early 1980s, journal articles indexed by Thomson Reuters that carried a Chinese author address were only 4 percent of the world's output. That number is now 10 percent, up from 5 percent only seven years ago. Today, China is second, behind the United States, ... (China) is rapidly becoming a world power in research (Pendlebury, 2015: 6). These kinds of benefits were being used not only to induce overseas Chinese academics but also academics from elsewhere, for example, the USA, the UK, *etc.* Although such preferential strategies may be more efficient for attracting overseas academics, it may also arouse some ill-feeling among local colleagues. And such 'inequality' in treatment may stimulate local colleagues, especially young lecturers, to go abroad.

1.1.3 Brain Circulation

Although governments make every effort to reverse the tide of brain drain to brain gain, only half of international doctoral or post-doctoral candidates in the USA return to their country of origin (Saxenian, 2006). China has the highest stay rate, where 92% of the 2002 doctoral graduates stayed in the US for at least five years (Cheung and Xu, 2015). Data from Saxenian also shows that, of Silicon Valley's Asian population in the late 1990s, 77% of Indian residents held at least a master's degree, while for Chinese residents the figure was 86%, (Saxenian, 2006). Australian and Canadian data show similar figures (Li, 2005; Welch, 2007).

Between 1990 and 2000, approximately half of the doctoral recipients from China sought and received opportunities for further study and employment in the United States (Johnson and Regets, 1998). Notably, over 80% of the long-term Chinese immigrants to Australia currently have degrees, and significant numbers have moved into academic posts, usually after completing their doctoral degree at an Australian university (Hugo, 2005; Welch and Zhang, 2005). Similarly in the UK, ethnic Chinese remain the top group in terms of input of non-UK students (HESA 2013/2014) and non-UK academic research staff (Universities UK 2007).

Since the late 1990s, 'transnational' thinking has gained popularity (for example, Vertovec 1999, Meyer 2001). This thinking recognises that, in the current era of globalisation, creating transnational networks may be more important than human capital 'stock' in a particular country. A professional thus may contribute more to the home country by residing overseas than by returning permanently. With the recognition of networks of skilled worker circulation, many social scientists and national policy-makers have tended to shift from a discourse of 'brain drain' to the notions of 'scientific diaspora' (Séguin *et al.* 2006) and 'brain circulation' (Saxenian 2002).

Researchers also recognise that the emphasis on the importance of the highly educated in recent times is a further reflection of the change towards more knowledge-based economies (and arguably the further commodification of education) (Welch and Zhen, 2008). The global circulation of diasporic communities is also part of this new orientation, which challenges our notion of space and place (Said, 2000; Tsolidis, 2001; Welch, 2008). The Chinese knowledge diaspora arguably forms a subset of these global flows of academic migrants and can contribute significantly to both scientific collaboration and stronger cultural ties, and at the same time could contribute actively to the internationalisation of higher education (Hugo, 2005).

This multi-polar quality of the global knowledge network means that the diaspora option can be instrumental in narrowing the North-South scientific gap (Meyer and Brown, 1999; Brown, 2000; Meyer *et al.*, 2001, Zweig and Fung, 2004). To better explain expatriate knowledge networks, Meyer and Brown

(1999) identify various types of possible networks: (1) Student/scholarly networks; (2) Local associations of skilled expatriates; (3) Expert pool assistance through the United Nations Development Programme (UNDP)'s Transfer of Knowledge Through Expatriate Nationals (TOKTEN) Programme; (4) Intellectual/scientific diaspora networks.

1. Student/scholarly networks often facilitate studies abroad and/or reintegration into the highly-qualified labour market afterwards. This kind of network may be very important in facilitating knowledge transfer among countries. As Lowell and Gerova (2004) argue, there is a strong positive correlation between the number of foreign scholars with a US Ph. D and the extent to which scientific articles authored in sending countries include a US author. More precisely, Choi (1995) observed that many academics from an Asian background in American higher education maintain close contact with their countries of origin, notably scientific and academic relationships with colleagues and institutions at home. That means that if scholarly networks help link members of the knowledge diaspora to their home country, diaspora networks can stimulate collaboration and the exchange of knowledge (Welch and Zhen, 2008).

From this perspective, the Chinese academics who are highly skilled, can be seen as a potential resource, rather than as an instance of brain drain. However, some researchers also argue that, for Chinese overseas academics, their close relationship with colleagues and institutions at home should be questioned. For example, Welch and Zhen's (2008) study indicates that although all interviewees kept in contact with the home country, they did not have any concrete collaboration, or collaborative outcomes, from the professional contact with their mainland peers. Interviewees described multiple channels of communication, and painted a complex and uneven picture of scholarly relations.

2. The highly-skilled scientists and technologists, often with experience in

Silicon Valley, are busily creating far more 'complex and decentralised, two-way flows of knowledge, capital and technology' (Saxenian, 2006: 6). Local associations of skilled expatriates have fostered these kinds of knowledge networks. The Chinese created the Yuan Hua Science and Technology Association (Welch and Zhen, 2008).

3. The Transfer of Knowledge Through Expatriate Nationals, TOKTEN Programme was one of the pioneering programmes. TOKTEN assists expatriates living abroad to work for short periods in their country of origin. After that, the International Organisation for Migration replaced its earlier programme on permanent return in Africa with a new programme, 'Migration for Development in Africa' (MIDA, Migrations pour le Dévelopment en Afrique, in French) in 2000. The MIDA programme emphasises the importance of temporary, periodic returns or even 'virtual' returns (tele-commuting and Online-teaching) (Xiang, 2005). This kind of temporary return migration tends not to be short term: 'There is nothing so permanent as temporary migration' (Ellerman, 2006: 29).

4. Intellectual/scientific diaspora networks built by diasporic intellectuals are part of the wider phenomenon of increased global mobility, and the transnational networks. The hypothesis that diasporic intellectuals may generate positive externalities for the source country may be true, not only with regard to knowledge diffusion but also for other areas as well. In particular, knowledge diasporas to more democratic societies may have a positive impact on the social, economic, and political institutions in their home countries (by giving lectures and publishing papers or books). Moreover, they might transmit new ideas and behaviours prevailing in the destination countries, and as such, they may influence, for example, views on family structure in their origin countries and, consequently, the fertility rate in those countries.

1.2 International Student Mobility

Over the last 10 years, student migration has increased sharply and has become one of the major forms of contemporary international mobility (Bhandari and Blumenthal, 2009). It is estimated that there are about 1.6 million international students worldwide (Altbach, 2015). Consequently, the literature on international student mobility has also increased markedly (Guruz, 2008; Solimano, 2008; Varghese, 2008; Williams and Balaz, 2008; Beine *et al.*, 2014; Long and Day, 2015; Cummings and Bain, 2015). Extensive research on international student mobility has been conducted on 'credit mobility' (short-term exchanges) such as the European Erasmus scheme (King and Ruiz-Gelices, 2003; Byram and Dervin, 2008) but, overall, studies of degree mobility have dominated. Most of the current studies on degree mobility are contributing to a further understanding of how international student mobility is embedded in the complex relations linking globalisation, pedagogy and society (Brooks and Waters, 2010; Edwards and Usher, 2007; Gulson and Syme, 2007). However, some have interpreted international student mobility as an outcome of individual decisions reflecting personal particularities, such as gender, social class, language and personality (e.g. Dreher and Putvaara, 2005).

Furthermore, international student mobility has been structured not only by social class but also by the internationalisation of the education system (Yang, 2003; Teichler, 2004), by the rising economic competition for global talent (Kuptsch, 2006), and by the geographies of cultural capital (Ong, 1999; Murphy-Lejeune, 2002; Waters, 2006). For example, Noble and Davies (2009) have shown that cultural capital in the form of education is often a key marker of social inclusion and exclusion. According to Waters (2006), the growing middle class in China are seeking to maximise the cultural capital of the next generation by sending them to international elite universities.

It has also been pointed out that international student mobility should be analysed as a process linking three life-stage arenas (school, university and labour market outcomes) rather than as a one-off migration 'event' (Findlay *et al.*, 2012). To that extent, international student mobility, as one of many 'new mobilities' (Urry, 2007), is reshaping contemporary 'host' and 'home' society. It not only constitutes a critical means of intensifying social difference within the globalising higher education system (Marginson *et al.*, 2007) but also leads to questions about how the internationalisation of higher education is linked to the reproduction of unevenness in the global labour market (Findlay *et al.*, 2012).

Perhaps one of the most intriguing findings in relation to international student mobility is that 'failure' (or the anticipation of failure) in the domestic education system frequently prompts the decision to seek education abroad (Wiers-Jenssen, 2008; Brooks and Waters, 2009; Findlay and King, 2010; Deakin, 2011; Findlay *et al.* 2012). However, the word 'failure' has different meanings in different situations. For some, it can mean an inability to access any domestic university place; while for others, it can indicate rejection from the most elite domestic HEIs (Waters, 2008; Findlay *et al.*, 2012). Although there is research looking at some key motivations for students studying abroad, it could be argued that in some circumstances, 'victory' in both the domestic and international system may be also deployed as a strategy in a student's transnational life. Some elite students may successfully hold a domestic offer in one hand and several international offers in another, especially those seeking to study on the postgraduate level. So, studying abroad for them is like standing at a crossroads with many choices.

International student mobility does not, of course, stop with the journey overseas but also includes the return trip. It has been pointed out by some researchers that often upon bringing their 'international' qualifications home that their full value is realised—it is common that they are competing for jobs against locally educated graduates, usually with positive outcomes (King and Ruiz-Gelices 2003; Waters, 2008). Chinese student returnees used to be called 'Hai Gui' 海龟 (which means sea turtle in Chinese). In recent decades, they have also come to be known as 'Hai Dai' 海带 (which means seaweed in Chinese). It is a game of words: 'Gui' 龟/归 means 'return' but also has an extended meaning 'to come home with honour'; 'Dai' 带/待 means 'wait', and has a second sense of 'waiting for a job'. Overall, the image of Chinese returnees has changed a lot in recent years and not all of them can find a decent job with their international qualifications. There are two main reasons that can explain this phenomenon: one is that after the so-called 'failure' in the domestic education system mentioned earlier, some students from a 'middle-class' background are interested in 'spending money' (to buy articles of luxury) instead of 'receiving knowledge' during their overseas period. The second reason is that this group of people (Hai Dai) has overestimated the value of their international qualifications by asking for a relatively high salary during their job interviewing process, while practically they cannot accomplish the task due to a lack of knowledge of the current Chinese domestic situation. To put it succinctly, a proportion of Chinese returnees are living in an awkward situation and are inevitably pushed and pulled between the Eastern and Western world (Chen, 2015).

Overall, it seems, 'previously sporadic, exceptional and limited international academic links have become increasingly systematic, dense, multiple and transnational' (Kim, 2010: 400). Regional and national policies and the strength of particular institutions are combining with cultural and personal factors to create new patterns[1] of transnational academic mobility (Kim, 2010). The group of mobile British academics discussed in this research belongs to the 'new

[1] Kim (2010) develops a three-part typology of mobile academics: the transnational 'academic intellectual', who she differentiates from the mobile 'academic expert' and the mobile 'manager academic'.

patterns' of mobility that are stimulated mainly by institutional expansion (although there were British academics going overseas during colonial period and soon after, for example to Caribbean or the Sub-Saharan Africa), while Chinese academic mobility could be personally driven, institutionally organised (Language teachers in Confucius Institute, visiting scholars, and post-doc researchers, *etc.*) or policy determined.

1.3 The Important Position of the UK and China in the 'Global Market' for International Academics

The policies framed by the notion of the knowledge economy (Kenway *et al.*, 2006) have led most nations into an intensifying competition for high-calibre researchers (Kenway and Fahey, 2010). For example, the European Research Council's Green Paper, 'The European Research Area: New Perspectives' (CEC, 2007) stresses the crucial role transnational academic mobility played in the European Research Area and highlights the necessity for realising a single labour market for researchers:

> *A key challenge for Europe is to train, retain and attract more competent researchers. Moreover, the seamless mobility of researchers across institutions, sectors and countries is even more important than for other professions: it (transnational academic mobility) constitutes one of the most efficient vehicles for the transmission of knowledge. (CEC, 2007: 10).*

In Britain, launched by Prime Minister Tony Blair on 18 April 2006, the Prime Minister's Initiative for International Education (PMI2[1]) was developed in consultation with the education sector. Its aim is to bring more international students into the UK education system, in recognition of their importance in fostering international relations and bringing long-term political and economic benefits to the UK (British Council, 2008). As part of PMI2, a series of high-

---

[1] The PMI2 is a five-year project.

level dialogues took place in key regions around the world. Each dialogue focused on a specific area and brought together groups of policy-makers, senior managers and practitioners from the UK and overseas.

Apart from international students, the number of international academics in UK universities is increasing each year. Table 2 – 1 reveals that of the 194245 academic staff employed at UK HEIs in 2013/2014, nearly 30% were of non-UK nationality. International academics have under growth significantly, increasing by 2.5% from 2010 to 2012, and then 6% in the last two years (HESA, 2010; 2012; 2014). One reason for this fast-growing phenomenon is that the effect of the Research Excellence Framework (REF) on research-intensive higher education institutions seeking to improve their ratings by recruiting 'star' researchers from other countries (Kim and Locke, 2010). Another reason may be the shortage of UK domiciled post-doctoral students available to fill teaching posts in certain subjects, such as biological, physical and mathematical sciences, engineering and technology (Kenway and Fahey, 2010).

Table 2 – 1 Academic and non-academic staff by geographic region of nationality in 2013/2014

Region	Academic	Non-academic	Total
UK	137650	179310	316960
Other EU	29225	10570	39795
Non-EU	22140	7970	30105
Other Europe	2310	480	2790
Africa	1910	1635	3545
Asia	8335	2985	11320
Australasia	1800	640	2445
Middle East	1345	210	1555
North America	5675	1735	7410
South America	765	280	1045
Not known	5230	3685	8915
Total	194245	201535	395780

Source: Staff in Higher Education Institutions, HESA, 2013/2014.

It has been found that the most common region for the recruitment in the UK of all levels of international academic staff was the European Union (see Table 2 - 1). For professors and lecturers, the most common region was North America; for researchers, it was East Asia (HESA, 2013/2014). On the nation-state level, the main countries of origin of foreign academics working in the UK are Germany, the Republic of Ireland, the United States, China, Italy, France and Greece. Among them, China provides the largest single group of non-UK nationals among researchers, and this group constitutes approximately two-thirds of all Chinese staff in UK higher education institutions (UCEA, 2008). Besides this, with regard to the 49680 (HESA, 2013/2014) Chinese students in the UK, the UK is also well known as the largest 'importer of Chinese brains' in comparison with other European countries (OECD, 2012), meaning the UK has the largest pool of potential Chinese academics in Europe.

Internationalisation of higher education has not just brought in international academics to the UK, but also caused a considerable out-flow of UK academics. English-speaking countries, especially the US, are the most popular places to work and to build up cross-country academic networks for British academics, with EU countries close on their heels (Kim and Locke, 2010). However, Lehman (2015) points out that those countries' dominance has recently been gradually waning. New economic entities, such as BRIC countries (Brazil, Russia, India and China), are becoming the hotspots for Western expatriates. He also notes that well-educated British young professionals are taking emerging economies, like China, as an alternative potential job market to the UK, due to the more vigorous competition in the home labour market:

> *It is foreseeable that the numbers of young, professional migrants to Asian countries could increase. It is probable that in this current climate more people from the West will choose to leave home for career opportunities and work experience in Asia. The middle classes are more likely than ever*

before to pack up and leave their homes in the 'West ' for the lands of supposed opportunity in the 'East ' (p. 2).

China is not only one of the ' new destinations ' for British academic migrants, but also the most important source country for sending Chinese academic migrants overseas. When drawing a sketch of Chinese academic migrants' current trend of flow across borders, you can find that, China, being the so-called ' exporter of brains ', is one of the main sending countries of highly-skilled migrants (Giordano and Pagano, 2013). Since 1978, when China's reform began, the official number of overseas Chinese students and scholars has reached 1. 62 million (Wang, 2012). The number of Chinese applicants to US postgraduate education witnessed a 7-year continuous double-digit jump, making China the most important source of US overseas masters and Ph. D students (Cheung and Xu, 2015). The Chinese Academy of Sciences (CAS) also points out that about 87% of the Chinese science and engineering professionals migrated to the host country after their graduation (CAS, 2014).

Why is going abroad so popular among Chinese students? The shrinking job opportunities in the Chinese job market keep pumping undergraduate students into Chinese academia to continue their post-graduate study, making the already heated competition in postgraduate schools even more intense. The annual admission of doctoral degree research students in China has been rising at an average pace of 2000 per year, reaching a record-hitting 73100 by 2015. [1] The increasing level of competition and some existing structural problems in the Chinese scientific research system have further increased the scarcity of academic resources, meaning a postgraduate degree is less likely to guarantee its bearer a promising future. In this context, getting postgraduate education abroad has become increasingly popular among Chinese university graduates, as they believe

---

[1] Zhou Guangli, The Quality Investigation of the Ph. D Candidate Investigation in China [R], 2015: 8-9

the overseas experience can bring them a better future.

In this scenario, the outflow of Chinese domestic academics is far more than the inflow of foreign academics and Chinese academic returnees. For example, during the period of 2009—2011, China would have needed at least 700000 highly-skilled professionals, including academics, to balance the outflow and inflow of human capital (Giordano and Pagano, 2013). China, therefore, has to provide resettlement packages to encourage the return of foreign-trained academics and professionals in order to improve science and technology in China (Zweig, 2006).

1.4 A Comparison of Recent Trends in Talent Attraction Policy for Chinese Academics in China and the UK

Since the early 2010s, a widespread movement to attract talents has been promoted in China. In December 2008, the Central Coordination Panel Board of Highly-Qualified Human Resources[1], an affiliate directly linked to the General Office of the Communist Party of China (CPC) Central Committee, embarked on a Recruitment Programme of Highly-Qualified Overseas Talents (also known as the 'Thousand Talents Plan', thereafter called the 'Plan'). This aimed to introduce around 2000 world-leading scientists and experts to China within 5 to 10 years to boost China's research and innovation capability. This is a scheme of unprecedented scale of both involvement and devotion. The coordination panel board, which is chiefly comprised of the Organisation Department of the CPC and the Ministry of Human Resources and Social Security, is joined by another seventeen resourceful state-level ministries and commissions, including the Ministry of Foreign Affairs, the Ministry of Education, the Ministry of Science and Technology, the Ministry of Public Security, the National Development and Reform Commission, and the People's Bank of China, among others.

---

1. Know in Chinese as '中央人才工作协调小组'.

A youth version of the Thousand Talents Plan, which targeted a younger generation of scholars (35 as the age ceiling instead of 55), was announced in December 2010. The same authorities also put forward preferential policies to support lower-level overseas-educated returnees to set up their own business. ❶ Other central ministries also launched new plans or revised existing policies to encourage more high-quality talents to return. For example, in 2011, the Ministry of Education revised its Yangtze River Scholars Programme, seeking to contract around 200 professor-level scholars from Western academia. ❷Universities are also given more latitude to recruit scholars from abroad. The State Ocean Administration❸ announced plans to recruit, during the 12th Five-year Plan period (2011—2015), around 100 young scholars with Western university doctoral degrees. ❹

Local authorities also made considerable efforts to boost their research/innovation capabilities and their economy. All the four direct-controlled municipalities (Beijing, Chongqing, Shanghai and Tianjin) have put forward their version of 'Thousand Talents Plan', aiming at attracting Western-educated talents to contribute to their economic development. Among 28 provinces and autonomous regions, more than 20 have put attracting overseas talents as their goal for the next few years. Tens of thousands of posts are open to Chinese highly-skilled migrants, among which Zhejiang and Shandong provinces are planning to

❶ See official website of the Central People's Government of the People's Republic of China http://www.gov.cn/zwgk/2011-04/14/content_1843836.htm (14/April/2011).

❷ For the 2011 revised version of Yangtze River Scholar Program, see official website: http://www.changjiang.edu.cn/news/16/16-20070319-136.htm (25/June/2013)

❸ The State Ocean Administration is an administrative agency subordinate to the Ministry of Land and Resources, responsible for the supervision and management of territorial sea area and coastal environmental protection, protecting national maritime rights and organising scientific and technical research of its territorial waters.

❹ For recruiting plan of the State Ocean Administration, see: http://www.1000plan.org/qrjh/channel/312 (25/June/2013).

introduce a total number of 10000 returnee talents to stimulate local economic development. [1]

The nationwide implementation of the Thousand Talents Plan model has brought new trends in strategies to attract academic talents. These changes have made the pathway set by the Plan accessible to an increasing number of academics. Firstly, focus is extended from world-leading academics (usually in their 50s) to a younger generation of scholars, who are usually more eager for success, often more able to adapt to new circumstances, and of course, more cost-effective to Chinese authorities. Secondly, attention is stretched to relatively lower stratum of talents. Compared to their elite colleagues who already have a satisfactory position in world-renowned laboratories or research centres, they are less fixed on their career future and will therefore have higher mobility. Thirdly, as the recruitment of overseas talents was delegated to ministerial and provincial authorities, more mid-level programmes have been provided to accommodate these new generation of returnees. Lastly, in order to make the composition of imported intellectuals well balanced, many talent introducing programmes, especially those run by educational institutions, also began to benefit 'soft sciences' areas such as humanities and social sciences, which makes the route opened by the Plan also available for non-'hard science' academics. In summary, these new trends in talent introducing programmes following the Thousand Talents Programme have made returning to China an available choice to an increasing number of Chinese academics.

In contrast, recent adjustment in UK immigration policy rendered young postgraduate students' pursuit of long-term career in the UK increasingly difficult. In March 2008, the Highly Skilled Migrant Programme (HSMP) was

---

[1] For talents attraction plan of direct-controlled municipalities, provinces and autonomous regions, see: http://www.1000plan.org/qrjh/section/4 (25/June/2013).

replaced by a Tier 1 point-based immigration system. The new point-based visa system (which was in fact introduced as early as November 2006 under HSMP) shows a strong preference to young (under 28 years old), in full-time employment and well-paid (higher than UK average income) applicants, having a higher level of diploma does not make a considerable difference (30 points for a bachelor degree, 35 points for a master degree and 45 points for a doctoral degree). Moreover, the close of the Post Study Work (PSW) visa since April 2012 has made it ever harder for university graduates to settle for good in the UK. For those lucky ones who have already secured a place in UK universities and research institutes, they too have every reason to feel concerned. Due to the global economic crisis, science and research funding in the UK has experienced budget cuts since 2010. Such a heavy blow to the research sector of the UK forced many researchers, especially Chinese researchers, to have second thoughts about their future.

When comparing the recent trends of Chinese and British policy for talent, it is not difficult to find that the Chinese policy is not only wider in terms of reach (national and local), but also in age structure (See Table 2-2). Consequently, these new policies will affect individuals' choice of migration or return in different stages of their academic lives, and in the same way, consciously or unconsciously, realise the production and exchange of cultural capital across oceans. I will return to this point in Chapter Four with more empirical details.

Table 2-2 The key differences between Chinese and the UK policy for highly-skilled professionals

policy	China	UK
Key Requirements	Western degree; Title; Academic outcome	In full-time employment and well paid
Age Group	Professor under 55; Young academic-under 35	Graduates under 28

Continued

policy	China	UK
Accomplishment	Well formed and less well formed, but have international experience	Less well formed (comparing to professor), but professionals in short supply)
Policy Diversity	National and local policy/programs for talents.	National immigration policy for highly skills
Discipline	Science and engineering; social science	Science and engineering

1.5 International Branch Campuses in China as a Mobility Vehicle for British Academics

Transnational education is not a recent phenomenon and an increasing number of universities have set up their branch campus overseas as part of their internationalisation strategies. In 2014, the number of branch campuses increased to 202 around the world. Among them, 77 were launched by US institutions, and followed by 28 campuses set up by UK institutions and 18 by Australia universities (C-BERT, 2014). The UK has been promoting transnational education as part of its national strategy, with China as the main target country. In 2015, UK institutions have 12 branch campuses in China (MOE, 2015).

The primary aim of setting up international branch campuses (IBCs) in China is debatable.

The reasons for establishing IBCs, given demands for the provision of such university places from host countries, include generating revenue, creating international brand recognition, the appeal of 'soft power' through contacts with graduates and business in host countries and, more recently in the United Kingdom, the imposition of stricter home country visa regulations for international students (Salt and Wood, 2014: 85).

While, possibly from a different perspective, university authorities normally state several purely educational motivations, for example, non-profit, seeking balance, commitment to excellence. Fazackerley (2007) suggests that 'more negative speculation has inevitably been fed by a lack of readily available information about the exact nature of the deals and how they are performing, due to commercial confidentiality' (p. 3).

In the beginning, the UK educational providers were taking Sino-British partnership as a brave venture investment, because to some degree 'Britain remains unhelpfully squeamish about acknowledging difference within the system... overseas campuses are a leap in the dark' (Fazackerley, 2007: 52). Ian Gow, the founding provost of The University of Nottingham Ningbo, pointed out carefully that the risks of setting up overseas campus in China are very considerable. China might be a future threat by gaining more from the joint venture, if the UK educational providers are not well prepared for the unknown challenges of negotiating with the Chinese government and managing the pioneer model of an international university (Gow, 2007).

The current literature focuses more on oversight of IBCs and the growth of international education (Kinser and Lane, 2013a; 2013b) or the overall analysis of IBCs' management performance and leading issues (Lane, 2011; Lane and Kinser, 2011; Shams and Huisman, 2012). There are several articles which explore IBCs in particular countries, such as Malaysia (Lane, 2010) and Dubai (Lane, 2010), or at a regional scale in Africa (Lane and Kinser, 2013), and Latin America (Lane, 2013). But, there has inevitably been little research upon staffing issues until recently. Fielden and Gillard (2010) directly state there are problems in relation to secondments of academic staff from home to the host countries. More specifically, Salt and Wood (2014: 84) suggest that the current way of recruiting staff needs to be changed, as the 'mobility portfolios based simply on ad hoc secondments and business travel, international staff recruitment, and electronic communications will not sustain the quality-driven business model being adopted by UK universities'. Moreover, they consider IBCs as institutions that are close to consultancy sectors in commercial multinational enterprises (MNEs), because for both, the product is conceptual knowledge rather than concrete goods. So, the management of IBCs can learn from MNEs that already have mature international strategies to move and manage expert staff effectively. They suggest that international recruitment used by MNEs may potentially be the future direction of IBCs' staffing strategy. However, the activities of IBCs in China are, potentially, different from those of an MNE. In China, an IBC's image is highly related to the authenticity of British education and Chinese students/parents are normally reluctant to take lectures delivered by 'Asian faces' in an IBC—this is not what they pay higher money for. The Chinese authorities also require high proportions of non-local staff in IBCs, especially for teaching positions (Fazackerley, 2007). Thus, international recruitment cannot be truly 'international', the recruitment is still mainly focused on 'White' transnational academics. Moreover, IBCs generally receive global staff dispatched from the 'home' institution; there is little need to rely heavily on international recruitment in the host country (Fielden and Gillard, 2011). The arguments around this issue will be discussed further in Chapter Four.

Salt and Wood (2014) also do not consider the relationship between academics' experience and the potential changes of recruiting policies (they only interview managers), as indeed, voices need to be heard from both sides of managers and academics. So, the main concern in Chapter Four is located in the gap between the 'rhetoric' images created by official publicity and the real everyday challenges confronting British academics in 'reality' (which can alter their decisions of movement), which seems largely to have escaped attention from most of the IBC literature. By examining this issue, we can gain an in-depth understanding of the difficulties confronted by transnational academics, and this can be one of the 'grounded instructions' for explaining British academic migrants' motivations in their transnational process.

2 Transnationalism, Academic Mobility and Practices

As a direct outcome of globalisation, transnationalism has reached a certain intensity in the past two decades (Appadurai 1990, 1996; Glick Schiller *et al.*, 1992; Guarnizo and Smith, 1999). The concept of transnationalism provides a useful framework, it brings the strnctare of the context within which transnational academic mobility operates into focus. Glick Schiller *et al.* (1992) use the term 'transnationalism' to describe the 'emergence of a social process in which migrants establish social fields that cross geographical, cultural and political borders' (p. 1). The central element of transnationalism is the linkage and involvements between their country of origin (home country) and the countries of settlement (host country) (Glick Schiller *et al.*, 1992). 'Transnationality', for Aihwa Ong (1993), includes the complexity of cultural interconnections, networks and trans-border movements. Building on the definition of transnationalism, Kongeter and Smith (2015) suggest that migration has its own complexity that cannot just be related to national polices or conceptualised in the ideal of 'assimilation, integration or multiculturalism'. Correspondingly, Kongeter and Smith's (2015) work stresses the impact of transnational agency on 'power relations, cultural constructions, economic interactions and social organisations' (Guarnizao and Smith, 1999: 5) should be emphasised more in transnationalism. This study echoes their suggestion to advance a transnational approach, one that concentrates on the dynamics and implications of cross-border academic practices of individuals and groups.

It is noticeable that the more recent resurgence of interest in the international mobility of the highly skilled has been accompanied by a body of research that draws from studies of globalisation and transnationalism (Pherali, 2011). As discussed in the previous section, the process of internationalisation of higher education has resulted in the increased mobility of academic migrants across national borders, which has caught scholars' attention (Kim and Locke, 2010; Poole and Ewan, 2010). The connections between highly-skilled migration and transnationalism have therefore been explored more specifically within the theme of academic mobility and transnational education (see Hoffman, 2009; Kim and Locke, 2010). My study falls into this category. The transnational movement of academics, which has been closely observed in my study, can be attributed to both the educational expansion of Western universities internationally (British academic mobility) and the 'magnetic' nature of elite universities that attract international staff to enhance their academic strengths (Chinese academic mobility) (Bennion and Locke, 2010).

In this section, the review focuses more on the analyses of distinction between different academic cultures and academic migrants' offshore challenges in the context of transnationalism. After a brief review of transnationalism and academic mobility, I go on to address the major challenges that are faced by international academic migrants. I then narrow this down to the academic culture 'distinctions' between Chinese and British academia and challenges for Chinese academic migrants that have been reported in existing literature. The following part explains the different pedagogic cultures, which are closely connected to one of the main challenging practices of academic migrants-teaching. The last part is about academic accumulation, which indicates how academic migrants from different educational fields cope with the current transnational reality.

2.1 Connecting Transnationalism with Academic Mobility

Most of the articles related to transnationalism and international academic mobility come from the field of education (Fahey and Kenway, 2010). There have been no full-scale (or in-depth) investigations specifically of the transnational mobility of university academics. Apart from the foreign senior academic leaders who receive media attention, little is known about international academics' lived experiences (Kim and Locke, 2010). Fahey and Keway (2010) suggest that the existing studies can be classified into epistemological, ontological or ethical paradigms.

In epistemological terms, the existing articles offer and invite further consideration of the links between knowledge and academic mobility. For example, Terri Kim (2010) takes UK examples as the main case study and argues that academic mobility around the world is intensifying. She employs a concept of 'transnational identity capital' to discuss the position of transnational mobile academic intellectuals as 'strangers', as inspired by Simmel's sociology of space. To illustrate this concept, Kim develops a three-part typology of mobile academics according to their self-identification: 'academic intellectual', 'academic expert' and 'manager academic'. She then concentrates on the transnational 'academic intellectual' and explores the relations of mobile academics and their knowledge.

In ontological terms, current studies draw attention to what it means to be a mobile academic and offer insights into the lives of these individuals and to the ways in which mobile academics as a group are stratified internally. For example, Leemann's (2010) study is focused on the individual and institutional factors that affect transnational academic mobility in the postdoctoral period. She identifies four different mobility patterns based on four different constellations of academic entrepreneurs[1]. In so doing, she shows that a stratifying process is involved in the geographic mobility of academic career paths. It means that academic mobility is a complex notion that can be affected by gender, partnership, dual-career

[1] (1) Flexible academic entrepreneurs 'without obstacles to mobility set by domestic partnership and family'. (2) Flexible academic entrepreneurs who 'put all their eggs in one basket'. (3) Dual-career academic entrepreneurship as 'the impossible thing'. (4) Inflexible academic entrepreneurs, 'not without domestic partnership and family' (Leemann, 2010: 620).

constellations, social class, and academic integration. In a theoretical sense, those elements can largely decide the equality or inequality in the accumulation of 'transnational social capital' (which refers to the social capital that accumulated from transnational mobility) (p. 616), which is relevant for establishing status in academia through transnational mobility.

In terms of ethical considerations, research findings suggest the scholars need to be more conscious and critical of both the underlying assumptions of academic mobility policies and the global context that is driving such policies and contemporary universities themselves (Fahey and Kenway, 2010). The negative implications and inadequacies of the 'brain drain/gain' (Robertson, 2006) are more fully realised in the transnational era, as there are so many problems which are manifested globally as well as regionally and cannot be addressed within the restricted logics of 'national interest'. Singer and Gregg's (2004) discussion of the nation as a global entity, with reference to Australia, is particularly critical of narrow notions of the national interest, and urges Australia to 'take a broader and long term view' that fosters 'an ethical framework for international relations and global cooperation' (p. 43). And, this could be one way in which any diasporic sensibilities they feel might be mobilised without resorting to a strict sense of nationalism (Fahey and Kenway, 2010). 'Transnationalisation', particularly in respect of higher education, has taken on a new urgency, such that it is now frequently prioritised in the strategic plans and policy agendas of higher education institutions (Marginson 2008), although this is driven more by economic necessity than ethical reasons.

2.2 Academic Acculturation: Minimising the Distinctions between Transnational Academics

The concept of academic acculturation is understood as the process of students' adaptation to a new academic environment in the host country and their adjustment and integration in relation to local academic cultures (see: Elliot *et* al. , 2015). However, few studies have attempted to involve the opinions of academics (Robson and Turner 2007) and the notion of academic acculturation need to be redefined when international academics are being involved.

Jiang *et al.* (2010: 157) define 'academic acculturation' as: 'The processes by which one becomes a part of a group (for example, institution, department, *etc.*) and integrates with its members, while possibly influencing the host group with one's own life experience and academic expertise, with regard to academic practice such as teaching, research, administration, pastoral duties, supervision and management'. This definition focuses on the scope of the group rather than culture in general. Nevertheless, group and culture are not separate domains, but are interlinked with each other through life experience and academic expertise (Jiang *et al.* , 2010). By using the concept of academic acculturation, Jiang *et al.* study the experiences of Chinese academic staff in their process of academic acculturation, and explore how academic acculturation in UK higher education can be facilitated.

It has been pointed out by many researchers that becoming part of an academic culture for any new member of staff is a process of transition (*e. g.* Barkhuizen, 2002; Trowler and Knight, 2000; Jawitz, 2007). Whether this process is experienced differently by particular groups of staff is however unclear. Furthermore, the concept of academic culture is too vague and might be interpreted differently in various contexts. For instance, the academic culture differs across countries and in different educational bodies in the same country. In this sense, it could be argued in this research that academic acculturation is very different to traditional understandings of acculturation, as the host group is very diverse.

At the macro-level, it is important to examine whether academic acculturation is a process of one-way change (from guest to host culture) or two-way change (both guest and host culture). Among Jiang *et al.*'s interviewees, few of them felt that they had changed the host group, instead, they described making a 'contribution' or adding 'diversity' to the host group. However, Jiang *et al.*'s research is based on 8 interviewees from two research intensive UK universities. The research findings might be different in other UK universities, and it is possible that their influences on the host culture take time to appear since 'acculturation may be delayed'. So, it has been suggested that the colleagues and/or students of international academic staff would have valuable observations and insights to add (Jiang *et al.*, 2010), in order to fully understand any culture impact of international academic staff on the host academic culture.

At the micro-level, much more attention should be paid to disciplinary culture, when academic acculturation is considered. It has been pointed out in the existing literature that the main unifying concept amongst members of the multicultural 'host group' was their disciplinary identity (Becher and Trowler 2001). It is evident that disciplinary identity could smooth the process of academic acculturation. However, it could be argued that differences in academic practice between the UK and China in disciplines, such as engineering or science are much smaller than in the disciplines of social science. Therefore, it seems that disciplinary cultures and identities should be clearly addressed in any definition of academic acculturation (Jiang *et al.*, 2010).

The existing studies on academic acculturation showed that the level of proficiency in English language is often considered as a major criterion in assessing immigrants' acculturation (Zane and Mak, 2002), and language competence is central in the process of acculturation (Sercu, 2004). However, Jiang *et al.* (2010) argued that there were a variety of other factors influencing international academic staff members' acculturation, and the notion that language was central could be questioned. It could also be found that, as Hsieh (2011) did, that language abilities, socialisation patterns and ideas of pedagogy were considered the main influencing factors of academic acculturation. So, in my research, I argue that academic acculturation in transnational education is also a continually changing and creative process for individual academics, which can improve transnational teaching, learning and administration.

2.3 Academic Culture Differences and the Challenges Faced by Transnational Academics

Most international academics could be assumed to face many challenges in the new educational environment as they are unlikely to be familiar with the 'host' academic practice, teaching styles and most of all the students they will be teaching, including their academic and social background. A plethora of literature analysing the issues of teaching and research abroad mainly deals with potential challenges encountered by academics from English-speaking countries who are assigned offshore teaching projects (Garson, 2005; Poole and Ewan, 2010). A number of researchers have reported that some migrant teachers find their experience demanding, lonely and difficult (Mowbray, 2001; Ochs, 2003). De Villiers (2007) conducted a case study of South African teachers to the UK, and he found that difficult overseas experience caused them to lose all interest in teaching. Asmal's (2004) research also indicates that many South Africans who already have a teaching job in the UK choose to leave the teaching profession on their return. The academic difficulties they face include: lack of induction programmes (Mulvaney, 2005); teaching without Qualified Teacher Status (QTS) (De Villiers, 2004; Mowbray, 2001; Mulvaney, 2005) and language issues (Ochs, 2003). However, De Villiers (2007) also claims that most of the South African teachers experience no discrimination in the UK, have a good relationship with their colleagues, have no problems in teaching multiracial classes, and the teaching experience in England improved their teaching ability.

While, in terms of Chinese academics in the UK, Luxon and Peelo's (2009) study on the experience of non-UK staff in a British university observed that international academic staff thought the language barrier appeared to be a problem not only in terms of daily communication and relationships, but also one that influenced their choice of teaching style. Similarly, Jiang *et al.* (2010) identified three main categories of challenges faced by Chinese academic staff in the UK higher education institutions: (1) different academic practices in the UK and China; (2) disciplinary identities, *i. e.* the different ways of doing the disciplines in different countries; and (3) language obstacles and cultural affiliation. Building on the shoulders of Jiang *et al.* (2010), Hsieh's (2011) study investigated the challenges of ethnic Chinese academic staff in the UK to discuss how UK higher education institutions can provide better support to meet their needs in terms of language, relationships and culture.

2.3.1 Perception of Academic Practices in Different Cultures

1. Teaching and research

In terms of teaching and research, different countries/institutions have different requirements and academics have various responsibilities in their home educational systems. In the UK, for example, academics often take both teaching and research as their own duty; however, in South Africa, lecturers consider teaching and research as dichotomous part of their academic life, they believe that the teaching role and research role should be undertaken separately (Lubben, 2009). Similarly, as Jiang *et al.* (2010) pointed out, it is possible for Chinese university staff to focus more on teaching than on research; while in the UK, academics often have to keep up with research all the time, and this lifestyle may cause stress or illness (Chalmers, 1998).

However, the different degrees of importance on teaching and research for academics are, again, not totally dependent on the countries, but also specified by institutions. It could be argued that not all Chinese universities focus more on teaching than on research, because academics in China still have the pressure to publish a certain number of works for promotion. The promotion criteria in China make it impossible for academics to be promoted if they only focus on teaching. This is perhaps due to the rapid changes now occurring in China as a result of an emerging global standard of research practices (Swales, 2004) and by which Western practices may be influencing those in China. Moreover, some research led by institutions, academics, especially professors, only focus on research without doing any teaching activities.

In terms of supervision practice, Jiang *et al.* (2010) pointed out that supervision practice in the UK and China differed in Ph. D students' admission and management. Universities in the UK are concerned with the individual qualities of Ph. D students rather than seeking numbers. While in China, one supervisor will perhaps supervise 10 or 20 students at the same time, because only professors have the right to supervise Ph. D students in China. This is in contrast to the UK where junior academic staff are able to supervise research students who could greatly increase their research output.

2. Language issues

In terms of the main obstacle facing international academics, some studies suggest that the teaching role was perceived to require a more advanced level of English than some other academic roles. Jiang *et al.* (2010), for example, their study on Chinese academics in two UK universities indicates that the process of academic acculturation could be hindered due to language obstacles that initially affected their personal communication with colleagues/students. Similarly, in Luxon and Peelo's (2009) study, Chinese lecturers indicated that they usually needed to spend more time to prepare course materials than native English speakers and usually felt exhausted after concentrating on speaking English for more than 20 to 25 minutes. Hsieh (2011), however, expresses the view that language was not a serious issue while teaching for most Chinese academic staff. Although participants in her study thought it was very difficult to achieve near native-speaker level, their English ability was sufficient to deliver course content clearly. It is could be argued that the English ability differs according to different groups of Chinese academic staff. For instance, a Chinese academic who has spent more than 20 years in English-speaking countries may have less difficulty in teaching comparing to those 'newcomers'.

It seems that language issues can hide more profound and yet interlinked cultural difficulties. These include behaviours, attitudes, values and beliefs, of which discipline is one sub-set (Jiang *et al*, 2010). It is noticeable that most participants in Hsieh's (2011) study considered that a lack of background knowledge with regard to the cultural connotations in English was the main obstacle in communication and teaching. It has been confirmed that barriers are likely to occur as a result of having difficulty in interpreting colloquial language and cultural connotations in different cultures (Cortazzi, Jin, and Zhiru 2009; Edwards and Ran 2009).

3. Relationship with colleagues and students

Studies by Jiang *et al.* (2010) and Luxon and Peelo (2009) indicated that Chinese academic staff in the UK believed that their social life could be kept separate from their academic life. Their study also suggested that Chinese academic staff restricted their social circle to other Chinese people due to having difficulties making friends with British people, which is in direct contrast to the research results of the study conducted by Hsieh (2011). Unlike the negative intercultural experience described by other researchers, the participants in Hsieh's study generally had a good relationship with colleagues. In her study, the Chinese academic staff (especially those who are in their 40s and beyond) were found to purposely avoid establishing close relationships with other Chinese academic staff in their workplace. In addition, establishing a good rapport with higher-status people sometimes becomes more important than one's professional knowledge and competence. These factors prevent them from forming close relationships with Chinese colleagues at work (Hsieh 2011).

Some of Jiang *et al.* 's interviewees also mentioned the differing hierarchical structures with regards to research between academic staff in the UK and their Chinese counterparts. The relationship between colleagues was considered more equal in the UK, whereas it was more complex and hierarchical in China (Jiang *et al*, 2010; Hsieh, 2011). Linked to this, Ouyang's (2006) study has described the hierarchical relationship among academic staff in China by referring to the concept of *danwei*, which is similar to the Western concept of a 'community of practice'. In a *danwei*, academic staff were assigned to different groups based on their subject area, and that the relationship in a *danwei* is hierarchical rather than offering an equal basis relationship as in the West.

It is interesting that the research findings on a similar topic by two researchers lead in totally different directions. There are some points that need to be explored in the following empirical chapters: First, both of these studies have only 8 participants and they are all from science and engineering disciplines. The result may be one-sided, Chinese academic staff from other disciplines, such as social science and art, also come under consideration in my study. The more detailed information about the selection would be provided in Chapter Three. Second, Jiang *et al.* (2010) and Luxon and Peelo's (2009) studies also point out that Chinese academic staff restrict their social circle to other Chinese people as they have difficulty in making friends with British people. I argue that this kind of relationship may be possible in the context of a conventional Chinatown or ethnic enclave model, but it seems impossible for Chinese academic staff who live in a multicultural environment. More evidence is provided to support this argument in the empirical sections. Third, the phenomenon of Chinese academic staff avoiding other Chinese colleagues in their workplace described in Hsieh's study has not been described in other studies. It is unclear if this is a special case, or if it can be applied to other Chinese academic staff in the UK. It is important to investigate if Chinese academic staff in my study also demonstrate this avoidance phenomenon.

2.3.2 Distinctive Teaching Cultures

According to the existing literature (*e.g.* Jin and Cortazzi, 2006; Shaw *et al.* 2007), the basic distinction between China and the UK in teaching is that teachers provide detailed knowledge to students in China, whereas students are encouraged to research topics by themselves in the UK. In terms of language for teaching, in contrast to the analytic and deductive language used in the Western educational system, the explicit and inductive approaches are highly recommended by Confucian culture (Hsieh, 2011). Some Chinese learners, however, may interpret the British tendency to use concepts without explanation, assuming the students already understand them, as being too ambiguous (Gu, 2005).

Kelly *et al.* (1999: 56) were 'convinced that conceptions of effective teaching are deeply rooted in specific cultural values and social norms' as a result of their findings. There are some distinctions between the two groups in terms of teaching qualities. On one hand, in the Chinese group, teachers were more focused on students' need and interest, and they were willing to adjust their teaching content or teaching method according to students' feedback. The Western group, on the other hand, was much more likely to guide students via assignment making, and possibly provide teaching assistant jobs or chances for publication to help them with their further academic career. Additionally, Western academics took the ideal of critically challenging and mentally provoking students as a crucial teaching tool. Last but not least, in terms of being 'professional', Chinese academics were strict and demanding, but helpful and patient both inside and outside the classroom, while Western academics tended to be more aware of the boundaries of the classroom or working hours and not being too close to their students.

Very often the understanding of teaching styles in different cultures has been marred by stereotypical views of being didactic, stressing imitation and teacher-centred in the Confucian Heritage Culture, and more communicative, creative and student-centred in Western countries (Kember, 1997; Jin and Cortazzi, 2006; Shaw *et al.*, 2007; Jiang *et al.*, 2010). Kember's (1997) work on university academics' concept of teaching is a foundation stone in terms of university teaching styles. Based on interviews with faculty members from seven countries, the author synthesised teaching conceptions under two broad orientations characterised as 'teacher-centred/content-oriented' and 'student-centred/learning-oriented'. The 'teacher-centred' approach included transmitting structured knowledge and imparting information, while a 'student-centred' approach involved facilitating understanding and encouraging conceptual change or intellectual development. Student-teacher integration/apprenticeship acted as a bridge that connects these two broad orientations.

However, it could be argued that these two orientations of teaching conceptions could be equally important in the academic practice, and they may be parallel emphases instead of opposites (Brown *et al.*, 2009). Many studies suggest that the quality of teaching is based on the capability to engage students in conceptual understanding, analytical thinking and critical reasoning rather than conducting 'teacher-centred' or 'student-centred' teaching. For example, Biggs (1996) challenges the crude stereotype by demonstrating that imitation is only the first stage of the total teaching process rather than the only stage (in art and music teaching) in China. In fact, Western teaching considers exploring as an early stage of developing skills, while Chinese believe in skill development before the process of creation, where memorising may be considered as a beginning stage in the whole educational process rather than an end in itself.

Stigler and Stevenson (1991) further pointed out that the Western stereotype of the Asian teacher as a total authoritarian and a knowledge dispenser was one-sided. They not only expect their students to memorise but also to challenge existing knowledge. Moreover, they found out that the teacher also tries to apply student-centred teaching as an innovative teaching style in China, and Japan. Likewise O'Connor (1991) claimed in his descriptive analysis of Chinese teachers' thought processes that Chinese teachers are more student-centred and are always taking the demands of their students seriously. They appear to spend a good deal of time communicating with their students inside and outside the classroom.

Nevertheless, it is argued that teaching and learning in Confucian Heritage Culture[1] is not as ineffective as Western observers previously assumed. In fact, the student-centred approach is already mentioned in an old Chinese proverb: 'The master teaches the trade, but the apprentice's skill is self-made' (师父领进门，修行在个人). Similarly, there is another Confucius saying: 'To teach students according to their aptitude' (因材施教). The proverbs demonstrate that, even in Confucian Culture, teachers are expected to use a pedagogy that not only provides solid subject knowledge but also develops students' interests and talents. Contrary to Western stereotypes of Asian teachers as harsh authoritarian figures, most Asian teachers, especially the academics in university, are highly student-centred, always ready to help and guide their students, and carefully orchestrating the learning experience of all students. They are always trying to be 'a scholarly mentor and a beneficial friend' (良师益友).

So, the key point maybe lies in 'how to make transnational teaching more effective' rather than applying stereotyped pedagogies to certain groups of students. Pratt *et al.*'s (1999) study used a survey to identify conceptions of 'effective teaching' in Hong Kong universities and to explore teaching goals of

[1] Confucian Heritage Culture (CHC) such countries as China, Vietnam, Singapore, Korea and Japan are considered countries with Confucian heritage culture (Phuong-Mai *et al.* 2005).

Western and Chinese teachers. The participants were from three groups including: Hong Kong Chinese university students, Hong Kong Chinese and Western expatriate university teachers. The survey conducted in Hong Kong SAR. found out that there are many Western academics from countries like the US, Britain, New Zealand and Australia, who were apparently experienced and successful teachers in their home countries, but expressed feelings of frustration that they were unable to give an effective lecture to their Chinese students by using their own teaching style. In the survey, the majority of teachers believed that knowledge, skills, critical thinking and problem solving are the four most important elements in academic development. These points are similar to the opinions held by the Hong Kong academics in Kember and Gow's (1993) interview study. Furthermore, they all emphasised the importance of lecture preparation and presentation skills, followed by guiding students in their learning.

2.3.3 The Ideal of 'Excellent Teaching'

The concept of the very best teaching varies in different cultures. Jin and Cortazzi (1998) discovered that a good teacher in British society, from the perspective of students, is the one who is able to arouse students' interest, explain knowledge structurally and clearly, use effective instructions and organise activities. However, the image of a good teacher in China is one who has deep and universal knowledge, is able to answer questions, provide moral guidance and act as a mentor (Gao and Watkins, 2002; Watkins and Biggs, 2001).

Table 2-3 shows the differences in the expectations of a 'good teacher' in China and the UK (Cortazzi, Jin and Zhiru, 2009). According to the table, both Chinese and British students in two British universities expect a teacher to be a responsible person, caring and helpful, friendly, patient, able to arouse students' interest, able to help students study independently, explain clearly, and use effective methods. However, there are some differences between the two. Chinese students expect a teacher to have deep knowledge, to be warm-hearted and understanding, to offer a good moral example, and to be humorous. Yet those values are not ranked in the first 12 from the point of view of British students. British students expect a teacher to be sympathetic, lively, to be able to discipline students, and to be able to organise a variety of activities.

Table 2 – 3 Characteristics of 'good teachers' rated by Chinese and British university students (Cortazzi, Jin and Zhiru, 2009: 118)

Rank	In China, a good teacher...	In the UK, a good teacher...
1	has deep knowledge	arouses students' interest
2	uses effective methods	explains clearly
3	is a responsible person	uses effective methods
4	arouses students' interest	is patient
5	is friendly	helps students to study independently
6	is warm-hearted, understanding	is caring and helpful
7	helps students to study independently	is a responsible person
8	is patient	is sympathetic
9	explains clearly	is lively
10	offers a good moral example	organises a variety of activities
11	is humorous	controls student discipline
12	is caring and helpful	is friendly

In sum, the Western literature has identified the following main categories of excellent teaching: pedagogical strategies and skills (Zehm and Kottler, 2005), personal and professional characteristics (HayMcBer, 2000), subject and pedagogical knowledge (Kottler and Zehm, 2000), classroom climate, behaviour management and student-teacher relationships (Witcher *et al.*, 2001), professionalism (Onwuegbuzie, Witcher, and James, 2002). In addition, Watkins and Zhang's (2006) study points out that being a moral guide or caring about a student's personal life is an important aspect of teaching for good teachers across all school levels in Hong Kong SAR. and Mainland China.

2.3.4 The Role of Institutional Support

It is also important to recognise the fact that the problems international academics face cannot be solved without a mature institutional support system. In Chinese universities, for example, a Foreign Affairs office has been set up particularly to help non-Chinese academics to settle in, such as finding accommodation, arranging finance and so on (Ouyang, 2004). Some universities in the UK provide useful information through university official websites in order to help international academics both pre and post-arrival. Moreover, Pherali (2012) suggests that institutions could deal with the problems of cultural disconnection strategically in a number of ways. Firstly, a mandatory induction programme focused on the UK educational system can be an effective way to let migrant academics have a general ideal of the new environment and get ready for the further challenges at the beginning stage. Secondly, international academics, by getting the HE teaching qualification (*e. g.* Postgraduate Certificate in Learning and Teaching in Higher Education), which is increasingly becoming a requirement for HE teachers, can know more about social and cultural aspects of the UK HE system, and at the same time, understand their teaching/researching role much better. Thirdly, the standard support system should be improved by an annual appraisal process; only in this way can the system avoid the common problems of international academics.

3 Conceptual Tools—Connecting Pierre Bourdieu's Theory of Practice, the Notion of Place, and Transitional Academic Migration

3.1 Bourdieu's Theory of Practice and Academic Migration

Existing studies have identified that Bourdieu's theory can indeed provide provocative insights into the concerns of mobility. For example, Pherali (2012) noted that Bourdieu's notion of field and forms of capital are relevant in explaining 'disconnections between agents' (international academics) embodied dispositions and their new professional setting in the receiving country (p. 316). Oliver and O' Reilly (2010), in their research on Bourdieusian analysis of class and migration, found Bourdieu's concept of field, capital, the game, habitus, and distinction helpful in attempting to understand the (re) production of class in the self-making migration project of British migrants in Spain. More specifically, as Peay *et al.* (2009) point out, Bourdieu's work showed some evidence of habitus transforming or reinventing itself when the agent encounters an unfamiliar social field, which points directly to the possibility of habitus reinvention for migrants (Oliver and O' Reilly, 2010).

Here, it needs to be acknowledged that a number of migration scholars built up the connections between social capital, cultural capital and mobility before the engagement with Bourdieu's work. For example, Taylor (1986) observed that kinship, friendship, and local origin are the main elements that help migrants to solve problems in the new destination. Apart from the social network of academic migrants, Massey and his colleagues pointed out in their institutional theory that an institution can also facilitate the legal/illegal mobility of migrants (Massey *et al.*, 1993). Later, a comprehensive sociological theory on international migration was established (Portes, 1996; Pries, 1999; Faist, 2000). The theory highlights the cross-border links between migrants and their friends and family members. Faist's understanding of social capital specifies that 'those resources that help people or groups to achieve their goals in ties and the assets inherent in patterned social and symbolic ties that allow actors to cooperate in networks and organizations, serving as a mechanism to integrate groups and symbolic communities' (2000: 102). Alejandro Portes was key in developing the concept of transnationalism and transnational social fields in the field of sociology and then extended it to other disciplines, including geography (Portes, 1996, 1998, 1999, 2006, 2008; Portes and Zhou, 1999). By focusing on the migrants in the US, Portes and his colleges addressed the fact that those who possess higher levels of social capital are more inclined to make transnational ties than those who accumulated less social capital (Portes, Guarinzo, and Landlot, 1999). Putnam's theorizing of social capital has been very influential in the field too, but has been critiqued for paying insufficient attention to qualitative, temporal and spatial differentiations experienced by migrants (Ryan *et al.*, 2008). In recent years, there has been a growing concern in the topics of the social support, innovation, and models of behaviour in relation to social networks between nations and the conversion/accumulation of transnational social capital (Levitt and Lamba-Nieves, 2011; Krzyzowski, 2013).

Generally speaking, being able to move geographically and socially is regarded as a capacity that helps agents to gain capital in modern societies (Kaufmann *et al.*, 2004). Brown (1995) and Noble and Davies (2009) have shown that cultural capital in educational systems inevitably becomes a key factor in making social inclusion and exclusion. Murphy-Lejeune (2002) suggests that through spatial mobility, students acquired a crucial subset of human capital from overseas universities. Those international experiences of education may later translate into their future success in the 'home' labour market, and contributes to the reproduction of social privileges (Ong, 1999; Brooks and Waters, 2009; Findley and King, 2010) with their cosmopolitan identities (Beck, 2004).

In this section, I shall begin by sketching the notion of Bourdieu's 'field', acknowledging its weaknesses and limitations, and critically analysing the degree to which the notion of 'field' is applicable to transnational higher education. By briefly discussing the different forms of capital, I will then argue that each of these has an important contribution to the study of academic migration. In the third part, I will go on talking about one of Bourdieu's key concepts: habitus. Through an emphasis on its strengths and a number of limitations, I will explore habitus as a tool for my own research. Then, I will discuss the possibility of connecting the notion of habitus with 'place'. I conclude by suggesting that recent advances in Bourdieu's concepts (such as field, capital and habitus) may be generalisable and that this gives us the possibility of joining the analytic insights to a more grounded line of research in international academic migration studies.

3.1.1 Field

For Bourdieu, the conception of field is not understood as a field enclosed by a fence, nor in an American sense of domain, but rather as a partially autonomous 'field of forces' and a dynamic area of struggle for positions within it. These struggles are seen to transform or conserve the field of forces (Bourdieu, 1983: 312). Fields thus identify areas of struggle over the course of Bourdieu's work: at some times the notion refers to an overall social field together with the related elements of 'capital' and 'habitus' in order to explain the social structure and practice; moreover, field in his work also means a set of relatively independent but interlocking spheres in social space, such as the field of the French academic world, the field of literature, the field of photography and so forth.

A good example of Bourdieu's notion of field in his own work is his analysis of the French higher educational system, which he considered as a separate field. In his 1988 book *Homo Academicus*, Bourdieu focuses on the field of French academic life, analysing the system of higher education in France and exploring the strategies and struggles for position that take place within it. He wants to show that the French educational system is one of the fundamental agencies for the maintenance of the social order:

> *The educational system, an institutionalised classifier which is itself an objectified system of classification reproducing the hierarchies of the social world in a transformed form... The 'culture' which an educational qualification is presumed to guarantee is one of the basic components in the dominant definition of the accomplished man [sic], so that privation is perceived as an intrinsic handicap, diminishing a person's identity and human dignity, condemning him [sic] to silence in all official situations,*

when he [sic] has to 'appear in public', presents himself [sic] before others, with his [sic] body, his [sic] manners and his [sic] language (Bourdieu, 1988: 387).

As mentioned above, Bourdieu's notion of field appears to be applicable to many kinds of social space, and indeed in his own work he used it in various situations. In my study, I link Bourdieu's Franco-centric empirical scope into a larger transnational academic field, namely Chinese and British academia. By doing so, I consider Bourdieu's notion of field as a universally valuable, but not universally accessible concept. There are two tasks in front of this study: first, and the most important is to regard his work as a method to understand empirical data instead of a completed theoretical edifice; second, to link the notion of fields with transnational education (Harker, 1990). Bourdieu's work specific to the French educational system cannot be applied directly to my empirical requirements. Rather it is his underlying concepts that are valuable as a supplemental tool to interpret the data. In this study then, the Sino-British educational system is regarded as a single global entity, which is considered as a transnational field.

In times of internationalisation of higher education, the question of the relationship between fields becomes particularly sharply focused. In Rajani Naidoo's (2001) work about struggle in the South African university field, he pointed out a limitation in Bourdieu's work: its under-theorisation of the relationship between fields. Bourdieu does not sort out a conceptual apparatus or analytic strategy to explicate the detailed working relationships between fields. Because not all fields are isolated imaginary islands, the specific fields sometimes will not function autonomously in terms of their own particular habituses and capital. For example, in terms of Anglo-Chinese university joint ventures in China, Ewan Dow (2010) pointed out that many Anglo-Chinese university collaborations (joint ventures) to date have seriously underestimated the Chinese academic system, the Chinese university setting and Chinese national governmental steering as part of the process of 'globalisation'. That means Bourdieu's theory of field becomes problematic when the relationship of the political field, the field of Westernised university educational system and the field of Chinese educational system all join together. To address this, I ask how the Chinese local academic system and Chinese governmental steering impact upon the British university's branch campus, specifically when considering the movement and grounded experiences of British academics in 'the internationalisation of (a) Western educational system' (Pherali, 2012).

Bourdieu's (1984) notion of field explicates a distinctive cultural setting (university) created by the 'agents' (local academics and administrators) and their 'social positions' (class, educational backgrounds, gender, and race). In the case of my study, both Chinese/British administrators and academics create the offshore university 'setting'. I would not conceive the Sino-British academic field as a fixed 'distinctive cultural setting' that exists objectively (as Chinese academia for example), but as a global entity that is created by the changing dynamic of 'agents' (administrators, academics), and influenced by local, national and international forces. The transnational field is in a state of 'flux', rather than 'fix'. Thus, this research offers insights into the intensifying linkages between Chinese academia and British academia, and the role of the Sino-British transnational educational field in producing academic mobility and influencing academic migrants' everyday practice.

3.1.2 Capital

Bourdieu's work is characterised as having emerged from modern Marxism, but he also sets out to make two breaks with it. First, he enlarged the economic field in Marxism to the general social field, and redefined the concept of 'capital' to 'different forms of capital'. Second, he also tried to break with the materialism of Marxism, and pointed out that we should not ignore the symbolic struggles within the social world. Building upon Marx's concept, Bourdieu defines capital broadly as 'accumulated, human labour' that can potentially produce different forms of profits (1986: 241). For Bourdieu, the term is extended 'to all the goods, materials and symbolic, without distinction, that present themselves as rare and worthy of being sought after in a particular social formation' (Bourdieu, 1977: 178). The term 'capital' is expanded to include both material things, which can have symbolic values as well as intangible but culturally-significant phenomena such as status and prestige. The acquisition of these resources gives access to power and ultimately to material wealth (Leung, 2012).

Based on various topics, Bourdieu operated with different categorisations of capital. The key theory was elaborated in 'The forms of capital' (Bourdieu, 1986), where capital has principally been put into four categories (See table 2-4).

Table 2-4 Different forms of capital

Forms of capital	Meaning
economic capital	income and other forms of financial resources and assets
social capital	durable social relations, networks and contacts
cultural capital	culture valued taste and consumption patterns. It takes three forms: objectified (*e. g.* books, computers), embodied (characteristics of a person, *e. g.* accent or multilingualism), and Institutionalised (*e. g.* university degree or affiliation with prestigious research institution)
symbolic capital	the prestige or status value attached to certain competencies, values, and/or places of learning and research

In terms of social capital, Ben Fine (2008) believes that Bourdieu's ideas of social capital has strengths, but that the concept has been used inappropriately by other researchers. First, social capital is augmented by the notions of cultural, symbolic and economic capital. Researchers now often use the notion of social capital without engaging with these other aspects. Second, Bourdieu insists that the use of social capital is context specific. Thus he uses the concepts of field and habitus. This emphasis on context is again absent from others using the notion of social capital. Third, Bourdieu focuses on questions of class, power and conflict. He looks at how his different capitals create, reproduce and transform these. Once again, others working with the notion of social capital tend not to do this.

He also believes Bourdieu's idea of social capital has weaknesses. First, his understanding of economic capital is specific to modern capitalism. Thus his understanding of social, cultural and symbolic capital should really limit itself to this period (despite his notions of field and habitus, which take specific contexts into account). Second, social theory has understood capitalism in terms of the structures and processes which tie the social capital and the economic capital together. Bourdieu makes economic capital distinct from social capital (as well as cultural capital and symbolic capital). Thus his notion of economic capital risks being a thing in itself that exists outside the social capital. Third, Bourdieu's four capitals behave in a money like fashion, exchangeable with one another. The qualitative and quantitative complexity of these capitals and their relationships to one another make this seem unconvincing.

In sum, Fine's (2008) point of view about Bourdieu's social capital is as follows: First, the social capital literature uses Bourdieu's terminology 'social capital' without addressing the context of this notion in his work—Bourdieu's social capital was not intended to be isolated from his concepts of cultural, symbolic and economic capital. Equally, these concepts do not make sense if divorced from his ideas of field and habitus and his questions of class, power and conflict. Second, if the notion of social capital is to be used, it should be used in a way that considers more fully its context and how it is situated in relation to economics, culture, class and power for example. Bourdieu's work may be flawed, but it does address issues that theorists tend not to address now when discussing social capital. Finally, there is a danger that the use of Bourdieu's terminology gives a false sense of coherence in this field, when in fact the literatures are each talking about different, incompatible or incomplete understandings of social capital. Social capital would be discussed in Chapter Six in relation to academic migrants' social interactions in places in the transnational university.

Although Bourdieu's work has received much criticism, his contribution to educational research is still impressive. In his work about the French academic field, he tries to classify faculty members by their social origins and connections, economic and political resources, academic experiences, titles, professional practice, etc. After the data collection, he analyses his sources precisely, typifying them into different categories, such as 'educational capital' 'capital of academic power' 'capital of scientific power and prestige' 'capital of intellectual renown' and 'capital of political power or economic power' (Leung, 2012). One essential conclusion in his study is that distinctions in social class are more or less reinforced by the educational related capitals mentioned above, and the educational system is dominated by the elites.

Bourdieu's notion of capital also has an important contribution for the research on the Chinese educational system. In Joel Andreas's (2009) study, he employs a modified version of Bourdieu's different forms of capital to examine the 'red engineers' who were trained at China's elite educational institutions in the 1950s and early to mid-1960s to be both 'red and expert'. In the early 2000s, they began to enter the top positions in the Chinese party and governmental leadership (Li, 2010). Andreas's work demonstrates that although Bourdieu's conceptual framework was originally used to analyse changes in the class structure of stable Western capitalist societies, it has also been found to be useful in the research of class change in non-capitalist societies, such as China. In his analysis of the Chinese educational system, Andreas mainly looks at two types of capital, namely cultural (academic certificates) and political (party membership). In his assessment, only these two types of capital are influential in gaining access to higher-class positions in that period.

In terms of academic migration, there are numbers of scholars who have, from different perspectives, put 'international academic experience' and 'capital' together. Some conclude that the international experience is a kind of accumulation of capital that may contribute to the reproduction of social privileges (Brooks and Waters, 2009; Findlay and King, 2010). Liu's (1997) work on Chinese students and researchers illustrates how Chinese academics and students translate their international academic experience into wealth accumulation or permanent residence overseas. Focusing on transnational academic mobility, knowledge, and identity capital, Kim (2010) explores the relations of mobile academics, their embodied knowledge, and the impact of mobility on their future career. He employs a concept of 'transnational identity capital' to discuss the position of transnational academic intellectuals as a 'stranger'. By using Bourdieu's capital theory, Waters (2012) suggests that international education entrenches, and in some cases within emerging economies, actively creates social inequalities.

Maggi Leung's (2012) work on geographical mobility and capital accumulation among Chinese scholars in Germany is also a good example of the adaptation of Bourdieu's capital theory to contemporary Chinese academic mobility. Academic mobility in her study refers to 'the academically motivated geographical movements of students, faculty and researchers, generally in higher education, from their home institution to another one, either inside or outside of their home country, to study, teach or take part in research for a period of time' (Leung, 2012: 56). Based on academic migrants' life experience, her research centres on interrogating the meanings and impact of Chinese academic mobility in the German context and the perceived accumulation/shrinkage and conversion of social, cultural and symbolic capital. More specifically, she considers geographical mobility as a form of capital along with the other forms of capital conceptualised by Pierre Bourdieu. The capital related discussions in my study are related to academic migrants' contributions in pushing the boundary of the current Sino-UK transnational academic space, rather than focusing on a single national academic space that she explored in her study.

Many works on international student mobilities have discovered that obtaining an international education can largely enhance graduates' employment prospects and the advantage can accrue to both individuals and their families. The authors captured this advantage and theorised it in terms of accumulation of capital, after Bourdieu (Brooks and Waters 2009; Deakin 2012; Findlay and King 2010; Findlay *et al.* 2012; Murphy-Lejeune 2002; Xiang and Shen 2009). Embodied cultural capital (in an individual person) and institutionalised culture capital (in academic qualifications formally conferred by educational establishments), in particular, have featured strongly in these accounts. On one hand, embodied cultural capital refers to the capital accumulation that comes with international students' intercultural experience. Living in a foreign culture and new language environment can improve their language ability, accent, style of dress, sense of humour, and so on, deemed desirable by prospective employers (Waters 2006). One the other hand, institutionalised cultural capital is represented by an academic degree certificate conferred by higher educational institutions, university ranking or status is also crucial for gaining institutionalised cultural capital. 'The most direct and obvious benefit of cultural capital is enhanced employment prospects' (where cultural capital is exchanged for economic capital) (Waters, 2012: 128). However, it could be argued that social capital (durable social relations, networks and contacts) of the family can simultaneously play an important role in international students' job seeking process. Another recent project on the internationalisation of education in Hong Kong SAR. has showed that the least privileged members of society are opting for 'transnational' education programmes (where the foreign university comes to them), as opposed to studying for a degree locally or travelling to an overseas destination (Waters and Leung forthcoming).

Such an expanded concept of capital has relevance to international academic migration research, which operates with extended forms of capital when compared to Marx's concept, ranging from the intellectual, and educational, to the culture and language. The goal of my research, therefore, is to use Bourdieu's expanded concept of capital as a conceptual tool to discuss the empirical data and get a better understanding of the grounded information. Bourdieu's expanded concept of capital can help us to unify and explain the academic migrants' everyday life experiences within a unified term between scholars, which allows us to understand the experience of different groups of migrants. Here, I draw upon Pierre Bourdieu's concept of different forms of capital as a source of power and future opportunities.

My research focuses on the accumulation of economic, social, cultural and symbolic capital among Chinese academics in the UK and British academics in China during their offshore campus experience. It also explores how transnational academic experience can be accumulated into economic, social, cultural and symbolic capital which eventually can be converted and transformed into professional creditability, both in geographical (overseas travelling afterwards) and social (international academic network) senses. How overseas academic life experiences can be understood as a means of capital accumulation, as perceived and practised by Chinese and British academic migrants, will be one of the central questions in my research. It will use Bourdieu's theory as a tool for examining the nature of interaction between migrant academics and local academics. Migrant academics are found to occupy an ambiguous position: On the one hand, they are 'outsiders' with little familiarity of the nature of the local academic system. While on the other hand, the highly-educated profile of migrant academics means that they often possess the kinds of cultural capital valued by the local educational system.

3.1.3 Habitus

Habitus is a key concept to Bourdieu's originality and contribution to social science. Although the notion of Bourdieu's habitus had been used popularly, 'habitus' remains anything but clear, and it is also one of the most misunderstood, misused and hotly contested of Bourdieu's ideas. So, what is habitus? As Bourdieu (1994: 56) states, 'all of my thinking started from this point: how can behaviour be regulated without being the product of obedience to rules?' In other words, Bourdieu asks how social structure and individual agency can be reconciled, and how objective and subjective realities help to shape each other.

Formally, Bourdieu defines habitus as a property of social agents (whether individuals, groups or institutions) that comprises a 'structured and structuring structure' (Bourdieu, 1996: 170). 'Structured' means habitus is related to one's past and present situation, such as family background, childhood memory, educational experience, *etc*. While 'Structuring' refers to how one's habitus can shape one's present and future practice. In sum, nothing happens randomly, they are all related to one's history and habitus. That is to say, 'where we are in life at any one moment is the result of numberless events in the past that have shaped our path' (Maton, 2000: 115). The concept is very closely related to migration studies, as migration is very much a process in time that relates to people's pasts and to futures (Boyle, Halfacree and Robinson, 1998).

Generally, 'habitus' describes those 'internalised structures, dispositions, tendencies, habits, ways of acting, that are both individualistic and yet typical of one's social groups, communities, family, and historical position' (Oliver and O' Reilly, 2010: 55). The habitus, however, does not act alone. Practice results from 'an unconscious relationship' between one's dispositions (habitus) and one's position in a field (capital), within the current state of play of that social space (field). Formally, Bourdieu (1986: 101) summarises this relation using the following equation: [(habitus) (capital)] + field = practice. As Bottomley (1992: 13) points out in her discussion of the concept, habitus 'manifests itself in practice, in action and movement, in the way one orients oneself in relation to specific social fields.' There is a close dynamic between habitus and field:

> *Social reality exists, so to speak, twice, in things and in minds, in fields and in habitus, outside and inside social agents. And when habitus encounters a social world of which it is the product, it is like a 'fish in water': it does not feel the weight of the water and it takes the world about itself for granted. (Bourdieu and Wacquant, 1992: 127)*

For Bourdieu, habitus is a concept that establishes the relationship between practice and situation within which meaning is produced by 'perception and appreciation that are themselves produced by observable social conditions' (Bourdieu, 1984: 101). As Bottomley, one of the critic of Bourdieu's concept of habitus, points out, 'the truth of social interaction is never entirely in the interaction as observed, and we need to recognise the structural constraints on perceptions' (Bottomley 1992: 12). Apart from Bottomley, there are other researchers who also hold a critical view towards Bourdieu's notion of habitus. Cicourel (1993: 109) has argued that there is a need to expand the notion of habitus into a larger scale, and use it to explore gender and racial differences that can occur across cultures and social classes or ethnic groups in relation to larger nation-states. Years later, Andrew Sayer (2004) makes a criticism of Bourdieu that he overplayed the unconscious impulses (habitus) and neglected everyday reflexivity (as a kind of 'inner conversation').

According to Richard Harker, Bourdieu 'works in a spiral between theory, empirical work and back to reformulating theory again but at a different level' (Harker *et al.*, 1990: 3). In an interview with Beate Krais, Bourdieu suggested that the chief strength of concepts such as habitus lied in their empirical relevance:

> *Ideas like those of habitus , practice , and so on , were intended , among other things , to point out that there is a practical knowledge that has its own logic , which cannot be reduced to that of theoretical knowledge ; that in a sense , agents know the social world better than the theoreticians (Bourdieu , 1990 : 252).*

Habitus is a conceptual tool to be used in empirical research rather than a theoretical idea to be debated in texts, and it is also a way of understanding the world. Habitus provides a method for simultaneously analysing 'the experience of social agents and... the objective structures which make this experience possible' (Bourdieu, 1988, p. 782). So, firstly, in my study, I use the notion of habitus as a complex interplay between past and present. I use qualitative data from the study to show how educational habitus can be still embodied in academic migrants within the field of transnational higher education, generating uncertainty, ambivalence, and anxiety in their offshore experience. I also focus on academic migrants' educational history to show habitus continues to operate after the 'objective conditions of its emergence have been dislodged' (Bourdieu, 2001: 13). Secondly, I use the concept of habitus as a research tool to identify factors attributing to the varied mobility experiences among scholars of different age, gender, discipline, academic rank, and geographical background. Finally, I take habitus not only in the sense of academic migrants' adaptations, reactions, and resistance towards a new educational environment, but also of them struggling to make the 'home' institution a different place.

3.2 Place and Transnational Higher Education

Place is a key conceptual tool for understanding academic migrants' professional practices in this study and therefore it is necessary to explicate the notion of place at play here. Place has a societal dimension, it is 'constructed out of particular interactions and mutual articulation of social relations, social processes, experiences and understandings' (Messy, 1993: 66). Moreover, place has a concrete material setting for social relations (Cresswell, 2004), which reveal power relations and social exclusion (McDowell, 1999; Rose, 1999; McGregor, 2003). That is to say, place could be 'inextricably bound up with the people, materials, and forms of knowledge that help people locate themselves in both place and time' (Nuttall and Edwards, 2014: 104). Thus, place is identified as a rich and complicated interplay of people's social practice and material settings, and is employed as a way of exploring and understanding the micro-geographies of transnational academic migration.

Talking about place, there is also a need to mention the difference between space and place. Escobar defines space as 'absolute, unlimited and universal', while place is 'the realm of particular, the limited, the local and the bound' (2001: 143). Cresswell has further pointed out that, in distinction of place, space is a more abstract 'fact of life', a 'realm without meaning which produces the basic coordinates for human life' (2004: 10). That is to say, space is inauthentic, generic and merely a physical location; place is instead a place of authenticity and a 'humanised space' (Tuan, 1995) which is emotionally and personally significant for people. Although, since the 1970s, some geographers use the ideal of social space to play almost the same role as place in their works (See: Lefebvre, 1991, Smith, 1991), space and place's distinction is still under consideration:

> *If the spatial is thought of in the context of space-time and as formed out of social relations at all scales, then one view of a place is of a particular articulation of those relations, a particular moment in those networks of social relations and understandings (Massey, 1994: 5).*

So, rather than inauthentic space, place could be a more appropriate approach to look at the micro-geography of migrants' everyday life. For instance, focusing on Turkish immigrants' local attachments and transnational practice in a

German city, Ehrkamp supports the ideal that place forms an important component of immigrants' everyday lives: 'conceptualising immigrants' attachments through the production of place teases out the complexities of multiple and sometimes conflicting attachments of contemporary migrants, and of their engagement with the receiving society' (2005: 362).

However, it is noticeable that the importance of place has been largely sidelined in the growing literature in relation to geography of education. Coming from a transnational perspective, Leung and Waters' (2013) work on the role of place and space in shaping Hong Kong SAR. students' learning experience in transnational education argues that the importance of place and space in transnational education is not sufficiently recognised by transnational education (TNE) providers. By analysing research on space and place in education, they further pointed out that recent works in social and cultural geography journals focus exclusively on places in school rather than on university campus. Even the limited studies on university campus space, which emphasize the spatial and social segregation on university campus, have been predominantly driven by a student approach (Fisher and Hartmann, 1995; Koen and Durrheim, 2010; Alexander and Tredoux, 2010; Hopkins, 2011; Holton, 2013). The places in university for academics are still overlooked. Studying transnational education from the academic staff members' perspective might be meaningful for the whole TNE sector, because they are one of the most 'important stakeholders' in the institution (Waters and Leung, 2013: 46). Thus, the complexity of contemporary everyday micro-struggles over space and time of academic migrants requires more extensive study.

Despite the paucity of studies on academics' lives in university space, there are still some articles on the educational field that recognise that university space is difficult to disentangle from the practice of teaching and learning: 'Spaces are themselves agents for change. Changed spaces will change practice' (Oblinger,

2006: 30). For instance, by drawing together two linked studies on formal teaching spaces within one university, Jessop *et al.* gathered qualitative information from both university staff and students concerning the constraints and potentials of university space. They conclude that conventional spaces in university may 're-inscribe hierarchical, teacher-centred approaches' (2012: 189). Cox *et al.*'s (2012) study explores defamiliarised individual experience of university spaces at the University of Sheffield. They studied how university space shapes academic identity and everyday work, and conversely, how staff identity shapes space. Their way of theorising the university space as place is related to the discussion of identity and belonging, as I have done in Chapter Six. The limitation of Cox *et al.*'s study, however, is that their research is based upon a relatively small sample—three academic staff members' offices in different departments at the University of Sheffield, and the findings are based on the immediacy of the authors' own engagement with the university space, without any connection to the social interaction of colleagues.

Within Geography, the limited work on academic mobility is often conducted, for instance, through the lens of gender issues (Jons, 2011) or Bourdieusian capital accumulation (Leung, 2012). Moreover, academic migrants' everyday experiences have not been widely applied in connection with university space and related notion of place. As a result, Holloway and Jons (2012) call for more analyses of different cultural contexts, more examinations from comparative perspectives and greater attention to the world-class universities' proliferation of branch campuses. In Chapter Six, I address this call by elucidating the role of university space in the making of cross-cultural working experiences. The chapter looks more closely at the ways in which different places in university coalesce in shaping the everyday working of academic migration, 'thereby usefully complementing growing research on the transnational academic mobility of students, educators, researchers and academics' (Holloway and Jons, 2012: 485).

3.3 Connecting Habitus with Place

Bourdieu defines habitus as a property of social agents (whether individuals, groups or institutions) that comprises a 'structured and structuring structure' (Bourdieu, 1996: 170). 'Structured' means habitus is related to one's past and present situation, such as family background, childhood memory, educational experience, *etc.* (for individual or groups). While 'structuring' refers to how one's habitus can shape one's present and future practice. In sum, nothing happens randomly, they are all related to one's habitus. That is to say, 'where we are in life at any one moment is the result of numberless events in the past that have shaped our path' (Maton, 2000: 52).

To Bourdieu, the habitus predisposes individuals towards certain ways of behaving:

> *The habitus, as a system of dispositions to a certain practice, is an objective basis for regular modes of behaviour, and thus for the regularity of modes of practice, and if practices can be predicted... this is because the effect of the habitus is that agents who are equipped with it will behave in a certain way in certain circumstances (Bourdieu, 1990: 77).*

Arguably, defining British academic migrants' habitus from a collective or national angle could be problematic in certain cases in my study. As Kelly and Lusis (2005) note, 'the habitus is a social/collective as well as a personal phenomenon, but Bourdieu is often very unclear on the social boundaries of habitus formation—in other words, how we might identify the scale at which the habitus of a group or collective is defined' (Kelly and Lusis, 2005: 835). To Bourdieu, the term habitus could be used to understand various issues, such as class, ethnic identity, occupation, gender, *etc.* However, when you adapt this concept through an angle of individuals' everyday experience, it could be connected with his/her class, ethnicity, occupation, gender and the length of *stay*, *etc.* It is hard to define a person's behaviour as coming from his/her habitus as British or an academic or both, for example. Thus, the so-called 'British habitus' or 'academic's habitus' could be problematic in many cases, as it leaves undifferentiated other important axes of the structuring process of an individual's habitus. In this study, the concept of habitus is considered and discussed as a notion applied to individual academic migrants and groups of individuals rather than categories based upon nationality for example.

Moreover, I argue that the conception of habitus is not only closely related to time, but also place, meaning there is 'an inherent geography to habitus where a person's social disposition and the spatial location become intertwined' (Holton, 2013: 68). Following Holton's path on exploring university students' habitus and sense of place in Portsmouth, the entwinement of British and Chinese academic migrants' everyday working lives with campus space will be closely examined in this study.

To start with, there is a need to outline the complex ways in which the connection of place and habitus is located in the recent literatures. Bourdieu's work has been routinely criticised for not treating the concept of geographical space/place as central (Painter, 2000; Bridge, 2003; Hillier and Rooksby, 2005; Ingram, 2009). However, the absence of spatiality in Bourdieu's theory leaves more conceptual space for geographers when they interpret Bourdieu's social notions from a geographical perspective (Cresswell, 2002). Hence, a range of explanations has emerged to make sense of the spatial potential of habitus. For instance, seeking to develop a geographical approach for Bourdieu's theory, it has been argued by Casey (2001) that habitus could be understood as a middle term between place and the body, and it is closely bounded to agent's action and place. More specially, he indicates that the agent's social disposition in the given field and the body's spatial movements are crucial in how place is experienced. Easthope also suggests that there is a close link between place and habitus, as 'habitus is intrinsically connected to the concept of rootedness' (2004: 133). More recently, by examining the geographies of urban young people's aspirations for work in creative industries in England, Allen and Hollingsworth suggest that habitus has been used variously to examine 'the interpenetration of locality and identity' (2013: 3). They write:

> *Habitus can be understood to relate not simply to class—based dispositional understandings of what is thinkable for 'people like me' but also for 'people from round here'. We see young people's aspirations—their sense of where they belong—as being deeply entangled with their social and spatial location. (2013 : 3)*

In order to address the spatial process that comprises migrants' experience, I draw on different places on campus that are crucial to academics' daily work—office, coffee shop (common room/pub) and residence. The classroom or other teaching spaces are discussed in Chapter Five in relation to teaching practice and pedagogies. Accordingly, by utilising habitus as a particular way of seeing and knowing British/Chinese academics' working life, this work delineates how academic migrants' embedded habitus affects their way of using place on the 'new' campus, and how the 'old' habitus is unconsciously changed by local university space during their migration process.

The diversity of practice depends on different educational backgrounds, uneven expectations of the host university, uneven educational strengths between China and the UK, a divergence in language abilities, and so on so forth. Chinese and British academic migrants enact various ways of using their workplace on campus by navigating between the unfamiliar and the familiar, the strange and the domesticated.

Conclusion: Research Agenda of the Study

This review of the current literature on the internationalisation of higher education and academic talent flow reveals a distinct gap that this study aims to fill in. In this thesis, I go beyond the academic mobility discourses on migration policy and develop new empirical directions that consider the influence of grounded transnational academic experience on academic mobility. I argue that the future mobility of academics is not only directed by policy trends but also by their everyday negotiation with the current working environment. I will discuss this issue in Chapter Four, developing an understanding of the significance of everyday practical challenges and the value of emotional attachment on altering peoples' decision of move.

The pedagogical differences in different academic cultures form the context of Chapter Five, in which I explore the extent to which transnational academic mobility contributes to the broadening of the intellectual tradition and the introduction of new styles of pedagogy. It has been argued that the hosting higher education institutions should help and encourage international academics to embrace their prior teaching and researching experience in their current academic practice in order to enrich the host institutions (Tran, 2010). Others suggest that an internationalised institution should adopt cultural differences and change the one-way westernised teaching methods in the internalisation process (Turner and Robson, 2008). Chapter Five addresses the question of how academics educated by their home country pedagogies, engage with the host country pedagogies while teaching in the host country. The questions that are explored are: Do they adopt the pedagogies and teaching skills in the host country or continue to use their own teaching style while teaching in the host country? Do they try to develop a new style of teaching by combining the strengths of both pedagogies? How does one's country of origin affect one's teaching practice in the host country? These questions may help us understand how different educational experiences, cultural backgrounds, and teaching methods can lead to diverse courses of action, albeit in one environment. This will bring to light how teaching practices obtained in one educational culture can in fact be generalised to others.

Chapter Six focuses predominantly upon the connections between academics' everyday experience and university space. Understanding grounded experience through the lens of ' place ' is a prominent discourse in geography, but rather ignored in existing literatures in relation to higher education. My research brings these together and uses Bourdieu's notion of habitus as a tool for illustration, forming a solid structure of analysing academic's non-teaching practices on campus (practices in offices, leisure places, and university residences). This gives a deeper and more vivid understanding of academic migrants' overseas work life and contributes to the literature of academic migration.

Through an engagement with the existing works on transnationalism, this study produces an insightful understanding of everyday experiences of being 'here' and 'there' (China and the UK) from multiple perspectives (from British and Chinese academic migrants). It explains the differential impact of offshore experience on 'multiple forms of mobility' (Oackes and Schein, 2006), as the British and Chinese academic migrants in the 'transnational university' cannot be regarded as a single national group. Rather, they represent several sets of elements in transnational mobility: provisional and long-term; self-motivated and institutionally directed; early career and experienced, *etc.* The research also makes a connection between transnationalism from above, from below and grounded transnationalism. It links the grounded transnational practice in education with cross-country mobility and the ways in which mobility intersects with transnational institutions and national policies.

In conclusion, the overseas working experience can be regarded as an important part of an academic's career development and an essential condition for their professional identification. It can reconstruct their professional skills, and offers the opportunity to critically examine their academic acculturation process in the context of transnational education. This study develops insights into this process, critically developing links between the internationalisation of higher education, transnational academic mobility and academic migrants grounded experience.

Based on the three parts of the literature review, it should be mentioned that Bourdieu's theory, transnationalism and the internationalisation of higher education are linked with each other in the study. The internationalisation of higher education has set up a 'global' market for transnational academics and invoked a special form of university that has been built beyond national borders (for example the Sino-UK transnational university in the study). So, the ideal of internationalisation of higher education is used as an overall backdrop of the study, and is one which promotes transnational education and academic mobility.

In the 'transnational' era, being 'international' is not enough for academics. As academic mobility becomes transnational, the problems that accompany it are manifested globally as well as locally, and it is impossible to be restricted to the 'national interest' of 'brain drain/gain'. The ideal of 'transnationalisation' is also frequently mentioned in strategic plans of higher education institutions, and the power of those transnational bodies upon academic mobility cannot be underestimated. So, the theoretical concept of transnationalism will be employed in the study to structure the main empirical resources from 'above' and from 'below'.

Bourdieu's theory is used in the study as a tool to analyse academic migrants' grounded experiences. However, it also connects with the ideal of internationalisation of higher education and transnationalism, as the notion of field is enlarged and linked with academia in different countries and the relations between capitals, habitus and the dynamics of migration are explained under the logics of a transnational institution. The linkage between Bourdieu's theory, internationalisation of higher education and transnationalism will be illustrated more explicitly in Chapter Seven, drawing on the empirical data discussed in

Chapters Four, Five and Six.

The structure of the literature review is set up on the theoretical context of the research, with discourses relevant to each of the empirical chapters weaved in between. It is not structured to make a one to one correspondence between bodies of literature and the empirical chapters, but rather to pick out pertinent threads of research that relate, to a greater or lesser extent, to all of the empirical chapters.

Chapter Three
Researching Transnational Academic Mobility

Informed by the existing literature on academic mobility and the theoretical framework of transnationalism, this study adopted a qualitative methodology to explore the everyday grounded experience of British and Chinese academics in a Sino-UK university campus. 'The strengths of qualitative research derive primarily from its inductive approach, its focus on specific situations or people, and its emphasis on words rather than numbers' (Maxwell, 1996: 17). So, qualitative research is helpful in searching for something less mechanical and more in tune with the complexity of human existence and in gaining insight into what is going on and why this is happening. My intention of employing the methodology is to contribute to empirical perspectives about the ways in which 'global processes are experienced in localised, everyday, embodied ways' (Hyndman 2001: 212), as the strength of qualitative research is to fully explore the complexity of agents' interactions and practices in their daily life.

To tackle the intertwining of transnational space and academic migration, I conducted my fieldwork from March 2013 until the end of the year, and I went back and did more participant observation in the UK campus at the beginning of 2015. The data collection phase of the research includes: 4 months in the UK and 3 months in China. In this chapter, I first specify the rationale behind the site and participant selection. I then argue why my choice of qualitative research methods—namely semi-structured in depth interviews, participant—directed photo interviews and participant observation—were the most suitable for the purpose of this study. Then, I focus on my positionality as a Chinese researcher in conducting the research. The issues around data collection and ethics are then discussed in separate sections. Finally, I conclude with my reflections in relation to the methods I used in the study.

1 Site Selection

This study focuses on the daily working experiences of Chinese/British academic migrants in a UK transnational university, using both its main and branch campuses as sites for exploration. In this section my objective is to explain why I chose the university as my study site to research academic migrants' life experience.

The choice of China and the UK is laid out in Chapter One, so the key point to be explained here is the reason for choosing the particular institution. The sampling process of universities was based on the list of the major joint venture licensed universities under the 2012 legislation in China. The rationale for choosing the Sino-UK university as the main research site was based on the consideration that this institution is one of the most 'special' joint ventures between the UK and China: it is different from other joint universities in that it has independent campuses and corporate capacity. The independent campus in China gave me a chance to link the 'abstract' concept of transnational academic space with the 'concrete' local university spaces that are used by academic migrants on their everyday bases. Furthermore, it has a large pool of Chinese and British academic migration resources from multiple disciplines. This helps me get a more representative choice of participants in terms of disciplines and age groups, which fit with the discussion on the limitations of current studies on

Chinese and British academic migration in Chapter Two. I sent a few emails out to get in touch with the major Sino-UK joint venture universities, and 3 of them responded. The one I selected is my first choice and they agreed to participate, because they also saw the value in doing this research.

There is a need to clarify the specificity of the comparative research work that has been done (interviews on one branch campus and in one university in the UK). First, knowing that different universities in the UK has different administration systems, funding sources, and teaching/research, focusing on various university institutions would be likely to have a significant effect on the diversity research data, as academic migrants' experience might be different, or even contrasting, in different institutions. For this reason, I decided to choose one institution.

Second, the institution needs to be 'international' as a result of the internationalisation of higher education. Focusing on one university that has campuses in the UK and China can provide a suitable field for analysing transnational academics, as the ideal of 'transnational academics' in this research is closely connected with the nature of the institution. Although in some cases, transnational academics can move freely by individual choice, the existence of the branch campus can also have a large effect on their personal trajectory, choice of stay, transplantation and grounded experience. This shows a new angle from which to understand the complexity of international academic mobility when compared to existing literature.

Third, the differences and the interconnections between the campus in the UK and China need to be addressed, in order to show how this affects Chinese and British academic migrants' everyday working practices. The international university that was chosen has its main campus in the UK and one of its international campuses in China. The main campus and the branch campus have different characters. The main campus in the UK is a well-known British university that has top academic resources and a large pool of international students. Meanwhile, its international branch campus in China is a joint university with a local Chinese university where most of the academic resources, including teaching and learning resources and academics, are provided by the UK main campus. The campus itself however, including the layout of the campus, buildings, and other basic infrastructures on campus, are mainly provided by their Chinese counterpart. Moreover, most of the students and administration staff are from China. So, in a sense, the Chinese academic migrants in the UK are working in an internationalised British university that is waiting for their integration and negotiation, while the British academics in China are facing a particular academic environment that should be 'very British' in theory, but is actually 'more Chinese' in practice. The choice of the two campuses of one international university gives us the possibility of understanding academic mobility in a Sino-UK academic field, which provides us with rich resources for comparing the two groups of academics in transnational education.

2 Participant Selection

According to existing literatures discussed in Chapter Two, key factors such as discipline, gender, age, and length of sojourn in the host country, academic rank, and institutional type, influence academic migrants' experiences (Jiang *et al*, 2010 and Hsieh, 2011). So, when recruiting participating academics, I sought to have a diversity of participants, paying particular attention to discipline, gender, age, academic position and length of time overseas. Apart from that, four basic criteria were used in the study to determine the sample.

The academics were employed in the selected university and working in the host country (China/the UK) at the time of data collecting.

Their country of last residence was China for Chinese academics and the UK for British academics, and most of their present nationality status was Chinese (From Mainland China) or British. A Chinese academic who had taken British citizenship and was now working in the UK was considered as a Chinese migrant.

Taking Mainland China's special academic culture into consideration, host country-born Chinese or Chinese who came to the host country from Hong Kong SAR, Taiwan area or elsewhere were excluded. Although politically Hong Kong SAR is a part of China following the government handover in 1997, Hong Kong SAR's academia is more westernised in terms of English language learning, academic administrative structure, and government control, and with a Hong Kong SAR. passport, Hong Kong academics are freer to move. So, their working experience in the host country is quite different from that of Chinese academics from Mainland China.

The participants were recruited using three main methods.

Firstly, I searched the university websites. With the advancement of online information technology, profiles of faculty staff are now available in most universities in both China and the UK. By reviewing this, it is possible to obtain certain basic information about faculty staff, including full name, discipline, gender, academic rank, publication and other research activities.

It was not difficult to identify Chinese names, because they were spelled according to the Mandarin spelling (hanyu pinyin) system adopted in China. Generally, ethnic Chinese born in places other than the mainland could be easily excluded as they do not employ this system to spell their names (Tsang, 2001). Arguably, a small percentage of ethnic Chinese may have typical Chinese names due to their families' Chinese origin. They were excluded by sending confirming emails. Moreover, the details of universities from which they obtained their first degrees further can confirm their Mainland Chinese identities

(Welch and Zhen, 2005). However, in terms of British academics, difficulties were encountered when using this recruiting method as their names normally have little connection with their citizenship status.

Additionally, the list of potential academic participants was obtained by contacting the International Students and Scholars Office of the sample universities. At the same time, the Centre of International Service and the International Student Association also provided assistance in seeking Chinese and British academics' voluntary participation.

I also used snowball sampling. I used personal networks, such as schoolmates and friends, to introduce qualified scholars who might be interested in the study. Similarly, at the end of each interview, the interviewed scholar was asked to introduce at least one migrant scholar resident in the area who fitted the criteria. Finally, potential academic participants were also found through the 'academia. edu' and 'Linkedin' websites by browsing their personal profile.

After obtaining the contact information, an email request was sent to potential research participants. The emails (Appendix A) contained an outline of the research, the research methods being used in the questionnaire and the interviews, and what respondents would be expected to do. The volunteers were contacted several times and asked for more personal details, if they were interested in participating in the study. If no feedback was received within two weeks, the recruitment email was resent along with an official letter from the Geography Department of Royal Holloway University of London in order to confirm my research status.

To conduct this research, I started by contacting nearly 150 academic migrants listed on the university official websites. Their British/Chinese nationality was judged from their formal educational experiences and the universities where they had previously worked. Sixty-four people responded to my recruiting email, and their nationalities were confirmed by subsequent emails. In total, 42 participants were recruited via this channel, and then a snowballing approach was adopted. Ten participants were recruited by this method. Another 8 academics were recruited randomly when I was doing my participant observation by distributing my business card and information sheet. In sum, 60 participants were recruited, and then 80 face-to-face interviews were conducted, including 60 first-time interviews and 20 follow-up photo-diary interviews in the British main campus and the international campus in China (see Table 3 – 1 for an overview of demographic information and Appendix C for details of participants).

Table 3 –1 Demographic Information of the Participants

Gender		Number
Sex	Male	44
	Female	16
Location	UK	30
	China	30
Average Age	British	43.6 years
	Chinese	39.5 years
Academic Discipline	Social Science and Humanities	20 (16 British and 8 Chinese)
	Natural Sciences and Engineering	26 (6 British and 16 Chinese)
	Business and Management	14 (8 British and 6 Chinese)
Length of Residence	British	2.8 years
	Chinese	11 years
Academic Position	Professor/Senior Manager	19 (12 British and 7 Chinese)
	Reader/ Senior Researcher	9 (5 British and 4 Chinese)
	Lecturer/ Researcher/ Language Tutor	32 (13 British and 19 Chinese)

Notes: 1. All participants were either Chinese academic migrants in the British main campus or British academics who are currently working in the international university campus in China.

2. All academics working in China and the UK had Ph. D degrees, while language tutors in China who teach the first year students normally had a master's degree in English language and many transnational experiences.

While I sought to have a good distribution of participants across a range of categories, this was not always possible. For example, there are more male academics than females in the sample, due to the nature of gender imbalance in the academic field. Among British academics, the age group between 40 and 50 is largely absent (this issue is discussed in Chapter Four), and there are more academics in Social Science and Management departments; while for Chinese academics, there is a large group of researchers in the fields of Natural Science and Engineering, professors and lecturers are much less than researchers. It also needs to note that 85% of the Chinese informants were educated in the UK or other Western countries, but only 50% of them had long-term transnational working experiences, while 90% of the British informants had not worked in China before and 75% of them had worked in more than 3 countries in the past. As a whole, the participants recruited were representative of the population of Chinese and British academic migrants, as the imbalance I have mentioned was caused by the nature of academic migration structure in these two countries. This will be discussed in more detail later, particularly in Chapter Four.

The first challenge that I faced was recruiting Chinese participants (I had basically no problem recruiting British academics in China). Although I did a pilot study in London in March 2013, and my supervisors provided me with the recruiting letter that I sent to my Chinese participants, I did not received as many responses as I expected. Only 5 participants out of 50 responded to my recruiting letter. I made appointments with those 5 candidates and asked them if the recruiting letter had any problems. They told me that the letter was a standard recruiting letter that was well written, but they are regularly asked to be the subjects of research and that sometimes they do not bother reading them as they are very busy. They suggested that I rewrite a letter in Chinese and see how it would go. So, I wrote a less formal letter in Chinese saying I was doing research on Chinese academic migrants for my Ph. D studies in the UK and I was also an academic in China, and to see if we can have a casual chat in a café and make friends. Surprisingly, 80% of people responded. I asked them why they immediately responded my letter. Aside from the Chinese letter being very conspicuous among their many English emails, they also empathised with my situation as a Chinese academic doing their Ph. D in the UK and wanted to help me as someone had helped them before. They also wanted to share information, because they were curious about Chinese academia. Given that Chinese people generally set great store by friendships, even in working environments, I was then introduced to their Chinese colleagues, which meant I had no difficulty in recruiting more participants. The problems I faced at the beginning of the process led to a solution that reconsidered the complexity of academic migration in greater detail. The problems thus forced me to adopt a methodology that went beyond the constraints of the usual methodological models, which do not take account of cultural flexibility.

3 Research Methods for Data Collection

A mixture of qualitative methods have been employed to gain insights and knowledge of the British and Chinese academic migrants' everyday lived world in the 'host' country and the transnational academic space in which they are situated. Qualitative research, as Strauss and Corbin (1998: 10) suggest, refers to 'any type of research that produces findings that are not arrived at by statistical procedures or other means of quantification. It refers to research about people's lives, lived experiences, behaviours, emotions, and feelings as well as about organisational functioning, social movements, cultural phenomena, and interactions between nations' that uses intensive methods such as focus groups and group interviews (Cameron 2000; Crang 2001; Longhurst 2003), autobiography and autoethnography (Butz 2001; Moss 2001), interviewing (Dunn 2000; England 2001), participant observation (Dowler 2001; Kearns 2000) and reading texts (Forbes 2000). Although qualitative methods have been used widely in geographic research throughout the twentieth century, the last two decades or so witnessed considerable development in qualitative methodologies in human geography (*e. g.* Aitken 2001; Kobayashi 2001; Smith

2001; Valentine 2002). As suggested by Davies and Dwyer, qualitative methods are now mainstream in geography (Davies and Dwyer, 2007; 2008) and methodological questions are at the heart of contemporary theoretical debates in geography about how everyday life might be apprehended and known (Thrift, 2007; Anderson and Harrison, 2009), and so ensure a fertile ground on which to engage anew with qualitative methodologies.

In this section, I outline the rationale behind the choice of qualitative research methods I made—namely, in-depth interviews, participant observation, and visual methods (photo diary interviews). My decision to employ mixed qualitative methods was made for two reasons. First is that the qualitative methods have become an accepted and popular way for geographers to understand a range of migration motivations, processes and outcomes (Beaverstock, 2005; Clarke, 2005), which are highly related to the themes that I discuss in the thesis. The other reason is that a mixture of methods in migration research is necessary to capture the multiple meanings and interpretations of migration and place (Findlay and Li, 1999). The details regarding the choice and use of those methods in this study are as follows:

3.1 Semi-Structured, In-depth Interviews

The main data collection method that I used was interviewing. According to Rubin and Rubin (1995), interviewing is a way of finding out what others feel and think about their worlds, and through an interview, the researcher can understand experiences and reconstruct events in which he/she did not participate. Clearly, it can give eligible Chinese and British academic migrants a chance to detail their experiences, their personal feelings and their attitudes. At the same time, by 'talking out' about routine practices (Hitchings, 2012), interviewing allows them to see their reflection in the 'mirror' and to have a better understanding of the university internationalisation process they are contributing to. Because, '... how people respond is probably as much insight as obstacle in so far as the ease with which they become critically reflexive about their own practices says much about how contentedly practices were previously being carried' (Hitchings, 2012: 66).

In order to get rich and reliable data, the researcher's personal skills in conducting the interview are of vital importance. Interviewers should have superb listening skills and be skilled in personal interaction, question framing and gentle probing for elaboration. Judgement or criticism can act as barriers to communication, so it is important to maintain openness during the interview process (Wertz *et al.*, 2011). A good interviewer can also think on their feet, respond to challenges, and make sure that the core purpose is being served. Furthermore, they are observant, picking up subtle cues such as facial expressions, body language, and tone of voice (Friesen, 2010). As a Chinese academic, also as a current Ph. D student in a British university, I may have the advantage of understanding the non-verbal cues during the interview, although I must be careful not to take this for granted and remain mindful of the possibility of misinterpretation. In order to be a qualified interviewer, prior to conducting an in-depth interview, I practised active listening on a friend or colleague by instructing him/her to talk about a topic of interest. Afterwards, I asked for feedback and continued with different topics until active listening became a natural way of interacting (Burley-Allen, 1995).

Eligible academic participants were interviewed at a location of their choice. The interviews were conducted in familiar places on campus, such as their offices, coffee shops, restaurants, and gardens, in order to build trust and engage the informants in comfortable conversations. Most academics chose their office where interruption was kept to minimum. Those English tutors who work in a shared office space in China often arranged the meeting in a café in the main administration building, while some of them preferred restaurants or gardens, as they did not want to be heard by colleagues during the conversation. The details of the study (question list) were sent prior to interview. Informed written consent was obtained prior to conducting the interview. Eligible academic migrants were asked a series of questions developed by the researcher (see Appendix D). These questions were refined during early interviews and served as a topic guide to encourage participants to express their thoughts and feelings and to allow issues that were salient for them to emerge. All participants were provided with a summary report of the interviews and invited to comment on the qualitative findings. The average duration of the interview was approximately 1 hour. Notes were taken to avoid information loss and capture key themes, and all interviews were digitally recorded.

3.2 Participant-directed Photography

Participant-directed photography was used in this study to develop an in-depth understanding of Chinese and British academic migrants' everyday interactions in relation to the environment on the host campus. The literature on participant-directed photography emphasises the ability to 'see in' spaces that we might not otherwise be able to see in to (see, for example, Latham, 2002; Johnsen *et al*, 2008). Photographs are able to 'engage thought, extend the imagination, and to undermine the implicit authority of the written word' (Walker 1993: 73). Indeed, photographs require thought and choice on the part of the photographer, especially when he or she is asked by a third party to photograph representations of the photographer's life.

There are many advantages of using participant-directed photography as a main research method. It provides a unique insight into the local environment. Its 'unusual nature' includes seeking opinions from different angles and perspectives, renegotiating the power relations between the researcher and the interviewees, reducing language inequalities, and appreciating the value of a more transparent representation of the life experiences of the participants in the study. Moreover, by using this method, special training and professional communication techniques are not required in this study. Therefore, the use of self-directed photography as a research method can help participants to tell researchers what they really want to say in a simple way (in the form of photography) instead of what they think the researchers want to hear.

Participant's photo interviews were conducted in a week after the first semi-structured interview with selected interviewees. The reasons for using the method in follow-up meetings with participants soon after their first semi-structured interviews in this study are: First, the participants have time for in-depth reflection before the interview, so the photo involved interview can reveal some more detailed and refined information in comparison with their first 'traditional' interview. As Hamdani (2013: 385) points out, individuals' identities are revealed in 'their actions and talk, the places they go, the objects they treasure, the décor of their room', the visual method added some possibility of capturing the essence of participants' practices in relation to space that were not fully articulated during their first interview. Second, the photo itself is a useful tool to prompt participants to talk about their social interactions logistically and vividly, which adds flavour to the general information I obtained during the previous one. Third, the visual representation could also help the participants in explaining the importance of the places being shown in the photos provided, and allow them to reflect on how these places make them feel and how they affect their sense of self and others. This is crucial for providing empirical data for the discourse formed around campus space in Chapter Six.

As I mentioned, the participant-directed photo method is an empirically-engaging method to investigate 'social practice in the making' (see Pratt, 2000; Thrift, 2000; Latham, 2003; Hamdani, 2013). This was an important method that I used to collect empirical evidence to support the chapters in relation to campus space. The photo diary method in this study was aimed at gathering information about what the academic migrants do at different times of the day or night on campus. Selected participants were asked to use their cell phones or cameras to take photos of their activities and the places they visited on campus during a day. Photo-taking instructions were sent to them soon after their first interview, and they had at least one week to take photos on campus. This allowed them to have time to think and make amendments to the finished product.

In general, the participants were very curious about the photo interview method, especially the academics from an engineering or science background. They took between 5 and 20 photos each, with the average number being 13. With their own digital equipment, 16 participants took all of their photos independently, 4 participants took the photos having the researcher by their side during a campus walk. In addition, 2 participants submitted photos that they had taken prior to the study, including bars and restaurants in the campus that presented crucial spots of their social life with colleagues. Although I did not encourage all my participants to do it, as Gibson *et al.* (2013) did, I accepted these photos, because these additional images allowed me to get a more 'diverse and longitudinal picture of the participants' lives and identities' (Gibson *et al.*, 2013: 12).

During the research process, I found that this method helped develop rapport between the researcher and the participant, lessened potential self-consciousness, provided a point of focus in conversation, introduced potential topics to the researcher (Capello, 2005; Croghan, Griffin, Hunter, and Phoenix, 2008; Handami, 2013), and captured their stories in a more concrete and vivid way than semi-structured interviews. For instance, one of my British participants, Laura, told me that she did not have much to say at the beginning, while when I asked her to take some photos in relation to her daily life and see if she could notice something that she usually takes for granted. Then, she told me some extremely interesting stories illustrated through the photos. So, rather than seeing photo interviews just as 'a method of uncovering narratives of place', it may also contribute as a method of 'challenging and constructing narratives' for participants (Holton and Riley, 2014: 64).

3.3 Participant Observation

Another method, which has been popularised by geographers, is participant observation (Cook, 1997). Participant observation entails looking, listening, experiencing, and recording an observer's observations of daily life (Robinson, 1998: 422). McMorran (2012: 489) claims that 'participant observation allows one to conduct research through the body and enables geographers to take seriously the spatiality and creativeness of embodied work practices'. In order to study bodies at work and to fully understand the complex geographies of work, we need to devote time to observe and experience work. This is why the participant observation employed in my study is related to academic work practice on campus. Besides, participant observations can help to reinforce or challenge what participants said in interviews; it can improve the validity of data.

In utilising an ethnographic approach, this study involved observing people, participating in their lives and sharing some of their experiences whilst trying to understand their world and then represent it in terms as closely as possible to their own interpretations (Tuan, 1976). It aims to understand, describe, and interpret the complexity of people's lives, as well as capturing and discovering meaning (Newman, 2003). Conradson and Latham (2005: 229) add that investigating the life-worlds of mobile individuals provides a useful counter viewpoint to the tendency to exaggerate a somehow frictionless world in some writings on globalisation.

I employed participant observation in my study through living on or near the university campus, attending lectures and conferences and building personal relationships with scholars and students, in order to understand the everyday textures of transnational academic mobility. These observations are further based on my personal working experience as an academic at a Chinese university, and also as a current Ph. D student at a British university. As an 'insider' in both the British and Chinese academic circle, I have the advantage of context—specific knowledge gained over a long period of time and the capability to gain access to social networks for my study. I lived near each campus for at least three months, and put myself in the right position to study the 'everyday' experience of transnational academic mobility. During the participant observation process, I recorded my observations, recollections and reflections of these events in a research diary, which I used to facilitate my fieldwork analysis.

In sum, a mixture of methods can powerfully capture and analyse academic migrants' everyday experiences. In-depth interviews were used to capture the subjective aspects of their daily working experiences shaped by their 'new' campus, their relationships with colleagues and students during migration, and the challenges they faced. Additionally, I used participant directed photography as a visual approach to help better comprehend academic migrants' experiences and understanding of the importance of university spaces in their everyday working lives. Participant observation was employed to verify those issues that I had discussed with my participants, and capture several issues that might have been missed in the interviewing process. By adopting complementary methods, I aimed to develop a more nuanced and complex picture than was possible with any single method used alone. This approach helped to illuminate and resolve ambiguity and create a clearer understanding of the transnational academic world.

4 Positionality

It is important to mention that 'language' played an important part in the fieldwork. The concern about language translation in conducting interviews is specified in Müller's (2007) work. By going beyond the technical deficiencies of translation that result from insufficient proficiency in a language (Sidaway *et al.*,

2004), he stresses the importance of considering 'not only the polyvalency of concepts in different languages but also the hegemonising and de-politicising effects of conventional translation' (p. 206). In my study, the interviews were conducted in Chinese with Chinese academics in the UK, while in English with British academics in China. Using Chinese to communicate can largely avoid mutual misunderstanding. However, the disadvantage is also obvious: it was hard to avoid 'the lost in translation' when I translated the transcript into English. It was caused by the 'situatedness' of language, specified in Ruddick's (2006) research, whereby some language structures are difficult to translate from one language to another. The interview data with Chinese academics were in Chinese. I did not translate all the text into English; I just picked the quotes that I needed in the thesis and translated them into English, which saved a great deal of time in reading and writing. Among British academics in China, the language is not a big issue for conducting interviews; with many years teaching experience in China, they know how to explain their ideas or express their feelings in a professional and understandable way to non-native speakers. However, I needed to be alert to misunderstandings, and I always asked them again to clarify points that I thought might be misunderstood, as there are 'heterogeneity and hybridity of concepts across and within languages' (Sidaway *et al.*, 2004: 1046).

It is clear that being a Chinese academic interviewing Chinese participants turned out to be an advantage for me in some respects, as my participants were willing to recount their working lives, including more personal aspects, because presumably they did not regard me as the 'outsider'. A rapport with research subjects thus built up easily. The British academics treated me not only as a Ph. D student, but also an academic with international experiences. They saw me as someone who could understand the problems they experienced due to restrictions in local academia and differences between the UK and Chinese working environments. Taken together, such attitudes from my participants offer considerable resources for thinking about how I treat my personal identity as a researcher and how a close liaison between the researcher and participants can affect the final result of the data collection.

The more informal recruiting letter led me to many Chinese academics that wanted not only to help with my study but also to make friends. Some even invited me to participate in their own research projects and institutional activities after several meetings. I had been also invited to participate in British academics' Halloween party, home-warming parties, birthday parties, and regular gatherings every Thursday, *etc.* when I was in China. In terms of making friends, the benefit is mutual. I found most of my Chinese participants did not have close relationships with their colleagues and were eager to express themselves with someone with whom they could confide without causing problems in their working environment, but who could nevertheless understand their everyday working life. While for the British academics, chatting with me was a way to explore aspects that they might normally ignore in their working life, a process that could help them to have deeper insight in both their working place and the Chinese academia. Moreover, I also assisted them when they needed some help in relation to Chinese language and cultural issues or accompanying my participant Simon (pseudonym) to hospital for example. Apart from 'doing a favour', the process turned into a participant observation, adding vivid impression to the data I got during interviews on the 'health care issue' that is discussed in Chapter Four. In sum, one thing that really helped me during the interviewing process was to communicate with people in sincerity and professionalism. The former made people trust me and willing to share, the later made them share the 'right' information that I needed.

Participating in my participants' teaching practice also helped me develop a level of reflexivity in relation to how my position as an observer and a participant gave meaning to one another. Tim invited me to do 4 sessions of classes with him for undergraduates when I was doing my fieldwork in China. Each session was divided into two parts, he was in charge for the first part with the introduction and content of the class, then I did a speech in terms of research experiences and points that need to be noted during the research process. My position as a Chinese lecturer played a part in altering students' attitudes and practices in class. For instance, when I said 'first... you need to remember that...' many students automatically noted what I had said in their notebooks. Tim was really puzzled afterwards, saying he had never seen this before in his class with the same group of students. There was ample practical evidence in these class sessions of the students as 'listener' and 'follower' in front of me, but more or less as 'challenger' and 'questioner' when Tim was teaching. When I dig deep into the totality of the students' experience, I see many examples in which Chinese students alter from 'student-centred' into 'teacher-centred' learning practices, not only with two different teachers, but also with one when he/she was using different teaching methods. This particular experience of participant observation allowed me to 'get into the gaps' of transnational academics' teaching experiences, both theoretically and practically. It was true that the conventional ideal of certain teaching methods and teachers' identities were interconnected; however, it could be argued that the 'teacher-centred' and 'student-centred' pedagogies can be altered when you apply both of them to the same group of students in an internationalised teaching environment. So, my observations certainly do not refute the role of academics in changing the face of their own pedagogies in a new setting of teaching 'playground' by experiencing challenges and otherness. Only by participating in the mundane, everyday and unspectacular teaching activities of academic migrants can the researcher be more aware of his/her role as 'insider/outsider' (Kusenbach, 2003) and truly understand the participants' real 'thoughts of experiences' 'underlying tensions', or how 'motives may be obscured' (Holton and Riley, 2014: 63).

5 Data Analysis

The first stage of data analysis began with the beginning of the fieldwork. I wrote fieldwork notes during interviews and wrote down my reflections in a research diary every day as a conclusion of information I collected during that day. My reflections and observations were organised separately. This note-taking and transcription process helped me to frame the emerging themes to be discussed in the thesis. It also helped me to improve the initial research plan during the fieldwork process. For example, I had planned to link academic migrants' practices with all spaces on the 'host' campus. So, the early analyses enabled me to continuously refine my research plan and focus on the discourses in the thesis.

The detailed data analysis (the second stage) began soon after I finished the data collection in China and the UK. I manually coded my research diary for systematic analysis. All data are systematically reorganised according to 'name' of participants, date, place, and institutions. Then, the detailed data was analysed thematically by developing categories of key themes that emerged from the narratives of the participants. The analysis also uses Bourdieu's theoretical notion of 'forms of capital,' particularly cultural and academic capital (Bourdieu, 1984), to locate some of the tensions of transnational academic movement revealed by this study.

As a result, in the third stage of data analysis, a full description of the individual experience in regard to Chinese and British academics' life experience was obtained and well organised. The individual experiences were compared in different layers separately for the two groups: Chinese academics in the UK and British academics in China. For both groups, the individual experiences were compared in terms of gender, age, discipline, and university. In this way, a composite textual-structural description of the meaning and essence of Chinese and British academic migrants' everyday life on campus were constructed.

The 'coding' process was important for the analysis. I started with 'open coding', so I could identify the concepts, the properties and dimensions of the data (Strauss and Corbin, 1998). I read the materials many times in order to grasp the key statements in relation to current literature. The code comes from various sources, including the literature review and the 'analytical thinking' (Marshall and Rossman, 2011) of the researcher. However, I mainly employed 'emergent categories' (allowing the code or categories to emerge from the raw data) rather than 'preset categories' (using preconceived categories from literature review to analyse data) for categorising data in this research (Chen, 2015: 61). At the end of the process, 150 codes emerged in the code dossier.

The final stage of the analytical process is to consider linking the findings with the key bodies of literature. I put the different themes of findings in a larger literature context, specifically the internationalism of higher education, transnationalism and academic mobility. I tried to attach significance to the findings, make sense of the arguments based on scholar discourses, challenge the stereotyped understanding of academic migrants' practices, offer explanations to what I observed during the investigating process, consider the meaning to the discipline, and draw conclusions to the key discourses I was going to make in the study.

6 Ethical Issues

Qualitative research is always accompanied with ethical concerns, as discussed by Ely *et al.* (2002: 218): 'Qualitative research is an ethical endeavour... striving to be faithful to another's viewpoint is striving to be ethical. Striving to maintain confidentiality is striving to be ethical. Striving to be trustworthy is striving to be ethical.' In this ethical section, I specify the ethical issues from three aspects, namely consent, confidentiality and trust (Ryen, 2011).

In this case, consent means participants have the right to know the purpose of the study, why they are important in it, and that they have the right to withdraw at any stage of the research project (Ryen, 2011). Before I collected information about the personal daily working experiences of academics in the targeted transnational university, permission to conduct the research was obtained through e-mails. In order to get consent for conducting my interviews, I first emailed the selected academics, and asked them if they would agree to participate in my interview. The research purpose, methods of data collection, and the employment of data in my study were well explained in the recruiting email. If they agreed, I would ask them to fill the consent form (approved by RHUL) before each interview. For the follow-up interviews (in relation to photos), I had another copy of the consent form with me, to obtain the second consent soon after the first interview (not all the academics participated in the follow-up interview). I always asked them if I could record the conversation with my digital recorder before the interview began, and I respected their choice not to answer some of the questions. In terms of the photos, before using them in my thesis, I made sure that I had been given permission to reproduce them. For participant observation, I got the permission from the selected academics to observe them in their lectures and classes; I asked them for their consent to be observed. I also asked the academic to inform students why I was sitting in the class. I did not get the consent of each student to observe the operation of the class if there are a large number of students, but all materials I used from classroom observations were kept confidential and anonymised for inclusion in the thesis.

All data were treated with full confidentiality. Pseudonyms were used to protect my participants; the data was collected under their pseudonyms and all the data was anonymised. In the empirical chapters, I used given names in some cases and title and family names in others, in order to make my participant less identifiable. In terms of computer security, I set up a code for my computer and all the files were named with numbers or pseudonyms rather than their real names. The signed consent forms were stored separately from the responses provided by participants. I also considered sensitive issues (*e. g.* about criticisms of workplace). Sometimes, the interviewees said things negative about their department or university. In that case, in data presentation, I found ways to make the name of the interviewee or the institution unidentifiable.

This study is building on the mutual trust between the researcher and the participants. During the fieldwork process, I made many efforts to build a good relationship with my interviewees. This allowed me to follow the ethical principles and gain insightful understanding of the data through the process. There were no particular benefits for participants of taking part in this research. I always anticipate the fact that 'time is money', as some researchers have been directly asked by their interviewees for an 'envelope' of money in exchange for various information or for interviews with officials, professors or researchers in post-socialist context (Scott *et al.*, 2005). I did not offer my participants money in my research, and many of them offered me their friendship after the data collection. What might be beneficial for them is to gain a deeper understanding of the workplace during the interviewing process and to have the chance to widen their transnational academic network.

Conclusion: Reflections after Fieldwork

Many of the fieldwork participants came from introductions and impromptu meetings in various places. What became abundantly clear is that even though many of the participants were recruited through this process, rather than more formal routes, they made up an important part of the whole data collection. It not only includes what I have got from day-to-day observation, but also how these activities and other research methods were interdependently working together. Normally, it was relatively easy to ask people to participate in the first interview, more so than the second one, because they were more familiar with the semi-structured interview format than the second photo-diary based interview, which was less known and more time-consuming. So, nearly all of my second-interview participants were the ones with whom I had closer personal relationships that had been built upon by those invited activities I mentioned. (However, there is a particular bias in the sample of those that did these activities, because they are usually young academics.) Moreover, participating in these activities gave me a useful insight into how my participants do and do not want to be seen in the interviews and how the activity itself becomes a reflection of the information they provided. That is, the unexpected casual interactions with participants can be viewed not just as giving observational detail, but also facts about their expatriate experiences. This offered insights into how particular activities and their surroundings were enmeshed with each other and the academic migrants' ideology and identity.

Importantly, using different methods on different occasions/places might lead to very different interview dynamics, even within the same research encounter. This issue mirrored Holton and Riley's (2014) observation on undergraduate students that the micro-cultures may be place-cohort related, and the research outcome differs when switching places during the interview process. I remember Dr. Yang, who was one of my interviewees in the UK. When I did my first interview with him (we even had a coffee together before the interview), he gave me the 'official response' that what he thought would be safe to be published, because I was recording the whole interview. While, after the interview, when we had lunch together, we mentioned some issues that had been discussed during the interview, and he then told me what he really thought about the issues without any hesitation. In consideration of the ethics of the project, I usually gained oral permission to use the data from these 'informal' meetings.

Both the methods and also the interview data were thus interconnected, and this helped me to dig more deeply and understand the situation more clearly from different angles. Sometimes I needed to use some 'practical implications' to help strike up a conversation. For example, after conducting several interviews, I found that certain topics that had been regularly mentioned by different academics were very important for my thesis, and I would then use the information that I had already had to ask my next participant, to seek out their views. In this way, I could build up a larger picture. Often, when people found that you really knew about their situation, they would tell you what they really thought rather than using 'strategic answers' that would, in some way, protect the 'face' of the university. This gave the research data a certain 'truthfulness': 'a truthfulness consisting both of an intellectual rigor as well as a certain emotional resonance' (Latham, 2002: 2012).

In this chapter, I have explained the reasons for the mixed research methods chosen to generate my empirical data, and how these methods have enlightened and enlivened my research into the lived working experiences of Chinese and British academic migrants in an 'international' university. My own research experience has shown that employing a single research method would not really secure the empirical knowledge that I required. Taking a methodological approach that opens up multifarious angles and encounters, through an approach that may appear less formal, enabled me to 'get into the gaps' and influenced the richness of the final research data. For example, photo interviews not only allow participants to 'reflect on the particular places' and move away from 'superficial or rehearsed narratives of the place', but also 'in giving an understanding of the more everyday, mundane and less easily storied spaces, which might be overlooked within a more conventional sedentary interview' (Holton and Riley, 2014: 63). I have also argued that apart from the listed methods that I used in this research, accumulated personal relationships and activities allowed me to uncover academic migrants' dynamic everyday life. This in turn facilitated a deep understanding of the situation and allowed me to gather information that is both experiential and related to wider departmental dynamics. Thus, it could be argued that mixed methods in this research were not linear but intricately layered, overlapped and interconnected, and a slight move in one part may affect the situation as a whole.

Chapter Four
Switching Places: Offshore Working Challenges, Opportunities and Reasons for 'Moving'

Introduction

This chapter explores Chinese/British academic migrants' professional movements under two themes: cultivating transnational capital from 'above' and negotiating local restrictions from 'below'. Building upon the transnationalism from above literature, the first section identifies how transnational infrastructural set-ups (namely policy and institutional regulations) allow migrants to gain capitals through cross-country movements. It argues that addressing the national immigration policies and/or institutional regulations is an indispensable step toward identifying the capitals that can affect academics' professional movements. Then, by focusing on grounded transnationalism and transnationalism from below, I argue, in the second section, that academic migrants' reasons for moving are also closely tied to the way they experienced the transnational workplace at the local level. There is clearly a need to 'ground' transnational academic mobility by focusing on academics' everyday experiences as lived reality in the transnational workplace. The transnational academic practice in this chapter is connected to Bourdieu's notion of different forms of capital. Capital, a conceptual tool that runs through the whole chapter, can not only be accumulated through transnational academic mobility, but also can equally be devalued in grounded daily practices, such as teaching or socialising with colleagues. This combination emerges as a significant reason for stimulating academic migrants' future moves.

The chapter seeks to provide a novel angle for understanding how academic mobility can be shaped and produced through national or institutional regulations, grounded practical restrictions and personal considerations. In this chapter, institutions of higher learning can be (re) imagined not just as a transnational academic workplace, or a zone of capital accumulation, but also as an infrastructure that shapes academic migrants' everyday work life, and which in turn produces mobility among academics. In doing so, this chapter highlights inner-linkages between transnationalism from above and below.

1 Cultivating Transnational Capital from 'Above': Importance of Policy and Capital Exchange in Directing Academic Migration

This section shows how national policy or institutional strategy influences transnational academic mobility from 'above'. It needs to be specified that Chinese academic migrants are more directed by national policy for highly skilled migrants, while British academic mobility is mainly influenced by institutional regulations. As such, the section suggests that international educational working experiences (or spatial mobility) can actively create professional 'inequalities' across countries through the capital exchange process.

1.1 Chinese Academics: Transnational Capital Exchange and National Policy

As I mentioned in Chapter Two, the Central Coordination Panel Board of Highly-Qualified Human Resources[1] embarked on a Recruitment Programme of

---

[1] Known in Chinese as '中央人才工作协调小组'.

Highly-Qualified Overseas Talents (also known as the 'Thousand Talents Plan', thereafter the 'Plan')[1] which aimed at introducing around 2,000 world-leading scientists and experts to China within 5 to 10 years to boost China's research and innovation capability. The success of the Plan influenced the transnational mobility of talents. This established an effective policy model for channelling Chinese academic migrants returning to and working for their 'motherland'. Its popularity among its target group is clearly manifested in increasing numbers of returnees the Plan has brought back.

A closer look at the Plan shows that it is targeted at a specific group of academics-professor, Western educated (Ph. D), and younger than 55. It is clear that the Chinese government is taking the 'Western university degree' as an important form of institutionalised cultural capital. Several researchers have mentioned the significance of a 'Western degree' in an Asian context. For example, Ong (1999) suggests that for many Chinese, the American college degree is the ultimate symbolic capital necessary for global mobility. Waters' (2005) study also reveals that a 'Western' university degree can be converted into economic capital more easily back in Asia. Middle-class families regard it as a 'more valuable form of culture capital' in maintaining their 'class reproduction' and 'place-based transnational social networks'. In this regard, cultural capital (or academic capital) can be valued differently in terms of its credibility across academic fields in different countries, as Moore (2008) observes:

> *Culture capital, in terms of two dimensions, accomplishment and transposability, that, in a combined embodied form, give a social agent 'distinction', and that together, determine the relative values of instances of culture symbolic capital. In practical terms, some social agents might be*

[1] For more detailed information about the Plan, see the official website of the Thousand Talents Plan http://www.1000plan.org/qrjh/section/2? m=rcrd (2013/June/25).

high in culture capital (highly accomplished) but in a restricted number of fields —their capital has restricted transposability ('a big fish in a small pond')... Culture capital has its highest value when it is (a) most highly formed and (b) optimised in terms of transposability (2008: 114).

I concur with this view, arguing that (a) it is not only Western degrees, but also high-ranking Western job titles (*e.g.* professor) that can represent more valuable forms of symbolic culture capital in the Chinese academic field than Chinese local educational degrees and titles. (b) In relation to transposablity, forms of capital accumulated in a Western country could be transposed more easily into higher value in China through the Chinese policy for highly skilled migration. Thus, Chinese professors who have a 'Western' Ph. D degree and work at a well-known British university (field of symbolic production) could be seen as 'the highest in culture capital' (Bourdieu, 1988). As capital is 'accumulated, human labour' that can potentially produce different forms of profits (Bourdieu, 1986: 241), the acquisition of capital gives access to power and ultimately to material wealth.

As mentioned in the second chapter, there are a number of scholars who have, from different perspectives, put 'international academic experience' and 'capital' together. They capture the advantage of mobility and theorise it in terms of accumulation of capital, after Bourdieu. The cohort conclude that the international experience is a kind of accumulation of capital that may contribute to the reproduction of social privileges (Brooks and Waters, 2009; Findlay and King, 2010), the wealth accumulation or permanent residence overseas (Liu, 1997) and the future career of transnational academics (Kim, 2010). Correspondingly, my study has discovered that transnational experience in UK academia can greatly enhance Chinese academic migrants' future employment prospects:

Since I have been working in the UK, many Chinese universities came to get in touch with me. This is partly because I have old classmates who work in those universities and introduced me to them, partly because I am a reader who has a doctoral degree from a top level university in the UK and my publications in the UK are considered to be very valuable in China. This has made me more competitive than the local Chinese academics (Xie, researcher, in his 30s, in the UK for 8 years).

From this quote, we can see that embodied culture capital (in an individual person), institutionalised culture capital (in academic qualifications formally conferred by educational establishments), objective culture capital (published books or papers), symbolic capital (title and reputation), and social capital (international academic networks) are considered to be crucial elements for the transnational capital exchange process. Chinese academics who embody a high value of culture capital through working in the UK can convert this into different forms of capital when they move back to China. According to the guideline of the Plan, shortlisted candidates will enjoy a package of privileges that will not only greatly facilitate their research and improve their working conditions, but also promote their social status and the quality of their everyday life. Chinese academic migrants embody an institutionalised culture capital that can be transposed into different forms of capital through the 'Plan' (see table 4-1).

Table 4-1 Connecting capitals with benefits provided by 'Thousand Talents Plan'

Forms of capital	Benefits provided by 'Thousand Talents Plan'
Economic Capital	A. Working conditions and salaries as good as their previous affiliation B. Bid for major state-level projects and funding C. They will enjoy many substantial preferential treatments in terms of taxation, insurance, housing, healthcare, *etc.*
Social Capital	They will have preferential treatment in international travel (if holding a foreign passport), children's education and spouse's career planning, *etc.*

Continued

Forms of capital	Benefits provided by 'Thousand Talents Plan'
Symbolic Capital	A. Fast-tracked to obtain governmental prizes and titles B. Assume leadership in state-owned research institutes C. Take part in policy-making in relevant areas and Chinese national HE standard making D. Great efforts were made to build-up returnees' public image. Many of these elite returnees are highly praised by Chinese official media. They are depicted as a new generation of enthusiastic patriots following in the steps of prominent Western-educated returnees such as Qian Xuesen and Li Siguang,❶ who were respected as role models by post-1949 scholars for their contribution to China

Consequently, these new policies affect individuals' choice of migration or return in different stages of their academic lives, and in the same way, consciously or unconsciously, realise the production and exchange of cultural capital across oceans. For example, Dr. Lu, who is in his 30s holds a Chinese passport and has a permanent post in UK academia but is still keeping an open mind on going back. He expresses a strong inclination towards taking Chinese policy as a springboard to future successes:

Personally, I know I will go back to China some day, but I do not want to go back right now. I know that if I can work in British academia a little longer, I can fit in to the One Thousand Talents Programme for young researchers easily, and through that, I can get a much better post compared to my old classmates in China. Maybe they need 10 years to get to that post, but if I follow the new Chinese policy, I can get that post in 5 years. I will go back to China eventually. One Thousand Talents Programme for me is the

❶ For the image build up of elite returnees in public media, see among others: http://news.xinhuanet.com/comments/2013-06/08/c_116088908.htm (8/June/2013) http://www.1000plan.org/qrjh/section/2? t=9 (26/June/2013).

icing on the cake of my career. (*Lu, researcher, in his 30s, in the UK for 7 years*).

For more established Chinese academic migrants, the capitals accumulated in the UK can be soon changed into economic capital and professional output in China. Prof. Deng thinks that the current Chinese policy is a good starting for turning 'theory' into 'practice' and is going back in order to start his own company and produce more publications.

> *One aspect that the Chinese government is doing particularly well in is giving funding to applied research. With so much input, I am sure that the outcome can be better than ever. From my personal perspective, I do want to go back to China and join the Thousand Talents Programme, because it will help my research and put theory into practice. If I go to China, I will have more chance to do applied research and can establish my own company, making my research into direct products. In the UK, you can do applied research, but you have to do lots of paperwork and the efficiency is much lower. I think one of my major criticisms of British academia is that they are doing lots of fundamental research or 'pure research'. They are doing research just for publishing papers, and the findings might be left in the laboratory forever! (Deng, professor, in his 40s, in the UK for 20 years).*

Over the last decade, China's investments in research funding have been steadily rising. To date, China has invested 1.5% of its gross domestic product (GDP) into relevant sectors❶. This rate is much higher than other developing countries. The instant outcome of China's new policy is publications. Simon and Cao (2009) point out that in the last ten years, the number of papers that have been published by Chinese scientists has risen four-fold. And in 2007, the

❶ The back flow of top Chinese experts: http://club.china.com/data/thread/12171906/2737/28/80/7_1.html (27/June/2013).

number of publications by Chinese academics was second to the US. Prof. Deng also described this situation and saw it as the outcome of Chinese policy:

You can see that there are more and more papers in Science and Nature that are written by Chinese academics. I think that is the direct outcome of the huge financial input related to the Chinese new policy. Personally, I think in my field, China can catch up with the UK in 5 to 10 years. In some special subjects, I think, China is already in the lead. For example, Chinese transgenic research is more advanced than that in the UK. You will have lots of rules if you want to do it in the UK, while in China, you are more free. So, why I want to go back is because, as a 'foreign expert', I could easily get funding and a research team to support my final publications. (Deng, professor, in his 40s, in the UK for 20 years).

While for more privileged professors, who already have liberal income and successful academic attainment, the exchange of economic or social capitals are regarded as less important. Their choice to return to China is motivated more by a deep attachment towards their 'motherland' rather than income or recognition. Ning (2001: 165) highlights the emotional attachment to China felt by Chinese students abroad, arguing that 'the consciousness of being Chinese is cast deeply into their psyches by a lifetime of upheaval and suffering'. The findings of this research also reveal that most Chinese academics still see themselves as Chinese even if they have changed their nationality. So, the attractiveness of return not only comes from economic or practical considerations of further research prosperity, but also from emotional attachments to China. Taking Prof. Yang for example:

I am actually going back to China. I am going to work in the University in which I did my undergraduate study, which is also located in my hometown. They have built a Research Centre for Chinese Health Policy and they have appointed me to be their Director... I am longing to go back to where I am from. (Yang, professor, in her 50s, in the UK for 25 years).

This study finds that Chinese policy is not only focused on providing capitals, but also vigorously promotes patriotism as a strategy to attract Chinese academic migrants. It is interesting to note that on the official website of One Thousand Talents Programme, a big red banner is highlighted: '祖国需要你们，祖国欢迎你们，祖国寄希望于你们！'（Your motherland needs you, your motherland welcomes you, and your motherland has high hopes on you!）. The authority knows that the feeling of non-existence and irrelevance to the host society they live in might consequently lead highly skilled Chinese migrants back to their homeland and they use the concept of 'motherland' and an emotional trigger to attract Chinese migrants back 'home'.

In terms of theory, Bourdieu has long been criticised in his belief that all culture production/practice, including science, is directly pointed towards profit. Some critics（*e. g.* Gartman, 1991; Jenkins, 1992）say that his theory is economically determinist, and most notably Carllé（1992）suggests that Bourdieu's theory fails to make a distinction between profits that can be consciously or potentially calculated and other factors that could not be explained rationally. Human emotions may be one of the 'other factors' mentioned by Carllé. Prof. Yang's motivation, for example, falls into the 'emotional' category. In Prof. Yang's case, she is not taking this move to going back as a way to pursue a higher salary or better position, as she already has one; instead, she regards it as a realisation of self-worth. The main reasons for her return might be the patriotic sentiments long and deeply embedded in her mind and 'following reticence in the immediate shadow of Tiananmen Square, the option of return now appears more attractive'（Ley and Kobayashi, 2005: 156）. For example, she believes that with her professional knowledge and 30 years overseas working experience, she could contribute to her home country. She said:

The Chinese government's main purpose of building this centre is to realise the goal of fostering new types of talent in the new era. As you know, two current problems in China are the inequity of heath treatment and academic corruption. So , I am willing to go back to foster a new generation of Chinese academics , bring some 'fresh air ', and at least , I hope my attitude towards academia can affect the young generation. (Yang , professor , in her 50s , in the UK for 25 years).

Recently, a huge number of famous scientists, such as Shi Yigong❶ have returned to China with a mission: restructuring China's research culture. It had been pointed out that academic corruption and nepotism could be the biggest obstacles for effective scientific research in China. The more 'accomplished' academic returnees, who are usually motivated by Chinese patriotism, want to be a catalyst for change and hope that the Chinese government will support them❷. Prof. Cai holds a similar view, noting that Chinese academia needs to be changed, not only in terms of laboratory equipment, but also in relation to Chinese academics' attitudes towards their careers. And he could be the right person to change the status quo. He said, 'The problem with many of local Chinese academics is that we expect quick results. I blame this on our quick fix, immediate-gratification culture'.

In this case, this group of 'privileged' academics are found to occupy an ambiguous position: On the one hand, they are 'outsiders' with little familiarity with the nature of the Chinese academic system, While on the other hand, the high professional profile of these academics means that they often possess the kinds of capital valued by the local Chinese educational system. Their capitals accumulated in the UK can not only be transformed into economic or social capital (as for younger academics) but also symbolic capital, which is powerful

❶ Shi Yigong: Why coming back to China is my best choice (in Chinese). See: http://news.xinhuanet.com/school/2008-05/08/content_8127981.htm (08/May/2008).

❷ For details see: http://club.china.com/data/thread/12171906/2737/28/80/7_1.html (12/Feb/2012).

enough to influence Chinese academia.

In sum, it is clear that the capital transformation process is different for academics in different career stages. Figure 4 – 1 demonstrates how those groups of Chinese academic migrants in the UK try to transform the more valuable cultural capital they acquired there into other forms of capital through spatial mobility and national policy.

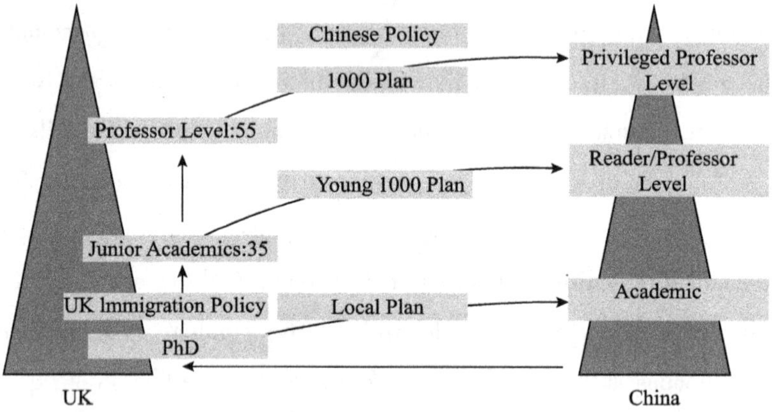

Figure 4 – 1 How different groups of Chinese academic migrants realise capital exchange through national policy

The figures show the possible major 'jumps' for Chinese academics at different stages of their life in relation to the current policy. The straight line at the bottom represents Chinese migration to the UK. After they get their degree, mostly Ph. Ds for academics, they have two choices to make which can realise the 'jump': One is to go back to China through a local or institutional plan and become an academic in China, another is to find a post in UK academia and stick to the UK migration policy in order to stay (or possibly go elsewhere). Under the age of 35, if they are 'good' enough, those who choose to stay have a second chance to consider their future—either go back to China through The Thousand Talents Plan for Young Academics and get into a higher academic position or stay in the UK. For more accomplished professors, the Plan will be a good option for them if they want to go back to China and that leads them to a more privileged position compared to local professors.

1.2 British Academics: Gaining Capital Through Institutional Regulation

One of the biggest challenges for UK IBCs (international branch campuses) is to surmount the insufficient number of core staff from the main UK campuses in order to keep the top teaching/researching standard in their Chinese campuses. Maintaining the same UK academic standard in the branch campuses is important as it directly links to student recruitment, institutional reputation and its future success. Many UK IBCs in China are now painfully aware that brief trips to China and captivating advertisements on websites or newspapers are all very well, but to continually recruit and maintain enough high quality staff in their branch campuses is not as easy. This issue was highlighted in the 2012 review of UK transnational education in China by QAA, and echoed in a report from the higher education think-tank Agora:

> *Many UK vice chancellors and other senior managers go over to China where they are wined, dined and courted, and given the impression that this is a wonderful place to work. They therefore tend to assume that everyone would think that going to China to work would be very attractive. This is an error. The day-to-day reality of working longer term in China is much tougher. There is a world of difference between a brief senior management tour and longer term working in China with all the difficulties that entails (Gow, 2007).*

Existing literature shows that UK IBCs have been 'beset by a reluctance of UK based staff to move abroad' (Salt and Wood, 2014: 92). There is a reluctance among British core academic staff to come to the Chinese campuses because of the educational resource imbalance between these two countries, ideological differences, the risk of less research output, or individual family commitments (Gow, 2007). Moreover, even among those who chose to work in China, it is quite hard persuading them to stay on a long-term basis (Salt and Wood, 2014), which means UK institutions in China are constantly losing staff with local knowledge accumulated on site who would be in a position to contribute to their further retention. As Rupert, observed:

> *Obviously, it will be extremely difficult to get somebody to do what I am doing, and people who now apply for those posts when we offer them are generally not even British! It's very difficult to get a British head of a department here; the head of × department is German, for example. (Rupert, senior manager, in his 50s, in China for 2 years).*

It is noticeable that academics from the home institution, especially British academics, seem to be preferred over others in UK IBCs. Salt and Wood's work (2013) highlights that the groups of academics who composed the main initial secondments from the 'home' institutions are senior managers, language teachers, postdoctoral researchers, and the researchers who might have stalled in the UK. While in my own research, participants identify an obvious gap among academic migrants: Most of them are either established senior professors/managers or academics at an early stage in their careers. Research active staff in their 'golden research age' (from 35 ~ 45) are relatively absent. Those academics from the main campus, especially those in the 'golden age', are considered to be the 'key' to keep the Chinese campus at the 'same academic standard' as the UK campus. This means the symbolic capital or academic capital embedded in those academics makes them more in demand than academics from elsewhere.

Salt and Wood (2013) further suggest that due to the lack of academics from 'home', international staff have often been recruited directly by the IBCs as an alternative option for the 'home staff shortage', and many of them are from India, Sri Lanka, Pakistan, Bangladesh, United States and European countries.

However, I was informed by my participants that this group of international staff so far appears to be ad hoc, which means they do not have the right to be redeployed by the home institution if random vacancies arise. Recruiting international staff could be regarded as an effective short-term method to solve the shortage of UK-based academic staff available for dispatching. However, it is possible that this 'emergency measure' might not be compatible with the long-term development of IBCs, as a manager suggested that this would affect the expected quality of teaching and research:

> *There is a consequence, and good for you to make it anonymous, that the people who applied are not as good as we expected. Most of the time, you only start to look for a job in Asia, if you have difficulty in finding a job in your own country. (Andy, manager, in his 50s, in China for 3 years).*

The quality of academics in IBCs is of vital importance. Based on research on policy and strategy of transnational education in China, Yuan (2014) suggests that the key to transnational education's long-term success is to keep the high quality UK teaching standard rather than being too obsessed with financial gain. Salt and Wood (2014: 89) echo Yuan, writing that 'success depends on an ability to continue recruiting staff with the right academic and administrative expertise, able to reflect the quality ethos of the parent institution while adapting to working in a non-UK context'. The current concern is that even using international recruitment, high standard teaching quality is at risk, because too few high-quality teaching staff (no matter where they are coming from) are willing to participate for various reasons as mentioned earlier.

The solution could be either to change the recruitment strategies or to improve the standard of management and make working in China more attractive for high calibre staff. One campus review report suggests that all the qualified members of academic staff in the case-study university need to have a Postgraduate Certificate in Higher Education or equivalent certificate. It goes on to say that the requirements of the Quality Manual need to be more formalised and staff training opportunities beyond the PGCHE should be provided for junior staff in the Chinese campus. Introductions are also recommended for newly arriving academic staff to make sure they know how to work with expected high efficiency in the new academic environment. Moreover, it is suggested that training modules, workshop sessions, project work, and a system of peer teaching observation should be continually provided and verified by the university. At the time I was collecting my research data in 2013, an improved version of the Chinese cultural training lecture was being given by an experienced senior manager from the main campus, in the creative form of theatre performance. However, the feedback I received from the interviewees was not all positive. Some of them suggested that it was 'amusing' rather than 'practical'.

In order to attract more 'staff of the highest calibre', the university offers attractive remuneration, welfare and a benefits package for relocation in terms of accommodation, travel, medical insurance, schooling for children and removals. Firstly, for accommodation, approximately 5000 RMB (500 GBP) allowance per month is provided for renting a place on or off campus. There are staff hotel rooms for single academics and apartments for family relocation on campus. Both Chinese and Western food is offered by a restaurant especially for international academics. For living off campus, the university support team is available to find a suitable place near the campus or in the city centre. Secondly, in terms of travel, air tickets are provided by the university for outward and return journeys to the home country. Moreover, there are several chances to fly back to the UK or other countries to attend conferences every year. Thirdly, as Chinese government health insurance is not available to foreigners, private medical insurance is arranged for academics and accompanying family members. Several hospitals in the city have a separate waiting room and the newest medical facilities for foreigners. For those who take up academic posts (lecturer and above), there is also support with international schooling for their children. Finally, the university assists with the removal of all personal belongings to and from China.

Most participants expressed their satisfaction in terms of financial gain whilst doing their current job in China. Indeed, that is one of the main reasons that many of them choose to come. The Chinese government's three-year tax-exemption policy for foreigners makes a huge difference to British academics' wages in China. Claire expressed the view that this was a strategic move for her to quickly realise the economic capital accumulation in her early career stage:

> *Among my colleagues, some are happy, some unhappy. It is really hard to say they are right or wrong, as one man's dream job is another man's nightmare. However, we all agree that the money is good. You get about 5000 RMB housing on top of your salary and you do not need to pay tax for the first three years. If you take the far lower cost of living in China into account, the three-year-tour in China can bring you a fortune that you usually need six years to get in the UK (Claire, lecturer, in her 30s, in China for a year).*

However, the advantage of high income is not as simple as it is shown in the university recruiting advertisement. The university adopted an annual salary based wage system, based upon three categories. Firstly, the standard academic staff wages for staff seconded from the UK main campus (detailed wage standard can be seen in Table 4 – 2). Secondly, expatriate staff wages for international recruitment—the wage scale depends upon the actual needs of the university and concerns a similar domestic and international university wage system. Thirdly, the university employs two different salary systems based on two national standard (China and the UK). The salary of Chinese administrative staff (who are directly recruited by the Chinese counterpart of the university), is indexed with standard Chinese university wages (approximately ten times less than British wages for administrative staff). In adopting the three dimensional system of staffing strategies, all recruitment is based on signed employment contracts.

Participants mentioned the salary differences depend very much upon the recruiting category:

To be honest, this is a good place to earn money if you get on the right contract. For example, one of my colleagues with a Ph. D from UCL is teaching a Master's level course and paid less than an English tutor with a Master's degree. It totally depends on where you signed the contract. If you signed in the UK and got paid in pounds, you would naturally have higher salary than your colleague who was recruited in China and earned RMB, even if he/she teached the higher-level course (Sara, English tutor, in her late 20s, in China for 2 years).

The holidays are great in this university for fractional staff. They work 35 weeks a year and get the equivalent of the full-time salary. This is better than the situation for the full time staff, as we work for the full calendar year rather than the academic year. There is holiday provision of course, but it is counted weekly. (Andy, senior researcher, in his 40s, in China for 4 years).

Table 4 – 2 Standard wage scale in a British IBC

Jobs by Type	Professional Stage	Annual Wages
Academic or Research	Professor/associate professor	Salary is negotiable depending on skills and experience and will be within the Professorial range, minimum £ 57031 per annum.
	Assistant professor	£ 33562 to£ 45053
	Senior research fellow	£ 36661 to£ 45053
	Research associate/ fellow	£ 25013 to£ 31644
Professional or Managerial	Head of IP commercialisation	£ 47787 to£ 57031
	Technical manager	£ 36661 to£ 45053
	Senior mental health adviser	£ 36661 to£ 45053
	Post graduate manager	£ 28132 to£ 36661

Continued

Jobs by Type	Professional Stage	Annual Wages
Clerical	Administration officer	£ 21597 to£ 25759
	Library advisor	£ 16705 to£ 19802
Technical	Technician	£ 21597 to£ 24289

Source: university official website, 25/02/2014

One crucial element that alters British academics' decision to stay or leave the branch campus is the balance between the university wage system and Chinese tax policy for foreigners. There are specific tax agreements between China and foreign countries such as the US and the UK. British academics in this IBC do not need to pay tax, if they are in their first three years of working in China. After entering the fourth year in China, British academics are required to contribute a certain percentage of their monthly wages for tax payment subject to a threshold set by local government (See: Table 4 – 3). As paying or not paying tax can make a huge difference in terms of personal income, many choose to leave in the fourth year.

Table 4 – 3 Income Tax Rates in China for an individual in 2013

Tax %	Monthly Income (CNY)
3%	1 ~ 1500
10%	1501 ~ 4500
20%	4501 ~ 9000
25%	9001 ~ 35000
30%	35001 ~ 55000
35%	55001 ~ 80000
45%	80001 and above

Source: China Tax Law official website

Interestingly, as reported by participants, some 'smarter' foreign academics learned how to get around the Chinese tax rules. Although tax-exemption only legally lasts three years in China and is non-renewable, in some cases, local government tax departments fail to trace foreigners' taxation history in other cities in China, giving people a chance to exploit a loophole in the legal system. So, they chose to leave China for some time, a semester for example, and go back working in another Chinese city, then, they can restart their 'duty-free' experience in China. However, the three years tax-exemption was removed in 2014, although a university was able to negotiate that those who had started their contract tax exemption could continue but new staff would no longer have the privilege.

2 Negotiating Restrictions from 'Below': How Is Academic Mobility Influenced by the Reproduction of Academic (Dis) advantage in Professional Practice?

Part one demonstrated and identified how academic mobility can be affected by transnational capital exchange (resulting from national policy and institutional regulations). This research builds on this, arguing that academic mobility is not only directed by the possibility of capital exchange, but also largely influenced by agents' grounded experiences in the 'host' institution. This is because although working abroad might be very attractive for academics, the day-to-day reality of working in the 'host' workplace is much tougher (Gow, 2007). So, this section mainly focuses on Chinese and British transnational academics' grounded experiences of working in the transnational academic workplace, to see how these two groups of academics negotiate with national or local restrictions from below, which in turn alters their transnational academic movements.

2.1 Chinese Academics

2.1.1 'Why Can't We Stay?' The British Political Restrictions for Chinese Academics

It is important to note that the back flow of highly skilled migrants to their home countries has been soaring in recent years (Fatiguso, 2007). This 'talent backflow phenomenon' is mainly caused by the restrictions of immigration policy and the reduction of government scholarship grants in the ' host ' countries (Zhang, 2012). China, as the biggest sending country of ' talents ', had also been affected by this phenomenon. For example, from 2000 to 2005, the number of Chinese academic returnees has almost tripled. (Fatiguso, 2007). The statistics in Giordano and Pagano's (2013) study show the backflow of Chinese intellectuals increased 25% from 2005 to 2013. This current trend of return migration gives us a reason to look at how new changes in British policy are influencing the migration decisions of academic migrants.

In the UK, the immigration policy for highly skilled migration (including academics) has been progressively restricted. More specifically, the recent policy adjustments render young postgraduate students' pursuit of long-term career in the UK increasingly difficult. In March 2008, the Highly Skilled Migrant Programme (HSMP) was replaced by a Tier 1 point—based immigration system. The new point—based visa system (which was in fact was introduced as early as November 2006 under HSMP) shows a strong preference to young (under 28 years old), in full-time employment and well-paid (higher than UK average income) applicants,[1] whereas having a higher level of diploma does not make a considerable difference (30 points for a bachelor degree, 35 points for a master degree and 45 points for a doctoral degree). Moreover, the removal of the Post Study Work (PSW) visa since April 2012 has made it ever harder for university graduates to settle in the UK.

Thus, for those early career Chinese academics who want a step into British academia, culture capital is acquired over time through a systematic process of inculcation. The relatively demanding British immigration policy acts as a barrier

[1] The new point-based Tier 1 visa assessment system (valid since April 2010) looks for higher ' quality ' migrants. In order to get 5 points, the applicant's income has to be at least 25, 000 GBP. While it is hard for young applicants to reach the requirement, as the median wage in the UK for all jobs is only about 20, 000 GBP. http: //news. bbc. co. uk/1/hi/8151355. stm (25/July/2014).

that they must 'jump over'. Bourdieu (1984: 208) suggests that this group of people tend to be those that belong to the ruled class, as they have not fully grasped the rules of the 'game'. Newcomers must buy a 'ticket' for their first game play, in order to fully understand the value of the 'game' and to get some practical information about it. Many of my early career Chinese participants expressed their views on the policy restriction and specified how it influenced their sojourn in the UK. Firstly, as mentioned, one of the main changes of the new policy is related to more restrictive revenue scores. Dr. Hu said, for most of the early stage researchers, it is really hard to reach the new immigration policy standard:

*Based on past income criteria, 20000 pounds is equal to 15 points*❶*. But now, if you want to have 15 points, you need to earn 30000 pounds, about 50 % higher. Now 20000 pounds is only equal to 5 points. So, young researchers like me will no longer comply with the new policy standards, because of my lower revenue score (Hu, researcher, in his 30s, in the UK for 3 years).*

Secondly, doctoral degree applicants will no longer be able to get direct access to the UK's high-tech academic immigrant visa. Thirdly, the age requirement is not suitable for most young Chinese academics.

Under the new policy standards, even if you have a British doctoral degree and meet the revenue criteria, you also need to be under the age of 28. In China, we normally spend 4 years on undergraduate study and 3 years on a Master's degree, while here, you only need 3 years for your undergraduate and 1 year for a Master's. So, that means if you did your Master's degree in China, it will be very hard for you to finish a British

❶ Tier one of the point-based system allows highly skilled migrants to come to Britain to look for work or self-employment opportunities for up to two years. To qualify, applicants must score at least 75 points based on their qualifications, previous earnings, age, language skills and have at least £ 2800 in their bank account.

Ph. D before the age of 28. In a word, it is much harder for us to be eligible to apply for UK's highly skilled immigrant visa. (Hu, researcher, in his 30s, in the UK for 3 years).

Those lucky ones who have got through the 'harsh' selection of the UK immigration policy and secured a place in UK universities or research institutes nevertheless have every reason to feel concerned. In terms of financial support, science and research funding in the UK has experienced budget cuts since 2010[1], due to the global economic crisis. Such a heavy blow to the research sector of the UK forced many international researchers, including Chinese researchers, to have second thoughts about their future. Apart from that, there are some practical issues related to the current immigration policy. Dr. Wen, who had already worked in UK academia for 5 years, pointed out his concerns about falling into the so-called 'naturalisation' dilemma:

I think I am now in a kind of 'naturalisation' dilemma. Chinese law stipulates that citizens cannot hold dual nationality. If you have the British passport, you can travel around the world, which is very handy for my academic career. However, you will have a lot of restrictions in relation to visiting relatives or long-term residence in China. My parents, my wife and kids are in China and I have to visit them regularly. Therefore, I choose to have permanent residency and it is only in this way that I can keep my Chinese passport. (Wen, researcher, in his 30s, in the UK for 5 years).

To summarise, an increasing number of Chinese students choose to go abroad for postgraduate education as a result of the relatively 'lower quality' of higher education in China; however, the increasingly harsh UK immigration policy and financial austerity have made survival in British academia and R and I (Research and Innovation) sector increasingly difficult. This may have gradually

[1] Wang Zhongcheng, UK's Resaerch Funding and Trend in the Post-crisis Era, Prospects of Global Sci-Tech Economy, (25/July /2014).

caused a higher out-flow of Chinese academic migrants from the UK back to China.

2.1.2 'Why Can't We Return?' The Restrictions of Chinese Policy of Talents

It needs to be pointed out that although the CPC Central Committee and the Chinese Government have launched the 'Thousand Talents Project' and relevant programmes for attracting Chinese migrants to return, 'among 50 million returned overseas Chinese, only 20 thousand have been identified by the government as highly skilled and leading professionals' (Wang, 2012). In other words, most Chinese academic migrants are not able to fit into the official Thousand Talents Project but join a relevant local programme. In this scenario, some of the participants who have joined the local programme expressed the idea that there exists a great imbalance in relation to income and benefits between foreign experts and foreign nationals (the one with a British passport). For example, based on his experience, Prof Zhen said:

At first I though I might fit into the Thousand Talents Project for the Foreign Expert, but then, I have found that they are only interested in foreigners. Although I have a British passport, I am not a 'pure' British, because I was born in China. This is a silly requirement. I just cannot join the plan because of my nationality. I know China better than they do and I have the professional expertise as well, but I have to join another programme just because of my nationality! So I get lower treatment (Zhen, professor, in his 50s, in the UK for 23 years).

Prof. Zhou also shared his experience of this 'unfairness'. He said:

I have a good example, one British expert applied for a post in the same research centre as I did, and the university gives him a higher salary. One day I met him and he knew that I was better than him in this particular field, so he wanted me to be the director and he could be the vice director. But still, our salary does not match with our post, just because of our nationality! It did hurt me because in some way I gave up everything for my home country and I have never thought I am a British instead of a Chinese. This is unfair. However, I know that I need to compromise if I want to go back to China. (Zhou, professor, in his 60s, in the UK for 28 years).

Although Chinese returnees can transpose their culture capital into more valuable other forms of capital through spatial movements, the inequality still exists. This, in Bourdieu's term, is 'symbolic violence'. The country of origin can play an important symbolic role in capital exchange across oceans, whilst the actual process of exchange creates social unfairness. So, this 'unfairness' and imbalance of capital exist not just between local Chinese academics and the Chinese returnees, but also between 'pure foreign' academics and the academic migrants. This illustrates one thing that was missed in Bourdieu's theory, that nationality itself could be regarded as a form of capital in the transnational education context. This argument is also supported by academic migrants' teaching experience, which will be discussed in Chapter Five. Here it is seen that Chinese students at the branch campus prefer teachers from the UK or other nations rather than Chinese academic migrants who have returned from the UK or elsewhere. So, I argue that there is a particular kind of 'nationality capital' that operates in the transnational capital exchange process, which results in unevenness between different nationalities.

2.1.3 Problems in Situ: Why Am I Considering Moving (or Not Moving)?

For those who have already settled in the UK, Chinese academic migrants at different career stages are facing different difficulties. Prof. Wang, who is in his 50s, is concerned about his retirement pension:

I have stayed in the UK for almost 30 years, but because I have not worked in UK academia for more than 30 years, I cannot get my full retirement pension here after my retirement. (Wang , senior researcher , in his 40s , in the UK for 24 years).

In contrast, Dr. Zhu, who is in her 30s, is more worried about her parents. Because of the UK immigration policy, she cannot move her parents into the UK. She said:

Talking about coming back , one of my major motivations is my parents. They have the right to come to the UK but only on a short-term basis. If they want to stay here longer for example , they have to go back to China and wait for a period of time and then come back again. As they are getting older , and my mother has heart disease , long distance flight is not suitable for them anymore. So , I am worried that I won ' t have the chance to take good care of them. Also , it is impossible for them to change nationality , because the UK policy has a restriction for a migrant's parents that only the parent or parents who have been unemployed for a certain number of years (i. e. without income and dependant upon their child) in China can have the right to be a UK citizen. Both of my parents are retired teachers. They cannot fit in to the unemployment category. (Zhu , researcher , in her 30s , in the UK for 8 years).

It needs to be mentioned that filial piety is playing a very important role in migrants' decision process. The concept of filial piety is related to the intimacy and quality of the parent—child relationship. If the immigration policy is in someway building barriers against 'gratitude and willingness to repay one's parents' care and sacrifice' for Chinese migrants, it will greatly affect the quality of favouring the intimate bond between family members (*qin qi*) and eventually affect academic migrants' plans.

Chinese academics who choose to come back to China, also have to make many 'compromises'. For example, although the Chinese academic returnees have substantial preferential treatments, such as taxation, insurance, housing, healthcare, children's education and spouse's career planning, *etc.*, if one goes through more detailed regulations or relevant local programmes, the Chinese policy fails to cover some important elements needed by Chinese academic returnees. For example, Prof. Li pointed out that healthcare is still a problem for her, as she did not join the national One Thousand Talents Programme but a local Scholars Programme. She said:

> *I have to give up my coveted tenure-track professor position in the UK and my wage/treatment is much lower than I can get in here. I will have no old-age pension and I have to buy medical insurance in China. Although the university does pay partially for my medical insurance, the problem is that I have diabetes mellitus and hypertension. As all the medicines I am taking right now are produced in the UK, I cannot apply for reimbursement for imported drugs by using my Chinese medical insurance. (Li, professor, in her 50s, in the UK for 19 years).*

Wang's (2012) research suggests that in the next 10 ~ 30 years the window of opportunity is closing, as the Chinese population is aging rapidly due to the implementation of the one-child policy. For example, some programmes fail to provide overall medical service for Chinese academic migrant returnees. However, as research indicates, 'the Chinese professionals over 40 years of age care about benefits and need a stable income' (Cai and Klyushina 2009: 39). China, therefore, even if it is capable of attracting a huge number of academic migrants from abroad, is not yet able to exercise the same kind of force towards substantial benefits to retain the talent pool in national bases. In that sense, 'the role of the national government is important because foreign talent is becoming more footloose, selective and demanding about which countries and opportunities will best suit its needs' (Harvey, 2013: 56).

When thinking about eventually moving back to China, there are some concerns too. My participants informed me that the symbolic capital entrusted to the Chinese government, university and the Chinese society provoked tacit problems between those elite returnees and local academic elites.

One essential conclusion in Bourdieu's study is that distinctions in social class are more or less reinforced by educational related capitals, and the educational system is dominated by the elites. However, when you use Bourdieu's theory as a tool for examining the nature of interaction between returned academics and local academics (for example, Prof. Yang's case), there are two issues that need to be considered. First, the lack of local educational knowledge/capital of most returnees, plus their ambitions of 'changing the rules', could provoke potential conflicts between returnees and local academics. In the process of 'bringing fresh air', it is hard to predict local academics' reactions, especially for those local elites (*e. g.* Chinese educated professors or head of the department), as the 'outsiders' are trying to change the 'rule' of the game. If this is the case, the situation will no longer be that the 'educational system is dominated by academic elites' but rather a question that the education system will 'be dominated by which group of academic elites'. Second, although these elite academic returnees have highly accomplished and transposable culture capital, they are mostly lacking in 'political capital'[1], as most of them have changed their nationality to British and China does not admit dual-citizenship. So, the UK and Chinese policy needs not only to consider attracting international academics as a group but also their subsequent integration into the workplace and society as a whole.

2.2 British Academics

Chinese academics mentioned relatively few 'problems' related to working

[1] In Joel Andreas's (2009) analysis of the Chinese educational system, he mainly looks at two types of capital, namely culture (academic certificates) and political (party membership). In his assessment, only these two types of capital are influential in gaining access to higher-class positions in China.

in the 'host' workplace but more problems with Chinese and British policy. In contrast, British academics in China did not tend to have problems with immigration policy; they were more concerned about their actual difficulties in terms of, academic practice and management, which are often the crucial elements that influence their future mobility. This empirical section seeks to provide a novel angle for looking at how institutions of higher learning can be (re) imagined as not just a transnational workplace, or a zone of capital accumulation for academics, but also an infrastructure that shape people's everyday working experiences, and then produce a very particular kind of mobility among academics.

2.2.1 Issues of Academic Practice

Although the English tutors in the university generally have a positive view towards the degree of educational freedom they get in China compared to other Chinese universities, there are still frequent attempts to 'bind their feet', and specifically problems towards teaching. One of the key problems reported by English tutors is that they have limited freedom to develop material for the class they teach, they cannot tailor the material to the needs of specific students, because they teach a prescribed curriculum with its own material approved by the administration office.

From the administrative perspective, the restriction of basic teaching materials for the preparation year is supposed to be reasonable and acceptable. However, from British academics' standpoint, the limited freedom in choosing teaching materials can cause problems in practice. Participants reported on the combined challenges of working with students from places that varied in English teaching standard, from rural parts of China, mega-cities, or foreign countries. Prescribed teaching material does not help this complex situation. There are some too who disagree: 'I just believe that everyone has expectations of work, they are interpreted negatively when their expectations are met. So the statement by those tutors is nothing to do with university, but only their negative interpretation of the situation'. (Jane, English tutor, in her 30s, in China for 3 years).

Nuttall and Edwards (2014: 103) suggest that places can 'offer a range of curriculum opportunities' and 'provide an anchor-point for teacher education'. It is true that transnational working experience can be a capital accumulation process that allows academics to make sense of the social and cultural connections that underpin their successful academic career. However, we should not overlook the point that transnational workplaces also have restrictions which mean academics' capitals may not only be accumulated but can also be curtailed, even devalued, in certain circumstances.

In terms of future development, capital could also be devalued for particular groups of British academics. As I mentioned earlier, for those well established academics who have been provided a senior manager position or young academics in their early career stage, their Chinese working experience would be regarded as a golden opportunity as they might get promoted faster either in the UK or China (the advantages vary across disciplines). However, among other research active British academics, some concerns are raised that the uncertainty of working at a primary stage IBC might risk their research reputation (Salt and Wood, 2014).

The majority of participants implied that although the university is providing them opportunities to attend international conferences, it is nearly impossible to keep pace with the intensive conference opportunities they have in the UK. It is mainly because of the physical distance and educational gap between the two countries, as 'research exchange has been predominately with universities in the developed world' (Salt and Wood, 2014: 88). As a result, it is also been reported that academic networks in the UK have also been affected, not just because of the inconvenience of attending a conference, but also due to the fact that the IBC's reputation in the UK is not as impressive as the UK parent university:

> *One academic I met during a conference asked me whether setting up IBCs is like building chain businesses like McDonald's. Well, to be honest, I was offended by that! (William, Reader, in his 40s, in China for 2 years).*

Among those early-mid career academics with support for project funding and local institutional collaboration, the quality of research facilities is always an issue, especially for those participants who need access to high quality laboratories. In terms of publication, the majority of participants noted that the quality and quantity of their publications have not been really affected because of the use of modern communications. Sometimes they even get more publishing opportunities from Chinese government projects or other Chinese research groups. Some academics, however, especially in the Humanities, are reluctant to accept the chances, due to the limited academic freedom and Chinese journals' lower international impacts:

> *I do get chances to get published in China. Last year, the local government contacted me and asked me to be the person in charge for one of their city-planning projects. The money they offered is good and they promised to help me get my related work published in Chinese. But, then I found they have their own ideals about the plan and I felt I was being restricted by their project framework. (John, Professor, in his late 40s, in China for 3 years).*

2.2.2 Management Issues

An important aspect of academics' overseas experience is to navigate a new management style that has been partly influenced by local systems and unfamiliar working mechanisms. The current management style in the university was reported as a major source of rising British academics' dissatisfaction. When asked about the management quality, these two participants commented:

The main problem was, and by all accounts still is, management. There is a delayed response to everything, as nearly all decisions have to be made first in the UK. (Henry, lecturer, in his 30s, in China for 3 years).

The management here is more or less on a major power play. I think the university is economically driven. They sell British education as a product in China, so they need to cooperate with Chinese. This might be a reason why they are increasingly promoting ambitious people with a lack of management skills in the academic field. I never understand this power hungry approach in our university. I have to say, although our university did lots of advertisements to promote its positive reputation, it is no longer on many academics' wish list. (Lily, senior lecturer, in her 30s, in China for a year).

In discussing the issues around management with the participants, 'power' was the most frequently used keyword in describing the differences they experienced in China and back in the UK. It is important to be clear that the 'power centred management style' (intensified hierarchical relations between colleagues) is not likely to be experienced by all staff, as managers in some departments are reported to be professional and thoughtful. However, many staff still report that management practices might operate according to very different logics that are not readily acceptable to them. As two participants put it:

In the UK campus, when the department arrives at a decision about what it is going to do, we get there in a very democratic fashion. We have meetings about it, committees, working groups, we vote on things. We usually make a majority decision. The head of the department does not say 'we do this', because other staff might have different views. The hierarchy is more informal in Britain. As a head of school, you have so many things to do and you need to keep your colleagues by your side. You cannot say 'I am the boss, go and do this'. This place is run a bit like a Chinese institution, it is more hierarchical. Even the same staff in the UK campus who would be very democratic became much more hierarchical when they get to China. I am not saying they give people orders, they do it politely, I mean they send you emails directly saying 'we are going to do this' no matter whether you agree or not. I do not understand, most of my colleagues are not Chinese, and they know it is crazy to make decisions like this in the UK, but they did not make any objections. Why are these guys from the UK giving orders and why are people choosing to obey them? That is why this place is very inefficient compared to our British university. (Amy, professor, in her 50s, in China for 4 years).

The head of the department here always sends emails to the faculty office when he wants to contact his colleagues. He does not send us emails directly...do not ask me why... haha! The result is, even though he is just around the corridor there, he feels much further away than he is, because his emails go down to the faculty office then go up here. You know 'deal with the faculty office'! If someone tried to do that in the UK the secretary would say 'go away, send your own emails, I've got too much work to do'. (Nick, professor, in his 50s, in China for 6 years).

These comments refer to a practice that most British academics are unlikely to be familiar with from their experience in the UK. However, as Amy mentioned, the fact that the university is in China means 'Chinese working styles' are to be expected. As both learners and practitioners, managers are in an inevitably awkward position: negotiating with Chinese government, British authorities in the UK campus, Chinese administration staff, and foreign academic staff from different countries. They are confronted with an array of different 'rules of the game' which determines the difficulties they found in making things 'right', as the word 'right' loses its meaning in this complex working place.

Pressure not only comes from senior British managers but also Chinese administrative staff. For example, participants reported that a few years ago the administration office sent an email to a group of academic staff to inform them of meeting on a fixed time and date, which raised some issues and most invited staff refused to attend the meeting, because they were not being 'respected'. However, for those administrative staff employed by the Chinese partner of the university, it is common sense that a group meeting time should be fixed by a manager rather than all the group members. Without acknowledging the local working rules, the majority of the participants felt dejected by the way they were treated, though all of them understood there was no malice on the part of their Chinese colleagues. This observation resonates with the overseas academic experience discussed in Dobos's (2011) study on international academics working at an offshore campus in Malaysia.

Indeed, although the initial plan of building the offshore campus in China was to protect the authentic character of the British university as a major educational force, in practice, this does not necessarily happen because the employees at IBCs need to be 'serving two masters' (Dobos, 2011). It will always be a puzzle for people working in that environment as they naturally reject things only because it differs from 'what it should be like', without realising that this does not necessarily need to be viewed in entirely negative terms. The working rules in the new working place have been changed without notice; however, one academic has opposite view towards the change:

This institution seems to have adopted a hierarchical working culture. A certain type of manager wants primarily to boost their ego rather than effect success and improvement. So, frustratingly our focus shifts from 'doing a good job' to 'being led and following regardlessly'. It is not negotiation, not consultation, it is not seeking agreement, and therefore, they make very bad decisions. If you do not discuss your decision with your colleague, they do not have the chance to tell you what kind of problems you would have from their practical perspective. So, a few months later, these crazy decisions end up like a disaster. They know that their decisions have caused the problems, but they continue to make decisions by themselves. So, you get lots of strange decisions. British university works better with the British working culture they normally have, but for some strange reason that culture does not exist here. This is not like our main campus at all. (Nick, senior manager, in his 50s, in China for 5 years).

In general, both positive and negative feedback has been received in relation to university management. It has been observed that the capacity for acceptance from individuals could greatly affect people's attitude in regards to changes of ' rules ' in their offshore working period. As an experienced professor stated:

In general, there are quite a few unhappy faces amongst the staff here. Maybe this is a stuffy British thing. I know they moan a lot just about everything... it grates sometimes... If you know enough about China, you will understand the things you thought unacceptable are nothing out of the ordinary here. You can never expect everything to run in the exact same way that it does in the UK, I do not think that is realistic to be honest. They look a little bit pampered, and forget they are overly paid for those inconveniences. (Paul, Professor, in his 60s, in China for 6 years).

Based on these different views on the issues around management in the branch campus, it is worth noting that the transnational academic workplace is a relatively more complicated space, which includes various academic, cultural, social interactions and conflicts among managers, international academics and other university staff. The grounded management difficulties do not just impact on participants' decisions to ' go back ' or ' go elsewhere '. They also have unpredictable influences on the academics at the ' home ' campus who are considering ' coming to ' the branch campus, as it usually travels ' by word of mouth '. (Derek, Lecture, in his 30s, in China for 3 years).

2.2.3 Personal Issues

As discussed earlier, there is a huge imbalance in recruitment between different age groups of international academics in IBCs in China. Salt and Wood's (2014) explanation of this issue, such as the perceived threat to career opportunities and research reputation on a relatively immature IBC (where there is possibly a lack of academic networks, access to laboratories or academic freedom) is also echoed in my research. However, one of the key reasons I found behind this age gap phenomenon is family commitment. A senior manager at one of the institutions commented:

> *So there are two types of person you get coming to China. One is the slightly older people like me. Their children are grown up, and they will be the most senior people. Or there will be younger people who have not yet got married or do not have children, so it is easier for them to come. But what is missing are people kind of in their 30s or 40s. It is very difficult to get the group in the middle. So, it is harder to get staff to come here for that reason, and fewer people apply for that reason. (Gary, professor, in his 50s, in China for 3 years).*

Although the branch university agrees to provide reward packages for family relocation in terms of housing and schooling for children, the real support facilities, like international schools, have not quite reached the UK standard yet. For example, many participants who have small children are concerned about the quality of the international school and limited educational resources for children in the region. There are only two newly established international schools in the city where the campus is located, one of them is close to the campus and the other one is one hour away by car (most British participants do not drive a car in China). Participants reported that the closest one cannot provide satisfactory education for children, and it would be inconvenient to go to the other one. Jack, a father of two young kids stated:

This is not Shanghai or Beijing. The English language schooling here is quite poor. There are only two schools in the city that are English speaking. They are really very bad. My son stayed here for 2 years, and went back because of the school. My colleagues in the UK know about it too, as people do gossip around. That is a problem for anybody who is moving here. (Jack, English tutor, in his early 30s, in China for 1.5 years).

In contrast to those mid-career staff that are constrained by research imperatives, well-established managers or professors' careers may prosper through their transnational experience (Salt and Wood, 2014). Logically, it would not be a big issue to second sufficient British senior leaders to China. However, one of the manager's long HR experience also suggests that actually, the education issue for children does affect anyone who has children and family commitments, even for senior managers in some cases. This is one of the reasons why the university suffers in finding suitable British departmental leaders. He said:

One of the main problems is about recruiting UK senior managers. They are going to be in their 40s or 50s. If they have small children, it is always more difficult to move to another country, and some of them do have small children. I have two sons, but they are grown up. They can live and work in the UK without me. (Rupert, senior manager, in his 50s, in China for 2 years).

Another unresolved problem is related to pensions. From 2011 onwards, the retirement age of British academics was raised from 60 to 65 years old. Moreover, for those who newly joined the pension scheme, their pension would be calculated on the average wage of their entire academic career rather than the highest salary before the retirement. As a result of averaging the highest and lowest salary, the pension is reduced relatively when compared to what they would have received before the pension scheme reform. This reform also caused concerns among British academic migrants in China, because the longer they stay in China the less pension they might get in the future, as the branch university is not responsible for their pension payments in the UK. Many of the participants, regardless of their age and gender were concerned about their pension:

The salary is not bad but on the other hand there is no pension in it. We have to pay our National Insurance contributions by ourselves while we are working in China , otherwise we will be destitute after the retirement. (Nick , professor , in his 50s , in China for 6 years).

British academics could not rely on their UK pension schemes if they continue to work in China, while the current Chinese pension system has proved to be unpractical for them too. Based on Chinese law, all institutions must contribute approximately 40 percent of the employee's basic payroll to the so-called ' five one insurance fund' that refers to endowment insurance, medical insurance, unemployment insurance, industrial injury insurance, maternity insurance and housing accumulation funds, ' unless an exemption is provided under an applicable bilateral social security tantalisation agreement' (Deloitte, 2013: 16). In practice, participants revealed that the above fund was actually useless. As the majority of them only stay in China for three to five years, there is no need for them to buy unemployment insurance and endowment insurance, as they will not retire in China. They are more in need of medical insurance. However, the Chinese health insurance does not reach the UK standard, so the university needs to buy extra business health insurance for foreign staff.

The university ended up paying a million pounds on unsuitable insurance policies. It is not only a burden on the university, but also aroused dissatisfaction among academic migrants:

The university says their packages include the health insurance , but when you look exactly what they are offering , it amounts to very little. (Andy , senior researcher , in his 40s , in China for 4 years).

The campus is fine , I mean , if you compare it with other places in China , but if you compare to what you can get in the UK , it looks like an unsafe place. The lack of fire alarms is an obvious issue, and the temperature in the building sometimes is inappropriate too. I know that one staff member got hurt while working. But the some management does not follow work safety or work insurance laws, which means he would get limited compensation or pension, which they are entitled according to the Chinese law. The pension is equal to Chinese average salary, which you cannot survive on anywhere else other than in China (Mary, lecturer, in her 30s, in China for 1 year).

Conclusion

In the late 2000s, both China and the UK made adjustments to their migration policies vis-a-vis academics. China, on one side, is using its diversified scientific investment, long-term talent strategic planning, and effective stimulus package to attract Chinese academic migrants back to serve the country. The UK, on the other side, is using its immigration policy to act as a filter, in order to receive the 'best and brightest' (Cameron, 2011) among highly skilled migrants. It has, in some ways, caused Chinese academics' lower employment opportunities in the UK and higher settling possibilities in China, which in turn, promoted the possibility of capital exchange through geographical resettlement. To those Chinese academics who are not secured in a tenure position, it may be both psychologically and economically attractive to use Chinese policy to easily boost their career in China to a higher level.

The IBCs in China have also highlighted that the key ingredient of its international extension was its international recruitment ability. One of the IBCs in China stressed the importance of recruiting high quality staff in the overseas campus: 'Our staff are the basis of our success. Most of our achievements are down to the quality of our staff. Our ambition and vision for the future means that more than ever, we are determined to attract, retain and motivate staff of the highest calibre'(University Strategic Plan, 2010: 1). Although the preferential recruiting policies have not really solved the staffing difficulties, for those British academics who chose to work in China, their embodied cultural capitals are still valued and changed into mostly economical capitals.

In the first part of this chapter, building on a basic analysis of current national and institutional policies in Sino-UK transnational academic space, I extended Bourdieu's (1984) argument—that of taking the educational system as one of the fundamental agencies of the maintenance of social order in France—into a greater transnational academic space. I argue that, as educational standards and systems vary spatially, spatial mobility for academics can be seen as a 'short cut' for 'reproducing the hierarchies of the social world' (Bourdieu, 1984: 387) through the realisation of transnational capital exchange. It is clear that through joint endeavour of central governmental agencies and substantial devotion of institutional resources, academic mobility can be regarded as an efficient way for imparting capitals across nations. As shown in the first part, Chinese/British academic migrants, who have accumulated a more 'valuable' form of culture capital in the UK, can transubstantiate their culture capital as other forms of capital through spatial mobility and engagement with national/institutional policy. However, although Bourdieu's theory of capital accumulation can explain some of the Chinese academic migrants' motivations, it fails to illustrate the emotional and non-economic parts of their move, especially for those accomplished academics who already have adequate economic means to live on and want to pursue more in relation to 'patriotic sentiments' and self-worth.

After the discussion on mobility and capital exchange, the second part of the chapter built on a key idea that, in a transnational era, current settlement only represents one point in migrants' lifelong trajectory of cross-ocean moves, as 'immigrants never quite arrive at their destination because they never quite leave home' (Ley and Kobayashi, 2005). This part teases out some of the threads in the complex web of challenges related to Chinese and British academic migrants' response to the national and local restrictions from 'below', showing that the possibility of capital accumulation (discussed in the first part) does not automatically mean academic migrants will embrace their working life in the 'host' university.

This part of the chapter indicates that some disparity issues associated with 'rules of the game' in the 'home' and 'host' educational field, have prevented academic migrants' capital accumulation from taking place or devalued their embodied capitals in many cases. So, I argue that mobility, for academic migrants, is not just a one-way process of cultivating capitals, but can also result in their embedded capitals being devalued. This means that mobility can not simply be defined as a form of capital, as Leung (2012) did in her research on Chinese academic mobility in Germany, namely 'mobility capital'. In my research, mobility is a capital accumulation/devaluating process rather than a form of capital itself. The current grounded difficulties and potential capital devaluation might directly point to academic migrants' next movement.

In sum, this chapter has questioned how the national policy and Sino-British University has helped formulate a transient academic mobility in today's international higher education landscape; how these infrastructures reinforce the individual's aims of capital accumulation; and correspondingly how the grounded difficulties and tensions act as another driving force of mobility from 'below', which negotiate with the national/institutional regulations and transnational capital exchange from 'above'. By structuring the chapter with the theoretical framework of 'transnationalism from above' and 'transnationalism from below', I argue that academic mobility is a continuous process embedded not only with opportunities but also challenges. This inquiry points out the limit of existing academic discourse regarding ‘academic mobility solely as a way of capital accumulation’, and seeks to provide a novel angle for looking at how grounded transnational experience can be (re) imagined as not just as a particular professional process or a way of capital accumulation for academics, but also an important factor that shapes, directs and produces transnational academic mobility.

Chapter Five
Academic Challenges and Adjustments in Transnational Teaching Space: a Recreation of Pedagogies

Introduction

In this chapter, I systematically consider both the ways in which transnational teaching can offer a range of curriculum opportunities to academic migrants, and how transnational education can provide more possibilities for negotiating different pedagogies beyond the wall of the 'home' university. As most of the participants are affiliated to both 'home' and 'host' campus, one in the UK and one in China, this chapter reflects on the situation of an increasing number of university academics whose workplace is transnational. I consider first the influence of past teaching experience on current teaching practice, and to find out what kind of difficulties they face during off-shore teaching if they continue using their 'old' teaching methods. Correspondingly, I explore Chinese and British academic migrants' adjustment in teaching practice, and see if they have adopted or recreated a 'new' pedagogy which is particularly tailored for their off-shore teaching. I then focus on the identical teaching and learning environment of the university (transnational classroom), to see how transnational teaching space can alter teacher-student relationship in the 'host' university and in turn affect teacher and student's academic practices. I demonstrate that transnational teaching practice is inextricably bound up with people, place, and forms of academic knowledge that help academic migrants locate themselves in transnational higher education. I also challenge the traditional ideal of academic 'assimilation' and 'integration' to the 'host country' academic field. On the one hand, by demonstrating (with grounded empirical data of transnational academics) that the transnational academic space is a more complex teaching and learning environment than a single academic system that academic migrants need to be assimilated or integrated into; One the other hand, arguing that the academic migrants in this academic space can be regarded as 'pioneers' to push the boundaries of current pedagogic limitations or important 'contributors' for recreating the transnational academic space rather than passive 'adaptors' to the 'host' academic context.

1 The Emergence of 'Transnational' Teaching and Assessment Methods

1.1 British Academics in China: a Transplantation of 'Student-Centred' Active Teaching?

1.1.1 The Main Teaching Activities in China

The seminar, as an unfamiliar learning activity for Chinese students, is one of the key elements of the so-called 'creative educational practice' that has been transferred from the UK to China by this Sino-British university. This is a widely used method of cultivating skills and attitudes of critical thinking in many countries, but still has not become a widespread teaching method in most Chinese universities. So, the university, as an international educational provider, tries to promote the student-centred teaching and active learning as crucial activities for its students in China:

There are types of teaching that the university promotes. For example, active learning in contrast with homological lectures and passive learning, right ? The courses are different , so the course for master students called two hours seminar , while the undergraduate classes were split between one-hour lecture and one-hour seminar. But , for the lecture we have been told to encourage active learning , to introduce interaction activities into the lecture class , which then blurs the distinction between lecture class and seminar class. (Paul , lecturer , in his 30s , in China for 2 years).

In seminars, the teacher normally tries to combine theory with practice, knowledge with up-to-date cases, and individual ideals with collective debates. The teacher plays an assisting role to guide students' creative discussion in this student-centred teaching activity. Usually, in this case study, the teacher uses approximately 30 minutes to present the content or theoretical ideas of the course in a two-hour seminar. As active learning is promoted in the university, discussion time is not only open for seminars but lectures. For Simon, there are not distinctive differences between his lecture and seminar classes, where explaining, questioning and reframing are three main activities that he uses in both:

In both of them , I try to mix activities between formal instruction where I am the only one speaking , talking , and I am explaining some concepts , giving some examples or reporting some research , and then in more practical sections , where they working on a document with some examples , I am doing some analyses or there are questions I put on the PowerPoint that I ask them to discuss in pairs or in group of three. Then , in other types of activities where I try to reframe their answers and guide those questions towards the point of the class , towards the learning outcomes of the class. They are normally the issues that I want them to know by the end of the class. These are the three main activates that I have in my class , but in between there are lots of improvisations , things work and things that do not work. (Simon , lecturer , 33 years old , in China for 4 years).

1.1.2 Difficulties in Conducting Active Learning

Student-centred practice has long been regarded as an effective pedagogy for deep learning, because it is a way to encourage students to think actively and seek knowledge by themselves (Kember, 1997). However, the transplantation of this teaching mode from the UK to China is not as smooth as the academics expected. The key problem is created by students (the main players in class) rather than teachers. This teaching method depends largely on students' interactive participation in class. However, many academics in this research pointed out that the Chinese students, (approximately 90% of the students in this university), are 'passive learners', as they are more reluctant to participate in class. (Jin and Cortazzi, 2006; Shaw *et al.*, 2007; Jiang *et al.*, 2010).

My participants often describe 'the awkward silence in class' when they have been asked about what is the biggest challenge of teaching on the campus in China. It is not the only downside of their teaching experience in China. The participants, especially those without Chinese teaching experiences, discovered that those Chinese students who were more inactive during the teaching process prefered to ask questions or express different opinions after class. My respondents reported that it was time-consuming from the teacher's perspective, as it takes lots of their time out of non-working hours.

The Chinese students' 'awkward silence' in and out of class is the visible part of the iceberg, whereas the reasons for this behaviour stretch far below the surface. One reason, has been clearly explained in Getty's research on the challenges and politics of teaching in China: 'in China, many of my students spoke to me quite earnestly outside class about how they were not accustomed to offering their opinions, for fear of offending the teacher by disagreeing (issue of 'face')' (Getty, 2011: 351). Moreover, for Chinese students, volunteering their own opinions in class would also risk losing their own face in front of their classmates, if the answer or question is not as wise as they expected. Asking questions after class can avoid the risk. Apart from the 'face' issue which has been discussed in many literatures in relation to Chinese people's behaviour, there is a more practical reason offered by one of my participants:

> *One of my students told me that the reason why she did not participate in the class discussion is because she did not prepare the reading before class, and why she did not prepare is because she knows this discussion would not be assessed. Why would they prepare for 3 hours to do all these readings, which have no influence on their final marks? (Nick, senior lecturer, 36 years old, in China for a year).*

Many students are pragmatists. They know why they are in this university and how they can get the 'most' out of it. Most of the Chinese students come to this 'international university' to accumulate academic capitals: studying in this university is cost effective, because as the university advertised, you can get the 'authentic British education' in China for 'half-price' compare to pursuing the study in the UK (see Waters, 2012). Simon summarised this when he said:

> *One of my students told me that he only needed to get the degree as soon as he could, and then he could be introduced to one of his father's friends' companies. You know, in China, even if you have social connections; working for a good company in China you need a good university degree and it's better with international experience. So, for him, to get a UK degree in China might be the most efficient way to realise his goal. Which means, for some of my students, how you get the degree is not that important as long as you get it eventually. (Simon, lecturer, 33 years old, in China for 4 years).*

So, getting good grades and then a British university degree is the crucial aim of Chinese students' university life. They know that this can give them a better chance to find a decent job, while simply being active in class, which usually is not part of their assessment, does not lead to this. This could partly explain why Chinese students give academic migrants an impression that they are inactive during class but active in asking questions after class. It must also be clear that the students who choose to ask questions either in class (it is possible) or after class are normally those 'good students' who are really concerned about their grades or really passionate about what they are studying.

Although they have their own ways to ask questions, it is noticeable that the majority of Chinese students were still identified to be more 'passive learners' not only by their behaviours in class, but particularly out of class. Rejecting the reading preparation is just one case, there are many other examples showed by my participants:

Most of my Chinese students are passive learners. They think they have nothing to do after class if I do not leave them homework! You sometimes got the impression that they are not working for themselves but for me or for their parents, I really do not understand this. (Lisa, English tutor, in her 20s, in China for 1 year).

The only time that they work extremely hard is before examinations, as the Chinese proverb says: Never burning incense when all is well, but clasping Buddha's feet in an emergency. Haha... you see, this is my biggest problem! My students, I mean, not all of them, do not have enough passion towards study, which means the driving force of pursuing knowledge in the academic field is not strong enough that you need to push them to make them 'run'. (Lucy, professor, 50 years old, in China for 2 years).

From my observation, I argue that learning actively is not an ability that most Chinese students lack, but a 'habitus' that most of the Chinese students have not cultivated throughout their learning path. 'In the Chinese cultural heritage... Chinese students tended to memorise the contents without gaining deep understanding of the actual meaning or development of practical skills. This means that traditionally, Chinese students tended to undertake surface learning rather than deep learning (Zou, 2014: 180). The Chinese students as a group approached the process of learning differently from students from the UK. The Chinese students are made to 'receive' rather than 'contribute' in the academic field. In the teacher-centred way of teaching, the instilling of explicit knowledge is emphasised, but an amount of tacit knowledge in the learning practice is neglected. They are good 'followers' rather than 'masters' in their educational path. This ideal echoed in Zou's (2014) research on Chinese cultural heritage and its influences on university learning and teaching:

> *One is the 'self-independence for one's own study' in Australia where the majority of students leave campus once classes finish and study alone; whereas in China students generally study and live on campus, where they support and help each other in studies and life skill development, with support and guidance from teachers. In other words, it is self-dependent learning in Australia, while it is teacher-dependent and peer-supported learning in China (Zou, 2014: 181).*

That is why they consider themselves to be free if the teacher does not leave them homework to do; they have been trained like this for almost twenty years. This is the habitus that British academic migrants are not familiar with; the students, likewise, do not understand the 'new rules of the game' in class brought in by the foreign academics. From here, it is not hard to understand why many Chinese students are puzzled at the beginning of their classes in this university. The direct transplantation of active teaching in China is like suddenly asking people who never heard of democracy to cast a vote. The academic migrants might take this teaching method for granted, because this is the way that they are used to learning and being taught. However, Chinese students might have difficulties in adapting, as they simply lack comprehension of this 'new' teaching method, which they have never experienced. As Getty points out: 'we do not like what we do not understand. It is human nature. Things outside of our experience make us feel insecure, and the easiest way to cope is to make a negative value judgment' (2011: 348). Take Mark for example, he reported that the misunderstanding or rejection of active learning from students often occurred in the first year:

I have found that most of my first year students did not understand my style of teaching at the beginning, because it is different from what they had in high school. Some of them felt a little bit lost, and they turned to me for help. I remember there was a girl in my class, one day she said to me: 'Mark, I know you are a good teacher, but I do not think I can learn much from you!' I asked her why, and she said she could not get use to my teaching method, which gives lots of time for self-learning and practicing. She told me: 'if we can learn by ourselves, why we need a teacher?' She believed that what she can get most out of a teacher is well-structured knowledge through well-organised lectures rather than the cultivation of independent learning and critical thinking. Honestly, I do not think she knew what critical thinking is; it is not in most Chinese students' blood. (Mark, 35 years old, English tutor, in China for 5 years).

The real difficulty is not just to point out those 'strange behaviours' of local students, but also to understand them, and find the corresponding solution. In a new transnational academic environment, it is not as easy as it sounds. Many academic migrants found it sometimes took them months to 'decipher' those activities that 'would seem to be basic and clear held meanings' (Getty, 2011: 349). Although the university did give academics training in these issues before they started, the problem still emerges throughout the real teaching practice. The different form of cultural capital from the teacher and the students, the different habitus of teaching and learning are the key to this issue.

This illustration of the difficulties faced by my participants in this section also showed the specificity of the transnational teaching and learning environment. I argue that this transnational teaching space in China cannot simply be imagined as a ‘transplantation’ of the UK institution in China, but a transnational space that has its own academic character. Logically, it is important to investigate the meaning of ‘transnationalism’ for those Chinese students even when not ‘moving’, and this will be discussed with more details in the second part of the chapter.

1.1.3 Students are not so Active in Class, What can you do?

Stepping into a new academic setting in the ‘host’ country is often associated with professional anxiety and practical problems for academic migrants (Sawir, 2014), such as problems associated with student-centred teaching. Much research indicates that it is of paramount importance for newcomers to get support from organisations or more experienced peers (Trice, 2004; Chapdelaine and Alexitch, 2004; Otten, 2009; Sawir, 2014). Searching for institutional help could be a significant step that enables academic migrants to develop relevant pedagogic skills to engage successfully with different classroom cultures.

In the university where I conducted my research, there is a teaching association particularly organised to solve the problems encountered by foreign academics teaching on the campus in China. The guidance leaflet of the association specified four steps of solving teaching problems: First, the teacher should try his/her best to solve the teaching problem. Second, if the problem can not be sorted out individually, the teacher can seek helps from group leaders and solve the problem with help from colleagues. Third, discussion in a workshop with experienced colleagues. Fourth, if the seminar is not so helpful, the teacher can apply for professional guidance from the ‘home’ university. In terms of teaching method, the university did not provide academics the opportunity to systematically learn teaching theories, but there is a seminar held bi-weekly by the teaching association, which aims to help academic migrants immerse themselves into the new and different teaching and research practice.

Adapting a personalised teaching strategy is relatively free at this university. The teaching materials provided by the university are not commonly used. Among British academic migrants, they selectively choose teaching materials based on the teaching content and level of students rather than rigidly on textbooks. Textbooks are normally used for self-learning after class (Sun and Chen, 2009). However, by the time I was conducting my fieldwork in the university, my participants informed me that the university was planning to enforce a new regulation that they should use the fixed teaching materials for the preliminary[1] year students to cope with the majority of students' English level. As will be discussed in the second part of the chapter, one of the biggest challenges faced by academics in the university is created by the diversity of students. By using the same teaching materials in parallel classes, the university can easily estimate students' level of English to make sure that they are qualified to use English for academic purposes at the beginning of the second year. The teaching materials are also improving over time based on both teacher and students' needs. For example, in order to solve Chinese students' issue of being relatively 'mute in class', the English Teaching Centre added several questions in the teaching materials to help the student ask questions, and set many exercises to improve students' critical thinking ability. The key is to build up students' confidence, let students learn about their talents, improve their learning attitudes and enhance their achievements in the study. It is clear that the university has its own consideration on training students, and the justifications initially are made for teacher's own good, however some of my participants were reluctant to use the materials, as it 'imprisoned your creativity'. (James, English tutor, 26 years

[1] Students in the university can study a three-year programme or a four-year programme inclusive of a preliminary year. It is designed for academically able students whose English level or school qualifications do not prepare them for direct entry to the three-year degree programmes.

old, in China for 1 year).

Apart from support systematically from the university, such as providing academic support and teaching materials, individual schools also have several strategies to deal with the difficulties associated with the student-centred teaching methods. For instance, in the school of economics, students are encouraged to be more interactive in class by assessing their classroom behaviour. This strategy has received positive feedback from academics in the economics department; some participants from other departments expressed their feelings:

> *The big problem is all my modules are graded based on a written or oral examination in the last week of term; it just focuses on one aspect of the course. In the economics department, if you are active you can have 20% more on your final mark. I think they are doing that particularly for students who are not so active in class. They designed this particularly for Chinese students. It is a smart move. Their students reacted much better in class. I wish our department would have this regulation someday. (Paul, lecturer, 36 years old, in China for 2 years).*

Nonetheless, it is easier said than done. Although the strategy has been proved to be applicable, other academics imply that there is also an inevitable shortcoming to this move:

> *You know I could spend longer time preparing lectures and think more about how I can encourage active learning. But I have also got to do research and admin duty. That comes back to the assessment as well, although it could be difficult to change the assessment, you could possibly make a case for them wanting to integrate, or at least a portion of the grade belongs to classroom participation, right? To do that, I have to fill out an application form, send it to the UK home school and have that verified and everything, it would work in maybe next year or next semester. I could do it, but I did not. Because, it then means more work for me, you know! Maybe students*

will act well during class , but then I have to assess that ! It would be easier to say , Ok , I teach the class. By the end of the semester , there is an essay. Ok , I mark the essays. There are 60 essays , it take ages , but then it is done ! You do not need to think about how you gonna see who participates better. (Betty , senior lecturer , 33 years old , in China for 4 years).

The situation is however not one sided. The adaptation of pedagogy is not only from the university, but also mainly from academic migrants themselves. According to Betty, from an individual perspective, the pedagogic strategies should be neither static nor dispassionate in the ‘transnational era’. They need to understand their ‘target’ students in order to ‘serve’ them better. However, this depends on what the goal is. The issue with much university teaching is that the goals of the actors involved do not always match. Rational analysis of problems and self-adjustments are significant for British academic migrants’ personal and professional development, they are significant for ‘providing the impetus for professional insight and constructive change’(Reybold and Alamia, 2008: 56). I have been told that they often prepare several sets of teaching schemes, in case students do not respond to one of them:

Teaching in here , you need to devote yourself to the understanding of your students , and make changes to your teaching method throughout time. For me , the first semester is the most challenging period , because you need to have plan A , B , and C when you prepare your class. If plan A is not working for your students , you have to quickly switch into an alterative one. It would get better on the following semesters. I think teaching experience is vital in this case , you learn through your teaching. (Rupert , professor , 55 years old , in China for 3 years).

Actually, a ‘good’ teacher would hope that this is the case in the UK and other countries as well. You have to be flexible to the students you have in the classroom. Richardson *et al.* (2006) suggest that open character and willingness to change is the key to helping migrants to adjust in a new field. Many British academic migrants state that understanding how the Chinese students' 'old habitus' operates is a necessary condition to make sense of their pedagogical practice and make it function effectively in their class. For example, Carl noted that his Chinese students were not naturally active, but actually good at answering questions if you asked them by their name in class:

> *Maximal participation and interaction are very important in my class. This is what we do in the UK. Chinese students are not very active in class compared to my students in the UK, so my solution is to ask their name to answer questions directly, and you might find they actually know more than you expected. (Carl, professor, 50 years old, in China for 3 years).*

In this section, I discuss the ways in which British academic migrants adapt to the 'new' academic settings in the transnational university. The pressure comes from both the students and the institution, and the participants needed to take account of diversity in their teaching and assessment process. So, in order to improve the teaching efficiency in the workplace, academic migrants challenged themselves to prepare several plans for different teaching practices, and finally found the appropriate one in each case. I argue that academic migrants' pedagogical approach is gradually changing in higher education landscapes that are increasingly 'transnationalised'.

1.2 Chinese Academics in the UK: Teaching Difficulties and 'Recreating' Pedagogy

The role of an academic who is pedagogically radical is first to fulfil a dialogical duty in their own class. Among those Chinese academics in the UK, many of them suggested that it was really hard at the beginning to simply be a dialogical educator who can illustrate well the object of study. This is not an issue of professional knowledge, it is a matter of language:

> *The biggest challenge for me at the beginning was language. I was very*

talkative when I was in China. When I did my postgraduate study in London, I became more reticent, because you do not need to talk much for having a Ph. D. When I was recruited in this university, they let me prepare a 90 minutes lecture. I felt that my spoken English was really impoverished, and it was really hard for me to express my thoughts as clearly as I wanted. You do not have self-confidence, especially in front of 100 people. It had been a year that I had a nightmare nearly every day that I lost my voice during my lecture. (Xiwen, lecturer, in her 30s, in the UK for 7 years).

Prior academic experiences in the UK may not perfectly match the teaching practices in one's early academic career. As Xiwen pointed out she became more reticent during her few years Ph. D study in London, which meant due to the very nature of Ph. D study, she did not really get the chance to practise her oral English frequently, and this partly affected her later teaching practice. She worked extremely hard during her postgraduate study in the UK, rewarded by excellent grades, but had weak social ties with English speaking students, which minimised the possibility of practising spoken language. Apart from Xiwen, the information I gathered from participants reveals that nearly everyone had a period of so-called 'language-improvement nightmare' in their early careers. The problem is not just the language per se, but other elements such as limited understanding of 'host' academic culture, which leads to misunderstanding or ineffective communication. Sawir supports this observation in recent work: '... Operating in a second or foreign language constitutes the first challenge. This is not solely about linguistic ability in speaking and writing, but also about how cultural meanings and assumptions are shared and correctly interpreted...' (2014: 134). Using a second language for teaching and being influenced by limited cultural capital was a recurring experience amongst many Chinese participants, who shared their hard experiences in teaching. For example:

I remember the first time when I received the feedback from my students. There was some positive feedback, however most of them are saying they could not understand the accent of the teacher and they did not understand why the university recruited so many international academics, etc. You do not normally get this kind of feedback from your Chinese students in China; these comments were too direct for me and I have to say they hammered my confidence. (Yanhong, lecturer, in his 30s, in the UK for 5 years).

Self-confidence has a close link towards teaching and discourse practice. A lack of confidence in Chinese academic migrants in their teaching practice is still a relatively unmentioned topic in literature. The lack of confidence may be aroused by a shift in their personal identity from a higher academic position in China to a more junior position in the UK (most participants who relocate directly form China were lowered in their position); from a majority academic population joining a minority in a new institution (Howe, 2008); from a more fully respected and easily controlled situation to a uncertain 'transformative learning'[1] (King, 2004) stage; or, in Yanhong's case, from a full sense of superiority in language to being easily criticised by native students whose English is objectively better. In addition, as a teacher originally from a culture where teacher — students hierarchy is relatively highly valued, receiving criticism directly from students could be harder to cope with. These were all reasons that I gathered during my observations, and these had an accumulated effect on my participants' self-esteem and also affected their language improvement in teaching. My participants repeatedly informed me that they were evaluated less positively than others at the early stages of their teaching experience in the UK.

Fitting into a new academic setting, teaching a curriculum with strong

[1] The theory of transformative learning has been used in adult learning, to see how individuals critically examine their practice and develop alternative perspective to incorporate knowledge or skills. For transformative learning to occur, one has to change his/her assumptions, perspectives and behaviour in the new environment.

'Britishness' and in a foreign language is not an easy endeavour for Chinese academic migrants. I have found that the attitude of acceptance appeared to be relevant in moderating the stress associated with criticisms received by participants in their entry period. The more reluctant they are to accept the local standard of teaching, the harder and slower the process to becoming a good teacher in the UK. In order to reach the state when the 'host' academic capital becomes theirs, Chinese academic migrants must refine their attitude to language improvement, and eventually become culturally and pedagogically competent. In this process, the devotion of hard work is the key. Most of my participants were willing to tell me about their 'bad old days' in their 'transformation periods':

> *I devoted lots of time for preparing my PowerPoint, sometimes nearly a week just for one lecture! I normally needed a day for framing the whole PowerPoint, and that was the easiest part for me. Then, I would use 6 days for rehearsal. I just locked myself in my office and pretended that I was in front of my 100 students. Like you were an actor, you need to perform well on your own stage. It did work, you were more confident in class. It went much better in the second or the third year. (Lijun, lecturer, in his 40s, in the UK for 12 years).*

Lijun's experience is a typical example that describes Chinese academic migrants' struggling transformation possess in their early stage of teaching in the 'host' university. Nearly every participant had this period. However, it needs to be mentioned that existing literature on the topic of migration and pedagogy is mainly focused on how migrants adapted to local conditions (assimilation of migration) rather than how academics influence the local teaching rules by bringing in teaching methods form their 'home' academic environments. The latter had been largely neglected; the 'reverse influence of migrants' to the local culture calls for more academic exploration. In this research, I have found that Chinese academic migrants have a tendency to fit into the local academic rules and the ways of teaching at the early stage of their career (including their language improving phase), while later on, they tend to search for their own pedagogical solutions to handle thorny problems they discovered in class. Wenhui is one who has found a way to minimise the language disadvantage during her teaching:

> *When you are using a foreign language for teaching, you are nervous, and when you are nervous you speak fast, because you naturally want to end the course as soon as possible. But, when you speak fast with a Chinese accent, your students find it hard to follow you, especially in big classes. Later, I found out that it would be better to speak as slowly and clearly as possible, and I tried my best to put concise sentences on the PowerPoint to make them get a general framework of what I was teaching. Moreover, I wrote down those technical words for international students. (Wenhui, professor, in her 50s, in the UK for 23 years).*

Naturally, working in UK academia as a migrant is not just purely handling challenges but creating new teaching methods. Being an academic migrant in a UK university does not only have disadvantages but also advantages. Although many students, especially those in the Chinese Contemporary School, were reluctant to accept lecturers from China (mainly for language issues), a large number of my participants who have already passed their 'language improving phase' were more welcomed by international students, because they 'understand their needs' in many ways. Thanks to their learning experience in Western countries, most of my participants know how to stand in international students' shoes in their teaching. 'Write down technical words for foreign students' could be one example, easily communicating with students and telling them some tips for dealing with the curriculum difference between countries could be another. Moreover, for those Chinese academics that teach subjects in relation to Chinese language or culture, their Chinese identity is actually the trump card that they are holding to 'win the game'. In this case, Chinese academics' cultural capital accumulated in China or by their relocation experiences are activated.

If you ask in what way my Chinese identity helped me in my teaching, I would tell you that it helped me in many aspects. I once did a lecture about Chinese architectural history; I noticed that my students were really focused on what I was saying and they were always nodding when I was illustrating my key points. I felt that I had been giving some kind of authority towards that subject. (Yi, senior lecturer, in his 40s, in the UK for 15 years).

As I mentioned, the uneven procession of academic capital between Chinese academic migrants and local academics not only causes problems but also leads to the reshaping of pedagogy in the 'host' academia. In some cases, interestingly, the changes in relation to pedagogy are stimulated by limited local academic capital. The Chinese proverb: 'Make best use of the advantages and bypass the disadvantages'（扬长避短）is the strategy that is frequently used by my participants, resulting in the shifting of teaching practice.

For instance, one disadvantage of working as an academic in the UK for Chinese academics is their lack of proficiency in reading and writing. Without years of practice, it is hard to compete on this with local academics. So, correcting assessments is another challenge faced by Chinese academics:

For the big classes, the challenge is correcting assessments. I have 187 students in my undergraduate class. You see the trolley next to the door is put there for carrying their assessments... One big difference of being an academic here is that we promote subjective tests rather than objective tests as we did in China, which means we lecture 6 to 7 themes for each semester, the students then can pick one of them for their final assessment. This leads to two problems for me: Ffirst, some students are 'cunning' and only come to the lectures in relation to the theme that they chose for their assessment and tried to slip through the rest of the lectures. Second, at 3000 words for each paper, it would take ages to finish correcting their assessments, the process is super boring, and it is always a big headache for me to give them feedback individually. (Yi, senior lecturer, in his 40s, in the UK for 15 years).

This is a typical example of meeting the challenges of academic cultural adaptation (the different 'rules of the game'). The challenges come from different angles. First, as Yi pointed out in his interview, subjective tests were promoted in the UK, while he had been used to objective tests to assess students in China, which means this is not a practice that he is familiar with and he does not have enough experience to know how to deal with it. Second, apart from speaking, the language issues also include reading and writing—it is very 'time consuming' to correct subjective tests in a second language. Third, I observed that many of my participants were reluctant to write feedback too often, as they cannot accept the fact that the students' English is 'better' than theirs. There is a deeper sociological reason behind this: A good teacher in China should perform well in teaching and other academic aspects, and only in this way can they gain the respect of their students. In Chinese heritage, 'Teachers should position themselves as models in both academic capacity and conduct, both inside and outside the classroom, so that students may follow their lead and find the correct way in their learning and development, the so called '为人师表', which means a teacher being a role model for students' (Zou, 2014: 180). Ideologically, performing less well in any practice of teaching and learning than students is unacceptable for Chinese academics, so they need to find a way to 'hide' their 'disadvantage'. For example, Hua stated:

When you are reading an essay of an undergraduate student, in most of the cases, you generally get the impression that what they wrote is superficial and sometimes identical. So, after reading for example 50 essays, you may find out that your brain stopped working, and it is really hard to judge which one is better, especially when you only have 10 ~ 20 minutes to read a 3000 words essay. As a result, in order to differentiate their grade, you end up focusing on those distinctive errors, such as reference and key words , rather than content. As a teacher , I know I can do better by devoting more time reading those essays , but the university has deadlines for handing in students ' grades , and correcting literally a trolley of essays in a week is just impossible. (Hua , Senior lecturer , in his 40s , in the UK for 18 years).

Focusing on distinctive errors can largely raise the effectiveness of correcting essays, but it is hard to predict the impact of such practice on the quality of teaching and learning. I cannot simply say such action is somehow irresponsible, because this would be considered to be understandable in a Chinese educational context and many Chinese academics would follow this way in order to save time even when they were correcting an assessment in Chinese. It is also hard to say whether or not academics among other ethnic groups do this too.

When I was in China , you know we all have standard answers for each question ; even for students ' essays , we have a list of key points that needs to be elaborated. It is like a checklist that allowed you to pick out the most important elements in the assessments during fast reading. (Xueke , Language teacher , in her 30s , in the UK for 2 years).

The key issue is that from these interviews I progressively find the ' way of thinking' that Chinese academics have adopted from their original culture was frequently used throughout their transformation as an international educator. For example, Xueke, a language teacher, told me：

In order to save time , when I am checking their assessments , I am always looking for key words. Normally , if the key elements that I told them in class are there , the mark will not be low. I think my Chinese education experience does have something to do with it , that is what we called : scoring points. (Xueke , Language teacher , in her 30s , in the UK for 2 years).

As correcting essays by looking for ' scoring points ', could result in a relatively unjust judgment of essay, some academics fundamentally changed their tests based on their previous Chinese working experience. This is not a case of making a 100% objective test, but to give the subjective test a certain level of 'objective' characteristics. This change shows that when a group of academics from different academic cultural backgrounds come into continuous contact with a different academic culture, there can be subsequent influence not just upon their original teaching and learning patterns, but also the local teaching and learning regulations. Wu gave me an example:

> *So, I find a way to solve this problem: for the first year students, I ask them to answer 3 specific questions in relation to my lectures in each semester and each question should be answered in about 400 words. That is to say there is a standard answer for each question, you can get higher marks if your answer is close to the standard answer that I had been prepared. I have to also make sure that the questions are appropriate so that only those who came to my classes could figure them out. Compared to 3000 words essay, this method saved tremendous time and made my students more serious in class. (Wu, Reader, in his 40s, in the UK for 20 years).*

In the case of Chinese academic migrants, one of the big differences between Chinese and the UK assessment system, as aforementioned, are subjective and objective tests. This distinction can be explained in a cultural value dimension—the so called 'individualistic' and 'collectivist' (Hofstede, 1984). The UK promotes individualism where social ties between individuals are relatively loose, and everyone is expected to have their own opinions and attitudes toward issues in life. In academia, an individual's creativity and critical thinking is regarded as the key ability that every student should possess. In contrast, China observes collectivism, which refers to 'a society in which people from birth onward are cohesively integrated and loyal to each other' (Sawir, 2014: 133) and an individual's interests are subordinate to collective interests. This means that the process of teaching individual ideals is also subordinate to the universal answers that had been set already. This is why subjective tests are used less in China than in the UK. Knowledge, especially at basic levels, is to be remembered rather than to be challenged. Similar ideals could be found in Zou's work on the topic of Chinese cultural heritage and influences on university learning and teaching:

> *Students were encouraged concurrently to think and seek knowledge: 'seeking knowledge without thinking is labour lost; thinking without seeking knowledge is perilous'. However, in the Chinese cultural heritage, studying implied careful, intensive reading and the depth of learning depended on the number of readings; therefore Chinese students tended to memorise content without gaining deep understanding of the actual meaning or development of practical skills. This means that traditionally, Chinese students tended to undertake surface learning rather than deep learning. (2014: 180).*

There are some successful strategies that were born from Chinese academics' 'original' academic capital, on the one hand and solved the time-consuming problem of correcting texts for migrant teachers, on the other hand, participants noted that these changes are also welcomed by students:

> *For postgraduate students, the fixed questions are not suitable for them. So, I figured out another solution for the assessment: I just let them to do an A2 sized poster in groups, including a designed work and 500 words comments in academic style. I received lots of positive feedbacks from my students, they suggest it is a good combination of theory and practice. It is also good for me, because I do not need to spend endless time on reading essays. (Li, lecturer, in his 30s, in the UK for 7 years).*

However, the strategies would not always leads to positive results. For example, one of my participants also found one of his assessments was not treated seriously by his students:

> *Of course, it was not always successful, I remember once I asked students to hand in a homework for which they needed to use professional software to finish their design work. I discovered later that some of them*

copied other peoples' work , just making some small changes and hoping that I did not notice. (Di , lecturer , in his 30s , in the UK for 7 years).

Existing research showed developed world education still has a stronger position: 'when I met the professor, he quite bluntly told me he did not have much faith in the quality of Third World country education... the incident left a permanent scar in my mind' (Razzaque, 2014: 107). Such a perspective partly explains why those Chinese academics that work in this world-class university cannot replant their original pedagogies in the UK, but rather try to select the positive aspects from both academic cultures in order to 'hide' their disadvantages in teaching and learning. It also demonstrates that the academic capital that has been accumulated in the original academic culture of migrants could be devalued in academic migrants' transformative process in the 'new' working field. However, it does not necessarily mean that this capital could not be the base of new pedagogies that are both acceptable for migrant teachers and their local or international students.

1.3 Discussion

In this section, I investigated the extent to which a transnational academic teaching space, in particular one that is made by different academic traditions and cultures, influences transnational academic migrants' pedagogies and methods for assessment on everyday basis. I looked at how the 'foreign academic culture' confronted the 'imposed local constraints' in grounded transnational teaching and learning practices. Generally speaking, the development of pedagogy in a transnational context deals with issues such as rethinking curriculum content, altered teaching conditions and the redefinition of transnational learning.

The findings suggests that British academics in China faced the challenge of fitting the so-called 'creative educational practice' into the 'host' teaching field peopled mainly by local Chinese students. The pivotal concern for this group of academics is to gain the ‘cultural capability’(see Trahar, 2012: 47) that it is an ability to ‘understand different values and systems and to challenge one's own thinking and behaviour about them’. Many of my participants specified how they gradually understood the ‘locality’ of this transnational academic workplace and the learning habitus embedded in their students. In turn, they made efforts to cope with the challenge and produced ‘effective’ teaching in the transnational university.

For Chinese academic migrants, language ability offers the opportunity for cross-cultural teaching and learning practices. By knowing their disadvantages in lecturing, Chinese academic migrants are finding possible methods to circumvent their weaknesses in terms of language. In this section, I pointed out two aspects that have not been largely discussed in existing literature: one is that the language challenge also comes from reading and writing, their self-confidence towards teaching in English, how to cope with students’ negative feedback about their teaching ability, and dealing with the misunderstandings in teaching. The other aspect is that the uneven academic capital may not be the obstacle of being an international educator, but become an impetus for the further development of new pedagogy. However, in contrast to the British academics in the UK who push the pedagogical boundary by searching for appropriated ‘Western’ pedagogy that fits ‘local sensitivities’, Chinese migrant teachers were improving their teaching by creating ‘new’ pedagogies which were inspired by the ‘Chinese pedagogies’ they were familiar with.

Most of the academic migrants I spoke to welcomed the greater diversity and dynamics in this transnational teaching space. Although the multi-layered complexity of the ‘host’ educational field had caused them problems, I was impressed by the time and energy they devoted to create a productive academic environment for students that they were not particular familiar with. It is clear that the development of transnational education has brought academic migrants opportunities to improve teaching and assessment with the inclusion of academic culture diversity. Thus, the involvement of transnationalism in higher education is meaningful for individual academics' pedagogical innovation, knowledge advancement and long-term professional development.

The points elaborated in this section respond to Kim's call on the uncertainty about the impact that academic migrants can bring to the 'host' educational environment: 'It is not yet clear to what extent the new forms and types of transnational academic mobility have an impact on the recognition and promotion of diverse academic cultures' (Kim, 2009: 398). In the section, I focused not simply on the challenges and assimilation (or integration), but pushed the boundary by looking at the ways that this group of migrants influenced the transnational academic space. It is vital to understand how transnational migrants have become a 'precious international commodity' that they can 'bring fresh perspectives to learning, teaching and research in their disciplines and through their professional expertise and cultural backgrounds' (Handal, 2014: 27).

2 Teacher-Student Relations in the Transnational Classroom

2.1 British Academics in China: Responding to Student Diversity in the Transnational Classroom

The classroom in the branch university has its own 'transnational' character. Although the classroom in this university is mainly 'occupied' by Chinese students, it is important to take into account that this university is also a relatively 'cosmopolitan workplace', with academics, non-academic staff and students 'often bearing qualifications and experiences from a wide range of countries' (Welch, 2002: 433). Currently, 20% ~ 25% of students in this university are international students; they come from more than 30 different countries leading to complexity in the transitional learning environment. In this section, I explore the meaning of 'transnational classroom' for academics and the students. To understand the particular kind of transnational education Chinese students can get even when they are not 'moving'.

Operating classes with students with uneven English levels constitutes the first challenge for my British participants. Several participants noted that the students came to this university with different English levels, which could be an obstacle for their everyday teaching. In order to adjust pedagogy in the transnational classroom, the first step is to find a way to get the whole picture of students' language level:

Generally, international students' English level is higher than local students. They are free to talk in class, express their opinions and they know how to make an argument. (Jack, English tutor, 33 years old, in China for 8 years).

Among this culturally diverse academic community, the participants further recognised a clear variation of English levels even in the group of Asian students:

All my students at undergraduate level that I have are Asian: 95% Chinese, 5% from Singapore or Indonesia. Definitely, student from outside of Mainland China have higher levels of English. But some Mainland Chinese who lived in the US for years, for example, can speak better English, so it is hard to say (Eva, English tutor, 34 years old, in China for 2 years).

Interestingly, the diversity can be also found among Chinese students:

I realised that even among those students from the Mainland China there are differences in English levels; generally speaking, those from big cities are much better than students from rural areas. (Jack, English tutor, 33 years old, in China for 8 years).

It is clear that the diversity of students and teachers has created a multicultural environment and that everyone involved works under a form of international exposure. Specifically, as Jack stated, the diversity exists also inside a nation: due to the regional academic differences, Chinese students are at different English levels. The diversity of English levels for students has created serious problems during teaching. Mark, one of the English tutors stated the problem he was facing in his class:

In order to have a general ideal of my students ' English level , I asked my students to hand me some of their previous writings they did in high school. To tell you the truth , the gap is obvious. For those who are already in higher level , it is easier for me to find out a way to push them into a better level ; however , for those who are not so good , it could be really hard to see the progress , as they might abase themselves before good students and be reluctant to learn. (Mark , English tutor , in his 30s , in China for 5 years).

As a result, one of the pedagogic predicaments facing the British academic migrants is how to balance the different needs of students from different countries/levels in the same class:

We normally have a student survey every semester. One of the problems I have had is I have had different feedback from different groups of students. Some students say how we want more formal presentations , or they say , the discussion is good ; it helps good learning. The international students say there are problems in the classroom , because of the different levels of language. So when it comes to discussion there is a lot of talk about what the concept means , like what the word means , as opposed to using them and having a talk about them. A mix of requests based on discussions makes it difficult for me to decide on my teaching method and materials. (Mary , Reader , 40 years old , in China for 1 year).

In terms of offshore teaching activities, the existing literatures often compare the classroom practice between national groups. For example, Patron (2009: 45) writes, 'Classroom practice of the French and Australians are highly contrasting.

French students rarely raise their hands to participate in class, for it is simply not part of their academic culture, whereas Australian students are encouraged to be more interactive, as it is usually part of their assessment.' (Cited in Handal, 2014: 28). However, as I mentioned, many of the participants found that students' behaviours in class were not simply variable because of nationality. In practice, individual learning habitus and academic level should also be taken into account. Here, I argue that due to the transnational nature of the class in this study, academic migrants need to reimagine the student structure of their transnational class, not only based on nationality but also taking into consideration the diversity of academic levels of students as a whole, especially inside national groups:

> *We always say Chinese students are quiet and uncommunicative in class. It is partly true, but not exactly like the stereotype in many cases. For example, there are about six Chinese students who always answer questions in my class. They usually speak English at the highest level; they are the smartest as well. Many international students in my class rarely talk during class. I think the activeness depends more on their personality and academic proficiency rather than nationality. (Rupert, professor, 55 years old, in China for 3 years).*

Correspondingly, my participants noted that it is impossible for them to 'shoe horn' pedagogies into different cultural groups:

> *It is hard to say in France I teach like this because they are French students, but here I teach like this because they are Chinese students. That is a mix really. (Coco, lecturer, 28 years old, in China for 1 year).*

It is true that the students in the 'transnational classroom' are not only multi-national, but also have a high diversity of academic and language levels. In a transnational teaching and learning environment, the challenge for transnational academics comes from negotiating with various students' demands and finding the balance to lead different groups of students in the same classroom. So, the modification of pedagogy to adapt to the needs of diverse students is of crucial importance in academic migrants' everyday teaching practices. Surely, for British academic migrants, adapting to this new international academic setting is no easy endeavour. The transnational classroom in 'internationalised higher educational systems' (Welch 1997, 2002) is a challenge for them at the moment, but also can serve as a catalyst for their pedagogic and processional development in a long-term sense, which echoes with the discussion in the first part of the chapter.

After recognising the diversity of students in a transnational classroom, the question arises as to what extent this kind of student structure in class affects transnational teaching and learning. Is it true that what the students get from the branch campus is the same from the UK main campus? It is noticeable that many of my participants complained about the fact of Chinese students as a major group in class affected the teaching efficiency:

> *One of the main problems I have found in my teaching is that my students, well 90% of them are Chinese, have problems when I was conducting group discussion. I asked them to move the desks together so they can chat with each other face to face. But, the biggest headache for me is that they often chat in Chinese rather than using English. Because they did not really discuss when I asked them questions after the discussion, they often depended on the 'good' student to answer the questions for the group. It is a little bit waste of time. (Lucy, lecturer, in China for 2 years).*

Apart from the issue identified by Lucy, what I found during my class observation is that the Chinese student (as a major group in class) affect my participants' teaching practice. Chinese students' learning habitus is one thing that really challenged them. For example, Chinese students are still more focused on pre-given knowledge, such as outlines on PowerPoint and key points on their textbook; many students used their smartphones to take photos of the teaching materials and lecture notes during lectures in order to save time, as many students expressed their difficulty in listening the lecture and writing notes at the same time. Many of my participants expressed their opinions on this 'photo taking' issue:

You know the first thing that I really cannot get use to is that my students always taking photos in class. I was a little bit shocked at the first time because I thought they were taking photos of me, but then I found that just for copying my presentation slideshow. I really cannot understand this, students in the UK do not do this every often. This does affect my mood for teaching; I felt sometimes I couldn't focus because of it. (Lea, English tutor, in China for 1 year).

It is true that the effectiveness of teaching in the transnational classroom can be affected not just by academics' pedagogy but also by students' actions and responses towards the teacher. Transnational teaching practice is related to academic migrants' teaching habitus and students' learning habitus, as revealed in Lucy and Lea's example. Apart from that, some participants also noticed the differences that Chinese students brought to the classroom environment:

One thing that really amazed me is that when it was raining, you can see hundreds of open umbrellas in front of the classroom, of different colours. Those bright colours give me a really good mood. I do not know why, maybe it reminds me about the raining days in the UK. (Allen, English Tutor, in China for 1 year).

The international breadth provided by the complexity of transnational classroom practice leads to the question of 'to what extent the transnational teaching and learning practice resemble the classroom practice in the UK main campus' and 'how do students experience this home—based transnational classroom without moving'. My participants explicitly recognised that students in this Sino-UK university are situated in the intellectual life of 'double receiving',

receiving knowledge from foreign teachers and interactions with students from various countries (but the majority of them are Chinese). In this university then, what is missing is the aspect of an international learning environment that is provided by a significant body of students who are not from the host country. This in turn impacts upon academic migrants' teaching efficiency, which makes the class less 'international' than it 'should be'.

One big difference I have noticed in my classroom is the students. When I was in the UK, I have more local students than Chinese students. The class I am teaching now is not as internationalised as the UK one. The purpose of building this branch campus is to bring British education to students. But, you know, foreign teachers are just one of the key elements for authentic British education, what is really missing in the classroom is actually not teacher but international students. No matter how much effort you put in, what they get from the teaching is different from those who are actually in the UK, especially for seminars, because the dynamics of discussion comes from the students rather than the teacher. (Bill, Lecturer, in China for about 4 years).

One sensitive issue pointed out by my participants is that not only the learning environment but also the outcome and quality of the study are not comparable to the home institution. Due to the pressure of strategically promoting the university in China, they need to lower their academic requirements for their students:

This leads to another problem, by the end of the semester: for 'strategic' reasons, I sometimes have to let those 'bad' students pass the final assessment, although I know they are not good enough. If I do not let them pass, it would affect students' rate of employment, then the university's reputation would be affected, and it would be difficult to recruit more students in the future. You see what I mean, the degree looks the same, but I have to say, it is actually different from the one you get in the

UK. (Mark, English tutor, in his 30s, in China for 5 years).

In sum, the transnational learning and teaching environment is not duplicated from the home institution. This section reveals that the student diversity in the transnational classroom can be roughly divided by nationality, but there is also a need to consider the diversity inside a single national group, and transnational academics' pedagogic choice cannot just be bounded with stereotyped national groups of student. British academic migrants struggled with providing suitable pedagogy to meet the needs of diverse student populations, especially the 'new' learning habitus embedded with local Chinese students. The grounded description of this transnational learning space developed a critical debate surrounding the issue of 'authentic transnational education', which means the 'one-to-one transfer of institutional capital across space and an unimportance of space' (Waters, 2013: 43). I echo Waters' view by concluding that the transitional classroom does not always travel wholly from 'home' to the 'host' institution. It is a special space that is highly affected by locality and intercultural relations between academics and students.

2.2 Chinese Academics in the UK: Changing Position from an 'Academic Role Model' to an 'Inspirational Guide' in Transnational Teaching

Chinese academic capital, educational and cultural heritage have a significant impact on Chinese academic migrants' teaching rationale, methods and practices in the UK university. As I discussed in chapter two, according to Han Yu, one of the leading scholars in the *Tang* Dynasty, the fundamental roles of a teacher in traditional Chinese ideology are 'to propagate the doctrine (*Chuan Dao*, 传道), impart professional knowledge (*Shuo Ye*, 授业), and resolve doubts (*Jie Huo*, 解惑)' (Gao, 1998 cited in Zou, 2014). Consequently, education in China is more or less 'teacher centred' and Chinese teachers have a duty to be a 'role model' in the field in order to lead their students through the 'mysteries' of academia. My participants' journey begins with finding a suitable lecturing niche in the new working environment. The university where I did my fieldwork is an international university. The increasing flow of international academic migrants gives the university a reason to promote new regulations to adjust to the situation. Knowing the differences between academia in different countries, allows the university to try to give international academic migrants some spaces to find their individual niche in work:

> *I do not know if it is because I am a Chinese lecture or if it is their normal procedure that they let me try as many courses as possible at the beginning. I did not have fixed lectures until the beginning of second year. (Junyu, lecturer, in his 30s, in the UK for 10 years).*

This rotation system allows academic migrants to have a year to experience the direction and magnitude of the differences between academic cultures. It is clear that cultural adjustments of academic migrants are 'mediated by differences between pedagogical systems' (Handal, 2014: 28). In contrast to those British academics in China who constantly go against the ideal of using fixed teaching materials for teaching activities, my participants in the UK cannot get use to the 'less fixed' course structure of the seminars. This challenge arises between the 'home' and 'host' academic culture: In China, even at postgraduate level, seminars are not a widespread teaching practice. Chinese academics' teaching is mainly based on teaching materials and in the form of lectures rather than participatory workshops or seminars in small groups. As Feng (2008) argues, Chinese universities are more examination-oriented and less open to discussions in class compared to Western universities. So, conversely, the reality of working in a UK university might force Chinese academics to transmit their knowledge in a different form: As a coordinator of discussion in class rather than a 'role model' to transmit wisdom, impart knowledge and resolve doubts. Not everyone navigated this cultural difference easily at the beginning, as Tanlin highlighted in her interview:

One of the Master courses is really a headache for me, because it is a course that does not have any fixed discussion topics. Unlike in China where we have teaching materials and are given teaching schedules for each semester, here everyone can chose their teaching materials and teaches in their own way. I know it is good to have your individual teaching plan, but as a foreign teacher, it is easy for me to feel a little bit lost, especially at the beginning. (Tanlin, lecturer, in her 20s, in the UK for 5 years).

Many researchers highlight the paramount importance of continued support from organisations or peers in helping international staff in their adjustment to the new academic settings. (see, for example, Louis, 1980; Trice, 2004; Otten, 2009; Sawir, 2014). My participants, especially those who had accumulated less UK academic capital, suggested that they need more formal training before they could actually step into their teaching path. Although the university is highly internationalised, its lack of understanding of the academic migrants' perspectives and its lack of human resources with an intercultural perspective may cause the university to send academic migrants to teach without adequate training. This can be for a variety of reasons, including a mistaken belief that the academic migrants might not require such training as they already had some during their Ph. D training with their native classmates. A particularly prevalent issue that was pointed out by participants is they had been 'left alone' during their transformation process into the new educational system, as it is easy to find a colleague or administrator with international experiences, but hard to find one who actually know the differences between China and the UK. Although Otten (2009: 415) argues that an international institution needs 'skilled and passionate people who are intrinsically motivated to get engaged in all the cultural stuff', it is hard to achieve this ideal in real working procedure:

Your colleagues are very independent; they are nice people but there is no way for them to help you, because they do not know what you do not get in this environment. (Xiwen, lecturer, in her 30s, in the UK for 7 years).

It is an issue of capability rather than attitude, as the 'host' academic community certainly has 'an intellectual and aesthetic stance of openness' (Szerszynski and Urry 2002: 408) towards migrants, but still lacks 'global competencies and intercultural communication skills' (Sawir, 2014: 137). As a result, in the words of the Chinese leader Deng Xiaoping, Chinese academic migrants are 'crossing a river by feeling the stones' at the exploratory stage of their teaching practice. A large number of my participants noted that they had to try different teaching methods (or attitudes) towards students in order to find the most suitable one:

> *I treated my students exceptionally well at the beginning. Because you are too friendly they do not take you as a teacher but a friend or a brother. Then you find it is hard to keep discipline in your classroom, because they are too free. So, I learned that I should balance between strict and friendly. (Dali, Language teacher, in his 30s, in the UK for 4 years).*

In Dali's case, because he is a language teacher with relatively little academic capital in the 'host' academic culture (most of the language teachers were sent directly from China), he has to accumulate his capital during his teaching with his students. The longer he practised and the stronger his willingness to learn and to adapt to changes, the better and sooner he can appropriately and competently function in the new educational environment. In order to avoid the 'coldness' of using 'Chinese traditional pedagogies', he tried to be friendly with his students. However, due to the very nature of 'student-centred education' in the UK, he found the biggest challenge lied in students' discipline in class. So, his pedagogical attitude towards students has to be anchored between 'laissez-faire' and 'strict'. These kinds of personal adjustments were significant among my participants. This is an 'assimilation process' where 'role model' becomes 'inspirational guide'.

Those Chinese academics who have accumulated more academic capital in the UK, also acknowledged that they had changed their methods many times during their transformation period:

Last semester, I gave students an overall score for their finial examination. Judging form their feedback, many are not Ok with it. One student asked me why Peter, his friend, got 67, while he only got 60. It is hard to say; I just told him it is just a general impression. I know it is not convincing, so I changed my scoring method this year. 30 % writing, 20 % group work, and 50 % experiment compose their final score. I also emailed them rubrics of how to measure their learning progress. You may need to write them feedbacks on each section, but it actually saved time because fewer emails appeared in relation to questioning their final grades. (He, lecturer, in his 30s, in the UK for 5 years).

One thing that I really cannot get use to at the beginning is that students often argue with you if they are not satisfied with their grade. You would rarely be in this kind of situation in a Chinese university. My experience told me that you should stick to your original judgement in most of the cases, because students do gossip, if you change one students' grade, you would receive endless emails arguing for their grades. It also means that you need to be extremely careful when you are assessing their works. (Gaoyuan, Language teacher, in his 40s, in the UK for 3 years).

Assimilation is a capital accumulation process that academic migrants can benefit personally and professionally from within the 'host' environment. However, the other key issue that should be discussed in this section is how the dominant academic culture could 'adopt a humble posture of learning in relation to the immigrant academic' (Sawir, 2014), which has not been fully explored by researchers. In Sawir's (2014) work, he notes that cultural diversity can be regarded as a particular form of cultural capital that the international students can also benefit from:

I found that research students, particularly those from Asian backgrounds, were able to relate to me easily. They came and spoke to me freely about their personal as well as academic matters. Students with family resident in Australia particularly came to me for advice on matters such as the schooling for their children, part-time jobs for their spouses and other domestic matters. There were also times the students came to see me for emotional support as they found the multiple roles of mother, student and worker difficult at times (Sawir, 2014: 137).

In my research I have also found that Chinese academic migrants provided academic and social/emotional support to international students, especially to Chinese students:

We always say customers are 'god' in business, while in UK University I have got the impression that our students are 'god' for us, unlike in China where teachers are 'god' for students. It is not easy for those kids to leave their home at such a young age, and the majority of them might be spoilt kids coming from rich families. When they come to the UK, it is hard for them to understand my lectures. They might give up easily; their parents might spend their money in vain. Although a teacher in the UK does not have the responsibility for securing his/her students' educational success, I still try my best to help them out. (Gaoyuan, Language teacher, in his 40s, in the UK for 3 years).

Although Sawir (2014) suggests that institutional academic support may be available for international students, my participants point out that actually the support provided by the university is more focused on language ability and personal difficulties rather than pedagogy and course structures. Even the universities' own web sites and handbooks for international students were unhelpful for many students who did not have enough time to read due to the limited time and English ability. As a result, many international students would experience a moment of crisis in learning. In this situation, an emotional interdependence would naturally form between the migrant teacher and his/her international students. The migrant teacher could be regarded as the students' 'comfort zone', as they share a common cultural background and common experience of learning in a new academic culture. As such, Chinese academic migrants' capital accumulated from their past learning or teaching experiences functions as a valuable resource to help international students in reducing stress and saving time for adaptation into the new location:

Normally, I would not treat certain groups of students specially. But, as you know, there is only a year for those master students, which means international students do not have enough time to adjust to the new environment. They might begin to do a project in their first week, however the huge difference between the UK and Chinese academic regulations made them feel lost. So, usually we have an introduction course for international students to let them know the major differences. Native students can choose to skip it. (Qi, Professor, in his 50s, in the UK for 20 years).

We have assignment books in China, which tell you what to do and how to do it, while here, when you do a project you first need to have a original idea or concept, no one will tell you that. I find local students follow you quickly and actively, while Chinese students are slow in catching up. Chinese students are more dedicated to the project details rather than having a clear concept of the blueprint. Both the Chinese and the UK educational system have cultivated me, so I know exactly the source of my students' difficulties. While, you see, local academics cannot boil down to their bullet points very easily, because they have not been in their students' places. I think it is an advantage of me being a foreign teacher here, especially when the university is eager to meet the needs of the international students (Yituo, lecturer, in his 30s, in the UK for 2 years).

As the university has become more internationalised, understanding the international students' needs is of paramount importance. These two quotations highlight the possibility of regarding Chinese academic migrants as 'potential resources' for providing support that enables students to engage fully with the 'host' academic setting. Amongst those Chinese academic migrants who work in the Contemporary Chinese School, their identity and embedded cultural capital also especially helps them not only in communication with international students and gaining trust, but also enables them to teach their subjects with additional authority as they are 'insiders' in relation to Chinese culture. However, many participants noted that Chinese students always want to communicate with them in Chinese, although they are reluctant to do so. In this case, they usually put their working position in priority:

> *Among undergraduates 15% ~ 20% are Asian, while 80% of Master students are from Mainland China. Sometimes my Chinese students come to me during course gaps and ask questions in Chinese. In this case, I always told them to use English; because when I am working I am a teacher in a world leading UK University rather than a Chinese person whom they can make friends with. I am more strict with my Master students, as the majority of them are Chinese, I ask them use English all the time, especially when they are doing group discussion with their Chinese classmates. (Juan, lecturer, in her 30s, in the UK for 10 years).*

2.3 Discussion

This section draws on insights provided by British and Chinese transnational academics in terms of offshore teaching in the transnational classrooms, in order to explore the challenges of transnational teaching in connection to teacher—student relations. The first part of this section illustrates the current teaching and learning environment of transnational education in the Chinese context. It interrogates the ideal of 'relocating the home institution as a whole to the host country and providing authentic academic environment for students without moving to the UK'. The findings I obtained in this section, demonstrated that the transnational teaching space in China was not a 'duplicate' of the UK academic space (although it is also regarded as a transnational space in this study) that Chinese students expected to have.

The reflections of my interviewees have underlined the significance of student diversity and their learning habitus in influencing transnational teaching and learning practices in their classroom. The findings also underline the importance of locality in academics' teaching and students' learning experiences. It echoes what Leask (2015: 210) concludes:

Two of the major challenges for teachers in the transnational classroom are, firstly, identify the range and balance of knowledge, skills and attitudes, and the need to develop to be successful transnational teachers and secondly, balancing their own learning with what of their students-understanding and meeting the immediate needs of their transnational students whilst simultaneously developing the knowledge, skills and attitudes that will make them more effective teachers in this environment. (Leask, 2015: 120).

The findings reveal that the dynamic of transnational teaching and learning is partly dependent upon students' English proficiency that varies beyond national and ethnic differences. Group learning habitus of local students also affects academic migrants' teaching practices in the transnational classroom. In this case study, local Chinese students who act as key components of the transnational classroom are paradoxically preventing them from reproducing the 'authentic' British educational environment. I argue that what students can get from the Sino-UK university is not as 'authentic' as the education provider initially planned and the transnational classroom provides tremendous challenges for transnational academics. The 'transnational' quality of the classroom leaves huge space for transnational academics' pedagogical adaptation and innovation, which echoes with the discussions in the first part of the chapter.

For the Chinese academics in the UK, their position as a teacher in China gave them a certain level of authority that is hardly challenged by students. However, if the 'rules of the game' in the UK are not identical with those in China, the 'players' in the field should adjust according to the 'UK rules' (or 'transnational rules') in this transnational university. So, the question is how my participants transformed themselves from a 'role model' in China to a more suitable position in relation to the students in the new transnational academic field in the UK. The findings suggest that many Chinese academics feel lost in teaching activities during their first few years in the UK, having problems in terms of preparing teaching materials, giving appropriate grades to students, finding suitable training personnel with 'global competencies' or getting help from colleagues. Then, after a few years of teaching experience, they realise that their role in the 'transnational classroom' is 'inspirational guide' rather than 'role model' they played in China.

Likewise, this challenging process traversed by my participants doesn't just include their adaptation to a new academic culture in a transnational classroom, but also their contribution to the academic advancement of the new environment. The findings also suggest that cultural capital embedded in Chinese academics can be beneficial for international students. In recognising the academic culture difference between China and the UK, Chinese academic migrants provided international students support from various aspects, academically, mentally and practically. So, I argue that, for academic migrants who teach in the transnational academic space, their embedded capital not only causes problems during the teaching process and changing relations with their students, but also enables them to be a special contributor in transnational teaching.

In sum, I argue in this section that the teacher—student relationship in the transnational classroom is decided by a teacher's capacity in recognising the diversity of students' needs and in using their embedded academic capital to improve their teaching quality. It also implied the importance of agency in altering the ‘locality’ of the transnational academic environment, both from the students’ and the teachers’ perspective. I pointed out that academic individuals played a crucial role in the changing nature of transnational higher education. They gradually constituted transnational teaching—learning patterns, academic values, and classroom cultures. They re-conceptualised the tradition of teaching and learning in this culturally-diverse, but locality-specified academic context.

Chapter Six
Chinese and British Academic Migrants' Working Experience in Transnational University Spaces

Introduction

As the findings showed in previous chapters, as transnational academic migrants travel from one country to another, they experience an unfamiliar academic field, the local communication patterns, different teaching strategies, *etc.* However, in the host university, they live and work in particular spaces in the transnational university, but these are often taken for granted. Academic mobility researchers have often overlooked this point: We cannot fully understand academic mobility unless there is a place for 'place', as everyday human experiences are inseparable from places. (Tuan, 2001; Cresswell, 2006; Ho and Hatfield, 2011).

In this chapter, I interrogate how place matters to Chinese and British academic migrants' everyday working experiences. It examines the everyday experiences of academic migrants through the lens of various places on campus. Specifically, I focus on material spaces such as workplaces and public places for relaxation on university campus in shaping academic migrants' working experience—an aspect that has been overlooked in the existing HE literature. By specifying the importance of place, this work demonstrates that the university campus can play an influential role in academic migrants' working lives rather than being invisible or taken for granted.

Everyday experience takes place through materially-embedded and socially-performed practice (McGregor, 2003). Accordingly, bringing 'sociality' and 'materiality' together can create a meaningful approach towards investigating migrants' everyday life (Ho and Hatfield 2011: 707). Thus, the specific research questions I address in this chapter are: how academic migrants' place-making practice shapes and, reciprocally, is shaped by the materiality of particular locations on campus; and how academic migrants' social relations were intertwined with a selection of places on campus, and mutually affected each other. I will then use Bourdieu's (1977) notion of habitus to help consider the question of how the 'social and the material are constitutively entangled in everyday life' (Orlikowski 2007: 1437) in the HE working environment.

The empirical sections give evidence (in relation to academic migrants' spatial practices) to support the key argument. The research captures participants' experiences through three different places on campus-the office, residential homes, and the 'hanging out' spaces. It outlines the 'rules of the game' embedded in these places through daily interaction; the influence that each place made to academic migrants' social interaction; additionally, the differences that academic migrants made to these places. Then, each section concludes with some reflections drawn from empirical discussions and which underpin my main arguments.

1 Workplace—Office

For academics, offices are a significant location in the workplace (McGregor, 2003). In this section, the office space is neither taken as an unchanging physical container nor fixed institutional backdrop in understanding and shaping academic migrants' everyday working life. The office here is understood as a place being constructed by objects, institutional rules, and social interactions.

The power of materiality and spatiality in shaping the understanding of academic migrants' everyday experiences in the workplace will be discussed in this section. It will be argued that office space in university constituted a particularly productive field to deeply understand the diverse social, cultural and institutional formations that affect the working experience of those who migrate in the context of transnational higher education.

1.1 Materiality and Everyday Place-making Process of Academic Migrants

1.1.1 British Academics in China

As I have already discussed earlier in the thesis, the university where I did my fieldwork is one of the earliest Sino-foreign universities in China with approval from the Chinese Ministry of Education. It is run by a world-leading university in the UK in cooperation with an education group in China. The teaching material academics and the whole teaching system are driven by the UK partnership, while the Chinese education group is responsible for the administration and campus facilities. All basic infrastructure is provided by the Chinese partnership (including teaching buildings, restaurants, administration building, gardens, residence for students and staff, *etc.*), which objectively constitutes a 'fertile ground' for the (re) production of identity and belonging, because of its inevitable physical dissimilarities from the UK 'home' institution.

The transnational working life of my participants is shown mostly in their particular ways of place-making in their offices. Many participants showed me their family pictures, cards and gifts from their students, photos of their special research group, *etc.* Most of them expressed individuality in their immediate surroundings in the workplace, and in the objects and images they chose. Such individual place-making practice can transform their 'anonymous' office space into a place of meaning and belonging, as 'place-making practices, and a sense of belonging are closely connected' (Riemsdijk, 2014: 9).

Noticeably, there were two trends for office decoration. First, many participants showed me 'the objects from the past', these objects are normally small in size, easy to carry and significant to the participant. For example, some (re) produced their sense of belonging by putting images related to 'home' in the office. Allen (English tutor, in China for 10 years) showed me one photo of his office desk (Plate 6 – 1) and pointed out those pictures of his homeland taken by his father in his desk space:

Plate 6 – 1 Allen's office space, and his habits of putting pictures of 'home' on the wall (Photo by participant)

When I was in the UK, or when I was here, every time I was given a dedicated working desk space, I was just making it a little bit more lively and more interesting. So one of the things I am very lucky with is that my father is a professional photographer. A lot of my desks are covered with his pictures. So, that is beneficial in several ways, one is beautiful images to take me away from what I am working on; two it is more connected to Scotland, it reminds me of home; and three, it reminds me of my father and his skills and stuff like that. It is not homesickness, because I have lived in China for almost 10 years, but it's quite nice to travel back sometimes.

From Allen's narrative, I can see that, the notion of 'nostalgia' is embodied in his photos, which connected to an imagined and long-established image of 'home' in Scotland that he is longing for, but can never truly return to. The 'feeling of home' generated in Allen's photos turned those particular objects into a visible representation of history and culture embedded Allen's past memories. This practice could be seen as a recreation of sense of belonging through objects, this place-making process was not only found in Allen's case, but also in that of many of my participants.

The ideal of recreating a 'feeling of home' and 'sense of belonging' through everyday engagement with material objects during the migration process has been identified by many migration researchers (see, for example, Rosales, 2010; Conlon, 2011; Dudley, 2011; Ho and Hatfield, 2011). Similarly, the above narrative reflects the mediating role of pictures/photos in preserving migrants' memories of 'home'. 'Home' here, is made of emotions and feelings, rather than bricks and woods. Blunt and Dowling (2006: 212) write, 'Home is often understood as a site of memory, and it becomes a temporal signifier as an imagined point of origin and return that implies a longing for an unattainable past'. In Allen's case, the pictures represent his memory of his father, his home country and his past in the UK, which is in a direct contrast with his 'foreign' and 'actual' experiences in China. 'Home' is a special existence for transnational academic migrants. It is a 'weapon' that they use to against the rapidly-changing working environments from one country to another. As the backdrop changes, their 'home' is the only thing that always stays the same (even though it may actually be changing). 'Home', therefore, especially for migrants, could be a source of strength for helping them continue their transnational journey. It is not simply a symbol of identity and past, but also could be an excuse for return or a reason to stay.

Photos on the wall showed Allen's emotional attachment to his 'home' (Scotland), recreated a sense of belonging and stimulated a mental strength to cope with his new workplace. However, it is important to explore, not only academic migrants' individual memories recoded in particular objects, the material culture involved in the migration experience, but also to see how this inseparable relationship between academic migration and things can travel across time and space. I discovered that, by using similar sorts of materials, a sense of belonging could be produced transnationally. For example, Allen's following statements showed me his own way of decorating his office, once acquired, could be transferred to different national contexts, and provides him some sort of pleasure and fulfilment. He said,

> *Well, I have worked in many countries, like the UK, Australia, Japan, and now China. But no matter what kind of office I had, I always put these photos in front of my work desk... when I was having tutorials with my students, they always asked me about Scotland when they saw the pictures. I see this as an immediate trigger to start a conversation with my students.*

The first half of his narrative mentioned that the place-making practice has a transnational character. Regardless where you teach, your office can be decorated with the same key elements that show your personal preference. For example, for someone who likes flowers, a vase with a bouquet of lilies might appear in his/her office in London, Tokyo, Beijing or elsewhere. The second half of this narrative reflects how the recreation of belonging (place-making) is not only expressed materially and corporeally, but also socially functional. A similar point is highlighted in Latham's (2006) research on forms of urban living in the

Auckland suburb of Ponsonby and Collins's (2008) work on culinary consumption choices of Republic of Korea's international students in Auckland. In this case, the photos of 'home' on the desk space can be understood as 'visual business cards' that Allen intentionally put there to show people his origin. As Allen said, these photos could be seen as a conversation 'trigger' to stimulate his social interaction with students, because 'many times, people are unable to talk separately about their life stories and their possessions' (Rosales, 2010: 511). It shows that the interaction between Allen and his students is characterised by a significant degree of familiarity and creativity, which is achieved through objects.

In sum, Allen's narrative shows that the social implication of objects has a transnational character, and that is why he always brings those photos into his office no matter where the office is located. As Nukaga (2013: 68) states: 'a transnational habitus could be understood as a 'culture tool-kit' that individuals build and utilise to navigate transnational social fields', Allen's way of using photos from 'home' in different workplaces could be seen as a 'tool' in this so-called 'culture tool-kit' that facilitates his social engagement with local students.

It needs to be mentioned that the other key character of office decoration is the 'Chinese style'. Lucky knots, paper fans, red five-pointed stars, tea and calligraphy are the objects frequently seen in British academics' offices (Plate 6-2). However, different from those pictures of 'home', they were mostly not bought by the academics. In many cases, they have either been left by the person who used the office previously, and it 'could be a waste to get rid of' (Mike, professor, 50 years old, 8 months in China) or given as a gift by students. Participants normally treat them as an evidence of living and working in China, which can make their working space 'lively, colourful and exotic' (Mike, professor, 50 years old, 8 months in China). Moreover, it also shows that their Chinese students respected them in a 'Chinese' way. Consequently, This reminds them to accomplish their academic duties and work hard for students in return. In this sense, it is logical to bring those elements into a place where they might have a sense of 'not belonging'.

Plate 6 – 2 Chinese style decoration in office—a traditional Chinese paper fan (Photo by participant)

Many of the participants' Chinese gift-taking experiences were framed in relation to their 'assumed' foreign identities by Chinese students. Participants addressed how, despite having their personal taste, the gifts they received in China could be limited by how their national/social identities were perceived by others. Chinese people usually believe that foreigners like 'Chinese traditional stuff', as the saying goes: '民族的就是世界的。 (Of the nation, of the world)'. The small Chinese gifts received by my participants would not be sent to other Chinese colleagues, as the 'Chinese-ness' embedded in those objects would be devalued, which can be viewed as an example of how 'race' may influence social practice in a multi-national social background and how 'rules of the game' are demonstrated in those Chinese objects. The lifeless objects hanging on the wall or placed on the office desk are not simply gifts from students; they are the reflection of a particular social habitus that has been rooted in Chinese people's culture and everyday life for centuries. Habitus, in this case, is not just a matter of class or position, but also a matter of nationality.

In sum, empirical evidence shows that British academics' place-making process and the recreation of belonging are highly connected to objects in their work place. More importantly, moving beyond theinanimate role of objects, data also shows the active role of objects in promoting intercultural social actions and triggering spontaneous relationships in HE work practice. Here, 'objects do not only 'express' 'symbolise' 'reflect' or 'reify' social relations, they also make them' (Frykman, 2010: 8).

1.1.2 Chinese Academics in the UK

In this section, I will explain the different ways that Chinese academics experience their working space at a British university. It needs to be specified that, at an institutional level, China may be categorised as a 'learner' vis-a-vis the UK as a 'knowledge provider' in the global knowledge economy. It is understandable that sending Chinese scholars overseas could result in elevating the position of both the migrants themselves and their affiliated university at 'home' (Leung, 2013). The 'uneven academic terrain' between China and the UK not only generates capital accumulation across transnational space, but also changes academic migrants' expectation and attitudes towards university campus space in those two countries.

Generally, Chinese academics in the UK campus have a more positive view towards their office environment compared to those British academics in China. Because, at most universities in China, only professors or higher-level administrators have the right to get an individual office space, other academic staff need to share with their colleagues. 'Clean' 'tidy' 'roomy' 'comfortable' and ' humane design ' are the key words that frequently appear in Chinese people's conversation when they talk about spaces in Western countries. This is not surprising given that ideal of ' learning from the advanced country ' is deeply rooted in Chinese academics.

For my participants, the office itself is more than the physically enclosed walls that they work within. It could also be the product of different working rules in the new field that they need to adapt to. The objects in place are sometimes embodied with what is permissible and what is forbidden in the host academic culture. For example, the perceived integrity and honesty is an important point that was raised by my participants when they talked about their office space:

One cabinet in the office has a special place for office supplies. It is very convenient, when you run out of something you just simply take some from there, no need to register. I remember one day I ran out of batteries and I went there to take some, my boss saw me when I was there. Surprisingly, the next morning they put a whole box of batteries in the cabinet, because they know I might need them next time. How thoughtful is that! This is totally based on trust and self-consciousness, which is particularly lacking in the Chinese working environment. If we have one corner like that in China, it hard to say that no one would take advantage of it. (Wang Fang, lecturer, in the UK for about 8 years).

Wu Fei, a young researcher who had worked in the university for about 3 years in the physics department, agreed with Wang Fang by showing me the pigeonholes in his department (Plate 6 – 3):

I am always wondering if the foreigners do care about their privacy, why they do not have a lock on their pigeonhole? I sometimes see our salary slips in there, but it seems that nobody would be curious enough to take a look at others. I think this is because they are using their honesty as a 'locker' to prevent letter or dossier losses, while in China we need a real one.

Plate 6 – 3 The pigeonhole area in Wu Fei's department (Photo by participant)

Besides, Chinese academics in the UK showed fewer national identities in their workplace decoration and objects around them. Different from their British colleagues in China, these Chinese academics find their core value system in the 'host' university, so, they do not feel it is necessary to recreate their sense of belonging in their current workplace by emphasising their cultural background. In most of the cases, their office decoration tells more about their occupation than cultural identity. For example, a lecturer's office in the Contemporary Chinese School is likely to be more Chinese culture related; while, an office space of a Chinese professor in Department of Physics could have objects that represent his/her research or hobbies, instead of cultural identity.

Furthermore, being in a minority group, some chose to diminish their Chinese identity in workplace, as they do not want to be treated as the 'other'. The original cultural identity that is highly appreciated in the Chinese context for

British academics is devalued for Chinese academic migrants in the UK in many cases. Some of them might experience a painful dislocation in their early academic career due to the lack of cultural capital in the ‘host’ field. Similar with those students from rural areas of China who entered in an elite university in Li’s research (2013), the mismatch of being ‘academic star’ back in China (as most of them were elite students/academics), and the sense of being ‘cultural incompetent’ in their early career stage at a strikingly new space resulted in a certain level of ‘stress and identity crises’ for those Chinese academics (p. 835). By experiencing a period of frustration, they learnt to accommodate themselves to the temporarily devalued situation through self-regulation and professional improvement. As if they can make up their ‘cultural incompetence’ with ‘academic competence’. Hence, they prefer to be regarded or evaluated by their professional proficiency rather than their national or ethnic identity. This is true for Dr. Wang, he stated:

> *I think in this university, I see myself as an academic rather than a Chinese, my nationality is less important than my knowledge. Yes, I have to admit that we do have culture differences, but the longer you stay, the better you know your position and your duties, the less you feel it. (Wang Feng, Senior lecturer, in the UK for about 10 years).*

Chinese identity might be a ‘trump card’ for China experts, but relatively useless for academics specialised in other fields. For this group of people, the devaluation of Chinese cultural capital in the ‘host’ academic field can be a reason for them to renounce many of their traces of origin in office space. For example, when you step into a shared office in the Department of Physics, it is hard for you to quickly identify which space belongs to a Chinese academic. Hiding away (at least not emphasising) the personal cultural identity in their office space can be a strategy for Chinese academics to efficiently minimise cultural distance with other academics.

1.1.3 Discussion

Place-making is about the recreation of ' soils of significance' (Ahmed *et al.*, 2003: 9), and objects can work as ' translation tools of contemporary migration experiences' (Rosales, 2010: 511). By closely looking at the material implications in academic migrants' everyday working life, it is interesting to find that British academic migrants are relatively more attached to objects that they consider crucial to the maintenance of their everyday working in different geographic locations. For them, their material experiences reach further than emotional attachment to objects from home, because the objects they bring to the ' host' university could not only recreate their identity and sense of belonging, but also have an active function in their social relationships with local students.

Whilst, for Chinese academics in the UK, the objects in the office place can provide some positive social values. This restructured their perception of the ' host' working place, and recreated a sense of belonging based on the ' host' working rules. Likewise, for Chinese participants, apart from those who use Chinese as their teaching/researching subject, their Chinese identity could not be used as a ' culture tool' in the UK working environment, so many of them chose to ' hide' their ' Chineseness' and ' be professional' in the workplace.

Chinese and British academic migrants are associated with the same class, because they ' occupy similar or neighbouring positions' at the same international university (Bourdieu, 1989: 17), however, the problem is, due to their identical cultural origins they do not have similar volume and genre of capitals. Moreover, their embodied cultural capital from country of origin is revived differently in their ' host' field. The concrete materials in participants' offices revealed that British identity could be seen as valuable cultural capital embedded in British academics in China. However, Chinese identity in the UK could be regarded as capital for those China experts or Chinese teachers, but not for the whole group. This inequality between cultures is a very important element in Chinese and British academic migrants' place-making practice, demonstrated by an examination of office decoration.

This 'transnational academic inequality' could not totally engage in Bourdieu's thinking tools, as it was established particularly for a single culture condition—the French society. So, this is not a class issue as Bourdieu normally discussed in his works, but a geographical one. The empirical resources in this section can relate Bourdieu's theory of practice into a more transnational outlook.

In sum, the migration experience cannot be divorced from materiality, and cultural capital could be one of the logics that 'preside over the intersecting movements of people and things' (Rosales, 2010: 512).

1.2 Changing Office Space and Evolving Habitus

1.2.1 British Academics in China

In this section, the observation and discussion will move on to how moving into a 'strikingly new host institution' could change academic migrants' ways of using office space, through which I catch a glimpse of their evolving habitus. During my fieldwork in China, when conducting interviews, I frequently observed half-empty bookshelves and things left by the previous user in the office space meaning that they did not fully engage with office environment. Participants gave a number of reasons for not treating their office as seriously as they did in the UK. Lucy (Lecturer, 30 years old, 1 year in China) has her opinion towards the empty bookshelf (Plate 6 - 4):

Plate 6 – 4 Empty bookshelf in office. (Photo by participant)

It is too expensive to ship all my books here , and I do not want to ship them back later. Basically , I can get eBooks or papers on Internet , no big difference.

Lucy's attitude is reasonable: rich online library resources offered a solid foundation for her choice of not shipping many books from the UK. The international campus in China shares library resources with the main campus in the UK, the Chinese counterpart institution, and local libraries. The library on the Chinese campus has 7500 textbooks, nearly 250000 other selected books and Aleph/Metalib journal system. Plus, the main campus can provide 10500 online journals and millions of electronic books. Many participants expressed the ideal that current online resources can cover most of their academic needs on a short-term basis. For those 'China experts', the campus in China can also provide first-hand resources that could be hard for them to get back in the UK. Obviously, they can maintain their daily work in China without recreating a similar bookshelf in the office. The geographical distance and virtual technologies have changed participants' previous way of using office space.

In addition, the physical absence from the office includes not just books but also academics themselves. Many academics I interviewed reported that some academics choose to work at home most of the time, not bothering to go to their offices very often. David (professor, 48 years old, in China for 4 years) a British professor, for instance, comments on being conscious of using a coffee cup in his office everyday and on viewing it as a signal of frequently using his office in comparison with some of his colleagues:

> *You see that is my cup. I can use my cup for coffee everyday instead of using paper cups. Some of my colleagues want to be at the desk as little as possible, so they choose paper cups. As they are not planning to stay here for many years, there is no point for them to organise the table and use facilities as I did.*

Paper cups are not the only things that reveal peoples' absence. Interestingly, when I was conducting my fieldwork on the campus, it was not difficult to notice that many windows on the office door had been covered with curtains, paper or other materials. These windows were initially placed for security and morality reasons. However, a group of academics complained about the lack of privacy and expressed the feeling of 'being observed all the time' or 'being like a fish in a fish tank' *etc.* They may cover their office windows under consideration of privacy, but as I have been informed, many of them also used it as a 'self-image cover' for 'escaping' from their office out of office hours. 'If you cover your window, then people have no way of knowing what you are doing or whether you are in your office or not. It is a smart way to maintain your public image.' (David, professor, 48 years old, in China for 4 years).

Migrants may reduce their engagement with the formal workplace (office) by working more frequently in their home office or elsewhere according to their new circumstance. Here, the 'new circumstance' refers to the spatial organisation of this particular university that allows them to have other choices: as with other Chinese universities, many academics live on campus.

I can work at home out of office hours. As you know, I live in the staff hotel—only 5 minutes walk from this building. Sometimes, the distance between your home and office changed a lot. For example, if your office is 2 hours on train from your home, it will largely increase your time of staying in the office, as it would be unrealistic to commute between office and home by using the gap between classes or meetings. While, if you live on campus, you can leave your home place ten minutes before your class begins, which means you can stay in your place as long as possible. (Gary, reader, 38 years old, 2 years in China).

There are other reasons that caused the reduction of office space utilisation. For example, the rapid expansion of the university meant that language tutors needed to share office space, which is every common in Chinese universities. It received significant negative feedback from British academics; some even chose not to use it very often. However, the academics that have acquired different types of capital required to 'fit in' to the Chinese educational field normally responded more 'strategically' compared to their peers. For instance, Tony (English tutor, 35 years old, in China for 7 years) recognised the fact that his transnational experience had helped him to be 'rational' and 'productive' in China compared to his colleagues who have less experience.

He said:

Lots of teachers are not happy about the fact that we have a shared office. But it is normal for many Asian universities and even some UK universities to have shared offices, I have worked in such environments many times in China, so my experience does help me sometimes. While for some of my colleagues, before they had private offices, and they did not realise how lucky they were. Now it had been taken away, they just complain a lot. I do not care. I have my headphones. If I want to ignore people, I just put them on and I am then in my 3 × 3 foot kingdom (Plate 6 – 5).

Plate 6 – 5 An English tutor is using his headphones to prevent noise and distractions (Photo by author)

'The process of becoming an academic and socialising in the academic habitus involves the internationalisation and acceptance as 'normal' of academic conventions and values' (Bauder, 2006 cited by Sliwa and Johansson, 2013: 203). Koehn and Rosensau (2002: 112) also argue that 'transnational actors must be flexible and skilled at managing multiple counterpart identities' in order to integrate into the more complex social field. While for my participants in this study, their ability to accept the 'normal' local habitus and, flexibility in managing multiple identities are closely related to their cultural capital accumulated through their transnational experience and the length and depth of working in the 'host' country. Taking John (English tutor, 33 years old, in China for 12 years) for example, his past transnational experience and deeper understanding of Chinese society gave him greater abilityto accept difference:

> *This desk space is in an office with about another 36 teachers. It was set up, so the computer was in the corner of the desk space, when I saw it, I thought, well I do not really like that, I do not think it is particularly comfortable, but rather than bother anyone by requesting could you do this or could you do that, I'd like to solve my own problems as well. So I re-*

did all the wiring on the computer and moved it to where I feel more comfortable. I try not to rely on the help of the bosses to do that, I will show them I have the ability to do this myself. Without mentioning it to them, when they come and they see—oh! This guy has done this, and even without mentioning it to me, it seems obvious to them that I am able to do things independently. I think that is a big difference between me and some of my colleagues, they are always just complaining and waiting to go back home, no one ever thinks about changing themselves!

Another little thing is my friend here, an electronic mosquito killer racket—my mosquito light under the table, because this is in the ground floor, and outside the window is a river that does not really move, and lots of trees, so lots of mosquitoes, getting my legs chewed for few weeks. Other people have these lamps, but they waited until the university supplied them. They waited and said we need these lamps! While as for me, from the first days of getting bitten I bought one for myself because it cost, well, not very much money. I'd rather solve the problem quickly myself than being stingy and have the attitude of I have the right to this, that the university should find this equipment.

These two issues mentioned by John demonstrate that he not only has the ability of observing, understanding, accepting the 'rules of the game' in this 'mixed' field, but also navigating a working style that is different from his old-world habitus. John also mentioned in the interview later that one reason why he did not turn to the boss or Chinese admin staff to sort out these issues was his acknowledgment of the complicated bureaucratic structure of the Chinese administration office and his past experience of time—consuming paperwork in other Chinese universities. Moreover, his behaviour, in his words, might leave a good impression with his boss, owing to the fact that he created a new local habitus transformed though engagement with his transnational movements and he knows what he did would be at least implicitly agreed upon by his boss and locals. As we can see, John is structuring his own habitus in the Sino-British field, which is similar to local Chinese academics' reaction, but different from what he might do back in the UK and also distinctive from other British colleagues' behaviour under the same situation. This habitus, in his words, might have positive impact on his further career, because he is following the 'rules of the game'. This habitus transformation is closely connected to the capital accumulation that I discussed in the last chapter. The deeper understanding of local academic rules could be considered as an evolving habitus and correspondingly a way of gaining capital that fits into local academia.

1.2.2 Chinese Academics in the UK

Working in an office in the UK, for my participants, is couched in terms of fewer working hours, and more 'freedom'. Wei Fang, a 35 years old researcher in the medical department holds a positive view towards the relatively shorter working times in the UK. She said:

> *They do not particularly care about how long you stay in the office every day. I like this style: they give you a mission that you could work on in a certain amount of time, and you only have to hand it out to them before the deadline. The team does not care about your working process, you can do it wherever you like in your office or at home, but the outcome should be good. I feel they give me more space to be creative and the possibility of actually enjoying my work. While in China, the whole team often works in the lab until midnight.*

Lynton and Thogersen (2009) suggest that, compared to Chinese, Western leaders in labs put more emphasis upon individualism, feelings, reflection and rights, whereas Chinese are 'immersing the self in the collective' 'persevering through hardship' and 'using the energy of group' (p. 116). Therefore, it is not hard to understand how Chinese academics, who once expressed their spirit of work through hard work and long working hours, took their 'loose' working experience in the UK as a 'change of lifestyle'.

However, it is hard to say the Chinese academics' lifestyle had been really changed in the UK, although there is no need for them to be committed to long hours of working in the office/lab. Yang Weichun, a 38 year old senior researcher in the material institute, told me that he still had a great attitude towards 'hardship' even though he left China to work in the UK over 8 years before. 'Hardship' is still considered to be the key elements to success for many Chinese. Mr Yang found his diligence could be regard as his special competitiveness in British academia. He said he was always the first one to show up in the office every morning and he often went to the swimming pool before he began his daily work. In his words: 'The fox changes his skin but not his habits'. 'Hard working' is like a tag attached to Chinese academic migrants. It is hard to change by the working rules in the host university, because this is how they have been educated in China and this is how they find their feet in the competitive world of British academia. Possibly, the 'host' working environment has reinforced this habitus, because they believed in '笨鸟先飞' (the early birds catches the worm), which means in order to accumulate their insufficient academic capital, they have to devote more time into their research/teaching, as a result of their transnational migration process.

Moreover, Chinese academic migrants have their own strategies to 'fit into' the local academia socially. Brushing aside atheist thoughts, many of them tried to integrate with their local colleagues through Christian faith. Shao Hua, a professor who has lived in the UK for a longer period of time (30 years) showed me a photo of his office decoration with a story of adapting to the 'new' field (Plate 6 -6):

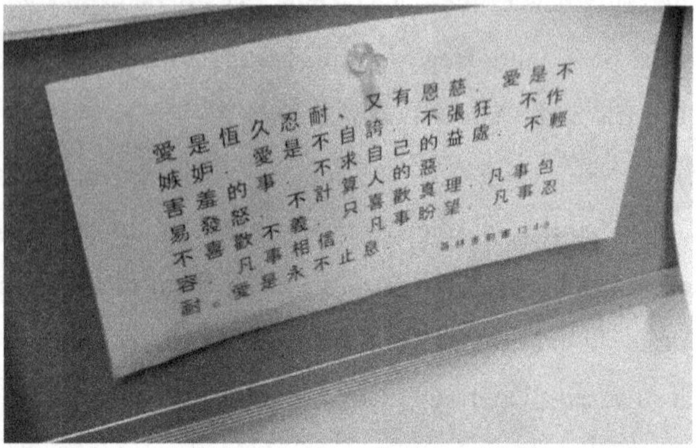

Plate 6 – 6　A note from the bible in Shao Hua's office. Translation: Love suffers long and is kind; love does not envy; love does not parade itself, is not puffed up; Does not behave rudely, does not seek its own, is not provoked, thinks no evil; Does not rejoice in iniquity, but rejoices in the truth; Bears all things, believe that things, hopes all things, endures all things. Love never fails (Corinthians, 13: 4-8) (Photo by author)

> *In the beginning, I found it was really hard for me to make friends here. You know, compared to China, the academics here work more independently, we do not have shared offices and everyone focuses on their own field—we do not have much to share. One day, a colleague asked me if I have religious belief. I said no. He introduced me to a local church. People there were very friendly, and some of them were also my colleagues, as we lived in the same area. Through studying the bible together, we shared our ideals, questions for life and personal experiences. Some of my colleagues became my good friends in this way, and little by little we built up a sense of understanding and trust, which allows us to cooperate in our work too. I found it was a win-win situation. That is why I put this note from the bible on the wall.*

Having a religious faith, for many of my participants, is considered to be not just a personal spiritual development gained from their offshore experience in the

UK, but more importantly, a practical way to practise English language and to bond with colleagues. Religious practice could be seen as an intermediary connecting Chinese academics with other colleagues who were predominantly British. This echoes Leung's (2013) finding of Chinese academics becoming churchgoers in Germany. She considers this fact as a way to accumulate social capital in the 'host' country. Habitus is thus not objectively given, but socially created, structured and reproduced by individuals in their working practices on day to day bases.

Rather than only focus on Chinese academics for a short period of professional motivated visit, such as Leung (2013) did, my study also include those who stayed for several decades. As a result, data generated from my participants point to a slightly different direction: Some said they treated their religious practice purely as a form of improving their social and cultural literacy rather than truly believing in it at the beginning; some said it was hard to get a profound understanding of Christian faith even after many years practice, but friendship accompanies them through the whole process. In those cases, we can see how habitus shifts for individuals following migration, and how the evolution of habitus changes for the 'rules of the game' in the 'host' workplace.

1.2.3 Discussion

For those British academics in China, lower office utilisation is compounded by the location of the university, the distance from home to the office, advanced communication/research technologies and the physical structure of the office itself. Many participants chose to spend less time in their office, while private places or public places on campus became their alternative working places. More specifically, the shared office for English tutors is still a concept that could not be accepted by many participants, and that is one of the main reasons for the change of working habitus. Whilst some participants (especially those who have more transnational experience) considered the shared office as 'no big issue' and 'still handy', many academics regretted the limited private space and time spent with students in the office. It is noticeable that those who are more experienced in overseas teaching and the local working environment are more 'flexible' in terms of facing changes and difficulties caused by local rules. However, for those 'less experienced' British academics, the curtailed physical attendance in office might have 'devalued their university life', which 'hampers the transfer and development of institutional social capital' (Leung and Waters, 2013: 48).

Interestingly, this different from British academics in China, Chinese participants considered the shared office space as 'convenient' and 'a place for communication between colleagues'. In China, the shared office is a social space rather than a working place. Chinese people normally do not mind other colleagues talking while they are working in the office, and they consider the office as a place that allows them to have a 'tea rest' and exchange 'gossip' during the ten minutes gap between courses. In this sense, the shared office in China functions more like a common room in the UK rather than an office purely for working purposes. After missing an important space for accumulating useful social capital, many Chinese academics use religion as a 'cultural tool' to cultivate their social capital.

For Chinese academics in the UK, based on the university rules, they do not need to work for extremely long hours in their office or laboratory as they did in China. However, their habitus has not been changed by the new working rules in the 'host' university. This is partly because, as non-native academics working in British academia, they have to devote more time and energy into their career, in order to keep their proficiency at an average or a higher level. Significantly, the local educational field has not changed their ways of working. In contrary, inevitable competition between colleagues and relatively limited social connections in the 'host' country reinforced the continuity of the old habitus. It is also needs to be mentioned that, in this section, I included people working in laboratories. Comparing to those Chinese academics that regularly working in office, this group of people are more closely tied to their workplace as they rely mostly on laboratory facilities. For those who work extremely hard, they even choose to sleep in the laboratory in order to observe experiments day and night.

From the above analysis on the interaction between habitus and place, I can see that first, academics' office utilisation is partly dependent on the material structure and geographic location of the office per se; second, the same office structure—the shared office—could have different interpretations from different migration groups. It is an inconvenient workplace for British academics, while it is a handy social place for Chinese academics. The key reason might be differences with regards to privacy and noise tolerance between these two migration groups.

In sum, the findings underline the importance of place in academics' offshore experience. The workplace can not be transferred wholly from the 'home' campuses to the branch campus due to the identified institutional, social and cultural factors. Which means academic's grounded interaction with their office space differs in different countries. I found a place-making process embedded in transnational mobility: Academic migrants' habitus could be affected by place, but place can also effectively altered by academic migrants. I argue that office space on transnational university campuses is key in producing academic migrants' sense of belonging and identity, as its materiality is important in terms of shaping academic migrants' working experience in the transnational academic space.

1.3 The New 'Rules of the Game' and Relations Between Colleagues

1.3.1 British Academics in China

Although several studies indicate that habitus is assumed to be affected by the place migrants newly moved to (see, for example, Friedmann, 2002; Marshall and Foster, 2002), Kelly and Lusis (2006: 836) argue that 'immigrants may indeed continue to judge their circumstances according to the rules of their place of origin'. In my study, communication barriers do exist if the British academic migrant continues to use his/her original expectations and preferences to judge the rules in relation to space use in the new educational field.

In the case of UK universities in China, a QAA report indicates that due to the university expansion, the university infrastructure and support services for staff are increasingly in demand among academics (QAA, 2012). The Chinese campus might look like the UK campus in many aspects, but you can still see the differences through details. Interviewees pointed out their daily inconvenience in terms of space use.

For example, Dick (Lecturer, 30 years old, 1 year in China) complained about the lack of central heating during the winter in his office (Plate 6 –7):

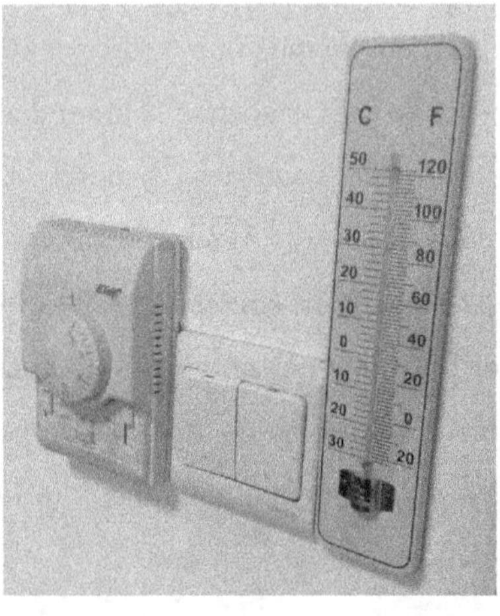

Plate 6 –7 The central air conditional controller in Dick's office—the highest temperature was at about 20℃ when the controller pointed to 30℃ (It could be much lower in winter) (Photo by participant)

I really cannot stand it , although we have central air conditioner , the temperature inside the office is still low , that is why I am usually not working in the office during the winter. Look , I switch it to 30℃ , but it is still only 20℃ at the moment. You can imagine it could not reach 20℃ in winter , because the temperature outside will be much lower in January.

Apart from issues around the central heating system, the study participants reported other barriers of adaptation in the 'host' field. Nancy (English tutor, 32 years old, in China for 3 years) stated:

Taking about using the office , our Chinese colleagues have a strange habit that I cannot understand until now... One day , I went to the admin office and saw that Lily had a cold , but her window next to her was wide open. It was winter and the air conditioner was on. It is not just Lily doing that , as I saw many Chinese staff offices were like that. This is not environmentally friendly at all !! Why does she open the window when she needs to keep warm ? Why doesn't she consider other people's feeling when they are in the same office ?

Kelly (Reader, 36 years old, in China for 1 year) and some other participants had similar feelings of inconvenience:

I usually have class until noon , and we normally have one to two hours gap before we go on teaching in the afternoon. But the thing is , that is the only time I have during the day to go to the admin office and sort out paperwork or ask questions. But I cannot , because they are not there !! I do not understand why my Chinese colleagues leave the office from twelve to two o ' clock. I so cannot get used to it !

The Chinese staff have different explanations towards the above issues. Lily said she opened the window because she is concerned about others in the office as she does not want to transfer her germs to them, and the reason why her and her Chinese colleagues are not in the office during the noon time is because this is what a Chinese administrative staff member's 'normal' schedule looks like. It is necessary to note here that as the Chinese administrative staff are employed by the Chinese counterpart of this Sino-British university, they always follow the Chinese work-and-rest system and have two hours free time after midday.

These narratives reveal that the habitus embodied in British academics is different from those of the Chinese staff. As habitus is formed by the individual or collective history in a specific field, lack of experience in the host field might lead to a certain level of misunderstanding between groups or individuals. In the above cases, local staff and British academic migrants act in two different 'structured frameworks of evaluations and expectations' (Kelly and Lusis, 2006: 833) generated form their previous dispositions and fostered in their earlier academic years. Those two identical frameworks lead to 'the conscious or intuitive prioritising of certain practices' (Kelly and Lusis, 2006: 833) that make both parties feel uncomfortable.

Distinctive institutional or individual habitus can stimulate social exclusion in the workplace. Bauder (2004) shows that immigrants are often excluded from the local Canadian labour markets, if they bring with them their own habitus from a foreign place. However, in this study, both British academics and Chinese administrative staff reinforce the exclusiveness. Because, if individuals' practices are determined by the 'rules of the game', there are at least two distinctive 'rules' in the Sino-British educational field, one determined British participants' practices, and another structured by Chinese administrative staff's practices. It is hard to say which could be the 'right' one to follow in different occasions, and which could be the more 'local' one, as it is a British university in partnership with a Chinese HEI. The existence of differences between groups is normal. It would be unrealistic to expect that the international campus in China can totally replicate its original campus in the UK.

Transnational workplaces are often 'the key location for the development of social contacts' (Willis and Yeoh, 2002: 558). However, the 'dispositions' brought by the participants and locals from their place of origin are proving exclusionary to each other, due to the unfamiliarity causing a certain kind of misunderstanding. On the one hand, embodied habitus from country of origin may result in the 'othering' of each other and the perception of each other as the 'outsider' in the transitional work place. On the other hand, such barriers or a feeling of discomfort towards local staff and the local working environment, for British academic migrants, could serve as a reason for them to be more actively connected to other international academic migrants that have similar experiences and mind-sets. This echoes Willis and Yeoh's (2002) study, as they indicate British expatriates' social networks established in the transnational workplace are often restricted to other expatriates or Western-educated Chinese nationals of the same level of income, language skills and forms of socialising, causing a lack of interaction with local colleagues (See also Cook *et al.*, 2011; Dudley, 2011; Tse, 2011).

1.3.2 Chinese Academics in the UK

For many Chinese academics the social contacts in workplace are not always easy to be build, because it 'comprises power relations' (Mcgregor, 2004) between different groups of academics. It has been pointed out in the existing literature that the relationship between colleagues is considered more equal in the UK, whereas it is more complex and hierarchical in China (Jiang *et al*, 2010; Hsieh, 2011). That is to say, the highly regarded status of the 'boss', which was the case in most Chinese universities, was found to be relatively less obvious (in most of the cases) in the UK educational field.

Interestingly, many British academics in the Chinese context talked about this issue. They found that some British academics became more 'bossy' when they were working on the Chinese campus due to certain 'mysterious influence' from other Chinese colleagues. They even pointed out that the same person would act differently when working in the UK. That is to say, the hierarchical structure does exist in the Chinese context and it even has an impact on those who work there temporarily.

In the British context, a 29-year-old Chinese researcher Wang Hui, who had worked in the university for 2 years after her graduation, pointed out the difference between the 'host' and 'home' working environment:

Generally speaking, the relationship with your 'boss' here (in UK) is more… 'informal', if you understand what I mean. They are not like those 'bosses' in China, who might have the power to give you benefits and change your academic future. My 'boss' in the UK, as far as I can see, is a person that willing to do something for the whole research team or department. Everybody is relatively independent; you can be successful in the field only because you are academically good enough. But in China, you also need to have a good personal relationship with your boss. This basically changed people's attitude. In China, you should always show him/her your respect by your words and gesture. While in here, there is no need to do that.

Nevertheless, Zhu Jianguo, a 32-year-old researcher, also highlighted the casual interaction between colleagues by showing me a picture of a lab door (Plate 6 – 8). He said:

Plate 6 – 8 The door of Zhu Jianguo's lab, with a note saying: 'this lab is now cold again'. (Photo by participant)

This is actually a joke made by my boss after we finished one of our important experiments. We successfully found out the second special gas that could reach an extremely low temperature, it might have some value in industry use in the near future. My boss was delighted and put this note on the door as a way of celebrating. Cool, right? I like the little tricks my boss made with us some time. He is an easygoing person who always has the ability to make our working environment delightful! While, my boss in China was more serious.

These two narratives indicate that relationships between colleagues are seen as more equal in the UK than in China. However, it is arguable that this 'non-hierarchical' impression could be a superficial phenomenon, as their judgment is purely based on the boss's friendly behaviour, attitude and gesture. His/her politeness could be understood as a social networking strategy or a certain working habitus cultivated in the UK educational field, not necessarily meaning more equality between colleagues in the UK. Moreover, some participants further pointed out this 'pure positive image' might be a façade, because:

Kind words do not cost much, struggle always exist. Sometimes, I know my colleagues are just feigning politeness, and I was misled by that ostensible friendly appearance at the beginning. (Zhang Fan, professor, 48 years old, in the UK for nearly 20 years).

Many more 'experienced' Chinese academics pointed out that the hierarchical structure does exist in this UK University, but it is 'carefully covered with smile and gentle attitude'. (Wei Da, Reader, 40 years old, in the UK for about 20 years).

This argument shows that the social aspect of power relations between colleagues in different educational fields might not have different structures but different forms of expression. Wang Hui's impression of equality in her department can be interpreted as a personal stereotyped view of the 'white' democratic country where everything is 'more equal' than China. This constructed perception of the West is deeply rooted in those Chinese academics that work in the UK for a relatively short period. Among these Chinese academics, the opportunity of experiencing the 'non-hierarchical' or 'simple' social relations in the UK was for some the main motivation of accepting a UK posting. This 'misunderstanding' is caused by their limited cultural capital and the unfamiliarly of 'rules in the new field'. However, it could certainly be argued that there are some elements of UK academic that are generally less hierarchical than in China, as I mentioned at the beginning of this section.

1.3.3 Discussion

In this section, I have focused on various kinds of social-spatial segregation of academic migrants. The findings reveal that social division between British and local Chinese administrative staff is commonly experienced among British academics in China, striking parallels with observation made in many studies on highly-skilled migration. It is clear that many British academic migrants in China have difficulty balancing the relationship with local academic staff, and balancing the differences between their expectation of the 'host' workplace and the reality. As it is impossible to duplicate the same working place as they had in the UK, they are paradoxically treated as both 'insiders' and 'outsiders' in a Sino-British university. The office space itself can be a problem for them. The other problem is the separated working rules between the UK campus and Chinese counterpart have caused spatial-social segregation in this transnational working place. While, among those Chinese academics in the UK, many of them expressed their feeling of the equality between colleagues, but this is just an impression, and this does not necessarily point to the less segmented relationship between colleagues in the UK HE system.

The different ways of using office space in highly connected to individuals' habitus and this can have some impact on their social capital. The unfamiliarity of the local working 'rules' directly causes misunderstanding between academic groups. In this case study, the social division between groups is more obviously shown from British participants. While looking at the relationship between Chinese academic migrants and their colleagues, it is not hard to find although they have relatively more positive feedback, the isolation and social segmentation with their local colleagues still exist, which caused some superficial understanding of the local field. Based on comments from those 'more experienced' Chinese academics they have not really had a chance to know the whole picture of social relations in the UK academia. Although the less hierarchical nature of UK academia in some places has been demonstrated, the Chinese academics' social segmentation could lead to the more one-sided, superficial, and imaginary understanding of the 'equal' relationship between colleagues. However, it must be pointed out that the social exclusion between colleagues does also not always happen between national groups. As academic work is more reliant on individual talents and teamwork, the reasons behind social segmentation in academia might not always be nationality, but might also depend on individuals' research field and personal interest. This will be discussed in more details in part three of the chapter.

2 Social Place

2.1 British Academics in China's Coffee Shop

In order to explore the social perspective of British academics' working experience in China, we need to have a closer look at the taken for granted texture of their leisure activities in workplace, 'coffee time' being one of them. The convenient coffee shop on campus fulfilled their basic personal, social and cultural needs during their working hours. This study reveals that British academic migrants' everyday social practice in China is closely bounded to their original distinctive 'social space' in the UK (Beaverstock, 2011; Waters, 2007), such as coffee shops and pubs. That is to say, in certain circumstance, the British academic's deep structure of the original habitus from the UK in social networking is never quite erased — even when they enter a new field in a new country.

The importance of the café in mediating social encounters and creating potential personal networks has long been acknowledged by academics (see: Shapira and Navon, 1991; Oldenburg, 1999; Laurier and Philo, 2005; Dines and Cattel, 2006; Simpson, 2008; Warner *et al.*, 2012). The café, in everyday social life, has been understood as a 'third place' of social vitality between work and home (Oldenburg, 1999), a place where the 'alone' and the 'together' are confused (Shapira and Navon, 1991: 122). Empirically, the importance of coffee shop could be reflected from Amy's (Professor, 55 years old, in China for 2 years) response when I asked about her dissatisfaction of the university: 'we need more coffee shops! The Aroma is the busiest one, because we have no choice'.

The Aroma coffee shop (Plate 9), mentioned by Amy, sits near the common room at the basement of the Administration Building, offering different kinds of coffee, sandwiches, bread, milk, *etc.* It is the place where I often interviewed my participants, and it is the only coffee shop in the teaching area. It charges a little bit more than the other two coffee shops in the High Street in the student residential area, which is about 10 minutes walk from the Administration Building. By asking participants about their daily interaction with Aroma coffee shop during working hours, major interlinked findings stood out.

Plate 6 –9 Aroma coffee shop (Photo by participant)

2.1.1 The Blissful Reminder of 'Home' in Coffee Place

Coffee plays a significant role in managing British academic migrants' transnational working, and most of my interviewees highlighted that coffee was a thing that could be regarded as an 'international ingredient' (Dick, Lecturer, 33 years old, in China for 1 year). Similarly, for Erick (English tutor, 36 years old, in China for 5 years), having coffee in Aroma is one of his daily routines:

The Aroma coffee shop is just down the corridor from our shared office. That makes it a quite handy place to go. How do I connect it to the working life... well... sometimes getting sleepy and getting tired, need a bit of energy, I go there buy a double espresso or Americano, when I need a little wake up.

Five of my participants who had experiences of teaching in China elsewhere were more aware of the difficulties of finding a good coffee place in Chinese universities. They specified that the Aroma had become a symbolic social and working space in this Sino-British university, as reported predominantly by international academics who live on campus, and due to their daily needs of 'real' coffee.

Moreover, echoing with Riemsdijk's (2014) work on the everyday place-making practices of highly-skilled IT migrants in Oslo, Norway, participants reported the importance of food as a major representation of home and belonging. My interview findings, coupled with daily observation in the Aroma café, showed this group of British academic migrants, in many cases, chose to live in a 'comfort zone' that this internationalised campus had well established for them before they came. About 65% participants make the conscious decision to eat food that reminded them of 'home', and they also regard 'good quality bread' provided by Aroma as a 'weekly celebration'. Will (Deputy of a Department, 55 years old, in China for 2 years) said:

You do get some kind of signals that came though emotionally and mentally you do not really know why, you really want the rice or you really want the particular type of milk or something. We are doing it as a weekly treatment or reward.

The important role of food from 'home' plays in migrants' everyday life has been established in previous literature on formation of belonging, and place-making (Fenster, 2005; Antonsich, 2009). Riemsdijk's (2014: 9) further suggests that Norwegian IT companies offer dishes that appeal to 'international taste buds' and encourage foreign employees to create a sense of belonging at

Norway through making dishes from ' home ' with the company chefs. It is nevertheless interesting to note that, similarly in this study, this Sino-British university also initially tended to establish the so-called ' affinity environments '❶ (Friedmann, 2005) for the recruited academic migrants, which made some changes to the coffee place on campus.

Although the institutionalised procedure of home-making created an intimate sense of belonging for many participants, some who have lived in China for a longer time have different views towards this. Dirk (English tutor, 35 years old, in China for 9 years) said:

Every Thursday, there is a delivery of those kind of Western or European style breads and things all these people go and buy them. It is not the quality. It is the closeness of style to what we can buy back home that made us so keen to buy them. For example, the quality of 'mantou' (the traditional Chinese version of bread) is very good, but they say it is bad quality, it is not bad quality, and it is just not what they get use to. You think the bread tastes good, is not because it is that good objectively, it just your brain established the judgment based on your eating history.

While for Erick (Professor, 54 years old, in China for 8 years), his colleagues have overly reproduced their own Britishness in the coffee shop in an irrational way:

We have a saying in Scottish: 'Fools and their money are soon parted'. It means it is very easy to get money from an idiot. It is a little bit harsh on my colleagues, but they are paying way higher prices than they should be for a product that they actually do not really need. They are quite

❶ ' Affinity environments represent a voluntary clustering of migrants in certain districts that, by virtue of migrants' proximity to each other, offer material and cultural support and eases the psychological pain of coping with the strains of surviving in a city where none of the familiar cultural cues are present' (Friedmann, 2005: 325).

happy to have something from home, but actually your are wasting your money and you might get stuck in this western 'comfort blanket' without tasting the real Chinese food outside of this 'British bubble'.

As Reay (2010) suggests, the movement of habitus across a new and unfamiliar field not only contains 'myriad adaptations, responses, reactions and resistances to the way the world is', but also the ways to 'make the world a different place'. Here, the coffee shop could not exist without the acknowledgment of Westerners' habitus (of coffee drinking) by the Chinese cooperative partner of this Sino-UK joint venture university. Thus, I argue that the notion of place is closely connected to everyday practice and habitus. On the one hand, British academics' habitus could be influenced by the specific place they came from, the different places they have been to; on the other hand, in this case, the 'host' place could also be affected by habitus embedded in 'the experience of social agents' as well as 'the objective structures which make this experience possible' (Bourdieu, 1988: 782). So, the findings remind us the importance of the 'agency' in transnational studies, and have provided some of the grounded insights from agents' perspective, in assessing the influence of academic mobility to the transnational academic space.

2.1.2 Chineseness in the Café is Like the Icing on the Cake

Although British academics in this study suggested that they are living in a particular space—the so-called 'British' bubble, their everyday experience is still affected by a sense of Chineseness, based on the fact that this university is run half by a Chinese institution. Mary (English tutor, 26 years old, in China for 1 year) told me how she finds 'China' in this coffee shop, she said:

We are living in a bubble, as we speak English on campus. The only thing that reminds you of living in China is when you go for a coffee in Aroma, you need to speak Chinese, as the support crew is recruited by our Chinese partner. Just some basic Chinese is enough. The old Chinese lady there is very nice , she sometimes corrects my Chinese pronunciation.

Another participant has a negative view of ' Chineseness ' in the coffee shop, he said:

Have you seen all these boxes in the corner of the smoking area (Plate 10) ? I think they are so unclean , and unsafe. It should not happen in our university , I have not seen a similar scene in the UK before... but no one does anything about it. (Emily , English Tutor , 34 years old , in China for 3 month).

Plate 6 – 10 Garbage in the smoking area outside Aroma
(Photo by participant)

Although the British academics working in the British system in China are assumed to have less difficulty as they could apply their habitus in this familiar ' bubble ', they still have to go through a process that somehow lowers their expectations, since the field is half designed by and inhabited by ' others '. Although the participant blames Chinese people for the making of unpleasant garbage area on campus, actually this is not a ' Chinese issue ', as this would happen in the UK in certain cases. While, it is understandable that personal standards could be restricted and limited to his/her previous experience and partial understanding. That could somehow explain why Emily said she had never seen a similar scene in the UK before.

2.1.3 Habitus Transformation in The 'Host' Coffee Place

For some participants, the coffee shop could also be imagined as an expansion of the office instead of a social place. Aroma uses its location in the heart of the main Administration Building as a drive to present itself as a place not purely for leisure, it is also a place for casual meeting and for practising 'boring' tasks as referred by Harry (Professor, 55 years old, in China for 2 years). A large proportion of participants stated that Café Aroma had its special function in relation to work. Take Rupert (English tutor, 32 years old, in China for 3 years) for example, he said:

> *It sometimes can be a peaceful place to work. Ironically, it is a lot noisier than the shared office, but in the office, colleagues are always asking questions or about to discuss stuff, whereas here, people do not stop you when they see you working. This is a quite interesting psychological twist. If you in the office busy, they do not see you're busy. They just come and disturb you. The other thing I like about noisiness is it stimulates you and helps to keep you awake. If I was making or doing boring tasks, I prefer go to the coffee place, as it turns out to be more efficient. So, the coffee shop which was probably designed for relaxation, is not the place I usually go to relax.*

It is noteworthy to point out that habitus of these English tutors is, in certain aspects, affected by spatial changes of their offices (from individual office to shared office). To avoid being interrupted by colleagues in the shared office, many interviewees turned Aroma into an alternative place for work, which is quite a distinctive transformation comparing what they usually did back 'home', in most cases.

Nevertheless, the smoking area of the café plays an important role in social capital accumulation. This observation is in accordance with the findings reported in prior studies (See: Chuang and Chuang, 2008; Brown *et al.*, 2006; Fang *et al.* 2003). It is similar in many countries, where smoking is considered as a social practice which serves to establish and maintain interpersonal relationships and social networks. By 'exchanging and lighting up cigarettes' (Mia, Professor, 49 years old, in China for 1 year), participants find a spontaneous way of socialising in this 'westernised' area, as the idea of the smoking area on campus only became popular in recent years in mega-cities of China as the law changes.

> *Smoking is a way of getting to know people. You just relax, and if you feel relaxed, it is quite easy for you to start a conversation. Smoking could be regarded as a social activity that promotes socialisation between strangers. You are kind of belonging to the same smoking group, no matter where you come from. (Nick, Lecturer, 29 years old, in China for 4 years).*

Data generated from my interviews show that the importance of nationality has been minimised in this HE organisation that act across borders. People in the study belong to the same group by sharing the same identity-academics. Different from most existing studies that focus on the social exclusion of highly-skilled transmigrants, this study suggest that, by sharing the same interest, academic migrants' social relations with colleagues could be bridged across their nations of origin. Other examples could be seen in 'residence' section of the chapter.

2.2 Chinese Academics in the UK: Common Room and Pub

2.2.1 Common Room and Habitus Transformation

Chinese participants outlined the importance of the common room as a place for socialising. The preference for the common room could be seen as a typical example to understand the relationships between habitus transformation and environment change for Chinese academic migrants. The existence of the common room is not taken for granted by Chinese academics, because it is not omnipresent in Chinese universities, and what happens in it thus becomes more interesting for them than for their local colleagues:

> *One thing good in there is that we have a common room for staff (Plate 6 – 11), and they have got free coffee and tea in there, the milk is free too. This is more communist than China, haha! Here is the place that you get to know people and it is good for us to have a chat during the lunch break. Some of my colleagues bring lunch here. I am starting to do this too. We do not have this in China, as you know, we often go to restaurants near campus. (Wang Qian, in her early 40s, senior researcher in Biology).*

Plate 6 – 11 Common room in a British University

(Photo by participant)

In this quote, Wang Qian highlights the unfamiliar but important role that the common room plays in her everyday working life. As an example, we might note, if the place is too small, too dark, too warm, or too far away, we choose and alter places to fit our needs and preferences; conversely, if the place is nice, creative and convenient, 'new' needs could be created to fit into the place. That is to say, from engaging with the sights, sounds, smells, tastes and touch of something that they know in the 'host' society (Collins, 2008), migrants also have the possibility of learning, changing, and switching from rejection to acceptance towards new practices under certain consequences. For many, the common room became an important place for daily socialising with colleagues during work hours.

Moreover, the different value of gift giving between different cultures has been noticed by Chinese academics in their common room:

> *We have 'table of joy' in the common room. There are littlesnacks on the table everyday. If our colleagues go out for a holiday, they would surely bring some sweets to share. I think it is really sweet, it is not about money, it is about people are thinking of you when they are not around. We give each other birthday cards too, but we do not 'Songli' (Gift-giving) to our boss, I mean expensive ones, as Chinese people normally do. I prefer the 'British' way.*

These different values have been discussed in Beatty *et al.*'s work (1993; 1996). They suggest that there is a huge difference in gift-giving behaviour between nations like the US, Japan, France, West Germany and Denmark. Among Chinese, the traditional concept such *renqing* (human obligations), *guanxi* (relationship), reciprocity, and *mianzi* (face) is likely to influence Chinese people's preference of luxury products as a way of gift-giving (Wang *et al.*, 2007). However, influenced by the local 'rules' of gift-giving, many Chinese academics are more or less doing 'what Romans do in Rome' and clearly showed their positive attitude of this 'relaxed way of living and working'. (Wen hui, 44 years old, a reader in Biology department).

2.2.2 Pub and Social Exclusion After Work

At first glance, the result of the Chinese academics' acceptance toward the new field appears to resemble Hsieh's (2011: 185) conclusion that 'Chinese academics generally have good relationships with colleagues in the workplace', in contrast to the 'clique' phenomenon among Chinese students (Edwards and Ran, 2009). However, the present research indicates that, although Chinese academics showed clearly their preference for socialising in the common room and their acceptance of the 'Western' style of gift giving, at the same time, they indeed have different social patterns in workplace, which, to some extent, might cause certain social exclusion in local social space. For example, the exclusivity of British social life centred on clubs and pubs in expat communities (Yeoh and Willis, 2010), had been reported by many Chinese as a 'social barrier' which is hard to cross:

The English people just love going to the pubs. Well, I know it is a very important way of socialising, however I could not get used to it. Partly because of the beer itself is not my thing, and I do not like holding an apple juice and acting like a weirdo. (Xiao Qiang, 33 years old, a statistician in medical department).

Or, as the participants indicated, gender could also be an issue that prevented them from going to the pubs. It could also be related to a Chinese social bias against women drinking alcohol and women's obligations in a traditional Chinese family, which is rarely mentioned in other studies:

You know my husband is Chinese and he do not like me drinking or getting drunk outside. He is very traditional. A woman who drinks and smokes is not acceptable for him. (Wen xiu, in her late 40s, professor in Chinese studies).

Some chose not to go to the pubs with their colleagues, simply because of the layout of the pub itself:

I cannot understand why the Britons like standing in the pubs while drinking and chatting. For Chinese, standing up is not the right body position for a real conversation, which means you just want a simple greeting and have to leave soon. (Li Hua, in his early 30s, a senior lecturer in

Contemporary Chinese School).

Indeed, the present study indicates that there are different cultural and gender norms surrounding drinking across nations and this phenomenon had been shown in Chinese academics' preference of social activity locations. Chinese do not go to the pub in China for many reasons: First, the English traditional pub does not exist in many cities in China. Second, Chinese people regard having meals together as a more acceptable way of socialising. Third, Chinese usually have their dinner after work at six to eight, which left them no time to have a drink in the pub. Similar with British migrants in China, who try to recreate their pub life from 'home' (Yeoh and Willis, 2010), Chinese academics have a tendency to 'replicate' their social life style in the UK. They normally enjoy 'friends gathering around table for meals' (Wu Xing, in her early 30s, a lecturer in Contemporary Chinese School) as a way of socialising with other Chinese. Most Chinese academics in this study tend to avoid or have a reluctance towards the British pub culture:

> *In the beginning, I was trying to follow them and tried my best to pretend that I liked going to the pubs. After a while I gave up, and I thought I have my own life and you have yours, there is no need to copy your life as long as I am comfortable with mine. (Wu Xing, in her early 30s, a lecturer in Contemporary Chinese School).*

Similar to other studies (*e. g.* Luxon and Peelo, 2009; Hsieh, 2011; Pherali, 2012), my participants' pub activity is prevented by some barriers in the form of language. Even those who have been in the UK for many years revealed that the cultural nuance of the language could be a key barrier for maintaining collegiality at workplace:

> *Language is another issue. I mean I am good at English compared to most Chinese, but I still cannot get their sense of humour. Sometimes I know every single word, but I could not understand the meaning of the sentence. It*

has something to do with cultural background , not just language itself. Now , I am making progress , I can understand 70 % normally. (Zhang Ming , in his early 40s , senior lecturer in chemistry).

However, the finding in this study suggests that there are a few more detailed language problems of intercultural integration. Many of my informants reflect that, in some case, it is easier to communicate with the locals rather than other nationalities, as the diversity of English pronunciations could be an issue for them:

I have a colleague from Northern Ireland. I am doing data analysing , and I do not even understand the word 'data' by his pronunciation , it sounds like 'hit him' (Da Ta) in Chinese ! Haha ! My name is Yue and he always calls me Yo... well... What is Yo ? (Xiao Yue , 33 years old , a statistician).

Moreover, there are narratives pointing to the avoidance of using second language (English) during work breaks, as a passive way of relaxation after intensive lecturing or marking assignments in English. Indeed, in Luxon and Peelo's study, Chinese lecturers indicated they usually felt exhausted after concentrating on speaking English for more than 20 to 25 minutes (Luxon and Peelo 2009). This could be an explanation for why many Chinese academics showed a certain level of exclusion from their British colleagues' social life, as the pub is not purely regarded as a place of 'joy' but 'pressure'.

Yet, this is not the case for everyone. Despite having the language barriers, those who are determined to improve their social/language skills often go to pubs with their colleagues. But, they are often more diligent and often put extra effort into the process of understanding and adaptation to the new social field:

I sometimes really do not understand what they are talking about , but I know I might feel embarrassed if I asked them to stop and explain. So , my strategy is to ask my English mate afterwards or Google on line. (Li hongzhi, at his early 30s, Chinese language teacher).

I find they do like non-academic gossip and small talk. If you do not watch TV, do not read books, do not have secrets, there is nothing to talk about. You always have something to learn from others, it is difficult at the beginning but fun and fulfilling by the end of the day. (Wen Weiping, at his late 20s, a researcher in engineering).

In sum, the data in my study suggest that it is hard to say Chinese academics' social circles in the UK are particularly restricted to either Chinese colleagues or in preference of other nationalities, although exclusion in particular places, such as pub, have been shown in this study.

2. 3 Discussion

This part of the findings section explores how the social experience among Chinese and British academics could be enlightened or restricted by particular social places on university campus. The discussion has sought to move the analytical focus from the traditional social segmentation/integration approach to the social function embedded in the concept of place itself. Specifically, I tend to query the reasons hiding behind the social exclusion by analysing the changing process of informants' habitus transformation in place.

The discussion has deepened my understanding of academic migrants' social life-world in three aspects. First, the empirical evidence has provided some of the first grounded insights into the diversity of the same national group. This research intended to break down those 'monolithic dualisms' (such as local or non-local, traditional or non-traditional migrants) and to potentially demonstrate a 'set of more fluid, heterogeneous classification' (Holton and Riley, 2013). This, in turn, is able to draw out why there might have been contradictory findings in different works in relation to the same group. For example, the study by Jiang *et al.* (2010) on Chinese academic staff in two research-intensive UK universities indicates that Chinese academics limite their social space to other Chinese nationals, which directly contradicts the result concluded byHsieh (2011) also on Chinese academics in the UK. Judging from my research data and observation, both of these two conclusions could be true, as Chinese academics are diverse in their academic dispositions and outlook on life. This also pointed to the limitations of those two studies, as Jiang *et al.* only selected 8 participants respectively. By interviewing 40 Chinese academics of different age, gender, discipline, position and past transnational experience in the same institution, the current study is mapping a more sophisticated and complete landscape of Chinese academics in the UK. For example, as it had been shown in the Chinese case, the academics had divergent attitudes towards pub going; and in the British case, people also were having opposed view towards 'Western style' bread.

Second, I concur with Hsieh's (2011) claim that shared research projects, spatial closeness, and spending time with colleagues are more important elements in promoting academics' close peer relationship rather than nationalities per se in the transnational HE environment. Moreover, migrants could be bound together through sharing a common interest, like smoking for example in this case and religious case in the previous section. Arguably, through a spatial angle of analysis, this study finds that examining social segmentation through a national lens could be problematic in certain academic migration studies.

Third, The transnational debates about academic mobility and the significant of place and space focus mainly on student's experience in transnational universities (see Leung and Waters, 2013). It is important to ask 'what moves?' for transnational academics too. The reflections of interview data have given emphasis to the intercultural significance of concrete social places on campus, such as café, common room and pub, among Chinese and British academic migrants. Here, I have particularly unfolded the social interaction of academic migrants in place, and pointed out that place played an important role in transnational social relations. What really 'moved' in this transitional context is academic migrants' embedded habitus and social capital that might alter their choice of frequenting in certain places and ultimately bring changes to them.

3 Residence

3.1 British Academics in China

Prof. Hu, the head of the branch campus, holds a supportive view towards the residential college mode in Europe and America, which originated from Oxford and Cambridge — a group of renowned professors live close to their students. He said: 'the students are surrounded by many distinguished academics. They can explore and solve problems, boost the sparks of wisdom, and it is also how the young academics get trained'. He wants to fully employ the '*yu ren di yi*' (educating people first) philosophy in this university. Although due to the funding constraints, the residential college system has not been fully realised at the moment, but 'we are nearly there, because the teachers basically live on campus, and students can find various ways to find their tutor'. (Li hongzhi, at his early 30s, Chinese language teacher).

Likewise, this residential college system has been applied in most Chinese universities. The Chinese university is considered as a '*danwei*' community of practice (Ouyang, 2004: 102). The *danwei* has been examined extensively by Chao and Chen (1997): it is a fully developed society in miniature. Having lived within the walls of the modern Chinese university, Ewan Dow attested that it is an example of one of Urry's (1998) 'post-modern' gated communities, a 'live, tame' zone in the midst of the rapidly developing 'live, wild' zones that constitute the modern Chinese metropolis (Ewan Dow, 2010). Everyone lives on campus, including scholars, their family members and students. Thus, the community operates like a big, extended family where everyone knows everyone else. The 'Chinese university is enclosed by walls, with a personnel system that restricts free mobility of those who want to get elsewhere' (Ouyang 2004: 124).

Surprisingly, these comments about Chinese universities are similar to what I was told by my participants in this study; they refer their lives as 'living in a bubble' in many cases. Their basic needs can be fulfilled in this campus, as post office, logistic affairs centre, finance centre, shops, supermarket, barbershop, laundry, café, 24 hour clinic and ATM can be found in the 'high street' on campus. On top of that, they are working under a British educational system and they only speak English inside the 'wall', since the university had been advertised for its authentic English education. Basic infrastructures are provided by the Chinese counterpart, so Chinese shop signs could still be seen on the high street (see, Plate 6 – 12).

Plate 6 – 12　High street on campus (Photo by author)

Moreover, it needs to be noted that the university environment in these two countries is different. Chinese academics often live on campus in China, whereas British academics are used to living elsewhere outside the campus. So for those British academic migrants who live on the campus of this Sino-UK joint venture, this 'new' experience clearly provides a more intense and prolonged form of contact than ephemeral micro-scale interactions, which have been the focus of much literature on encounters. Thus, as a site of intercultural contact, a British university campus in China that operates a style of collective residence is interesting in relation to the debates around habitus in connection to place and space. As such the campus environment provides an interesting case study of the inevitable tensions between different lived experiences.

For those who choose to live on campus, they either live in a staff apartment (if he/she has family members with them) or staff hotel (if she/he is single). (Plate 6 – 13) They prefer to enjoy the 'comfort blanket' in this 'tame' campus. The main reason participants gave for staying on campus is the convenience. Anne (English tutor, 46 years old, in China for 2 years) said:

Plate 6 – 13 School bus and children of the academics in front of the staff apartment (Photo by author)

I think the good of living on campus is the convenience. It only takes 5 minutes from your room to the classroom and you can go home for lunch and then go back to the office.

However, unlike the expectations of the head of the University, empirical findings associated with the residential college system applied in this university suggest that there are also many academics who choose to ‘escape’ from the ‘bubble’. It is certain that there are a group of British academics who want to divide their personal lives completely from work and are reluctant to meet students after working hours. In addition, in most cases, they are motivated themselves to experience the ‘wild’ (Ewan Dow, 2010) Chinese city life. By living in a more ‘authentic’ Chinese resident area of the city, transnational academics can get the essential of ‘negotiate and navigate a transnational lifestyle above and beyond their Britishness’ (Beaverstock, 2011).

Most participants who live in different residential communities[1] near the campus, either cycle or use a scooter to commute, in view of the fact that the Chinese cars are all left-hand drive, but in the UK, all are right-hand drive. Some senior members or professors hired a car and a driver for themselves, as it is both ‘affordable’ and ‘handy’ in China, reported by Harry (Reader, 48 years old, in China for 4 years).

In terms of living outside the campus, participants gave different reasons. First, it is a good way to experience the real China.

> *I lived on campus for the first 8 months, so I have been off campus for a year now. You feel a little bit of relief leaving the campus at the end of the day. You do feel like there is a separation between your work and going home. So, that is the main difference, really. I suppose you are more like*

---

[1] In the mainland of the People's Republic of China, a community (社区, *she qu*), also called residential unit or residential quarter (小区, *xiao qu*) or neighbourhood (居民区, *ju min qu*) or residential community (居住区, *ju zhu qiu*), is an urban residential area and its residents administrated by a sub-district (街道办事处, *jie dao ban shi chu*). Every community has a community committee, neighbourhood committee or residents' committee (社区居民委员会, *she qu ju min wei yuan hui*) and every committee administers or dwellers living in that community. Different form western ideal of district or blocks, this residential unit often have many buildings and all enclosed in walls.

living in China, when you live off campus. Because, I know it is quite a multinational campus, but still, you are surrounded by generally not the majority of Chinese people. (Kitty, Lecturer, 33 years old, in China for 1 year).

The university is located in a less internationalised 'second tier city' (in comparison to the first tier mega-cities, such as Beijing, Shanghai and Guangzhou), which has received little attention in the skilled-migration literature. The lack of well-established expatriate community outside the university poses challenges to the academic migrants' communication and adaptation with the locals, if they move out of the campus, but also created opportunities for them to experience more 'real' local places such as restaurants and supermarkets.

Second, everyone needs freedom and privacy.

You feel like you've got more freedom, I suppose as well. Like I did not experience it so much but I think, some of my colleagues who are living on campus always feel people know where you are going. It is perhaps a little bit intrusive, and yes, it is just great to have that feeling of freedom when you live off campus. (David, Professor, 50 years old, in China for 6 years).

Many of my participants pointed out the main reason for them to chose not to live on campus was the privacy issue and the 'feeling of lack of freedom'. It is not hard to understand their choices, because the university campus is a relatively enclosed space that they work on daily bases, and their choices are limited by the people they know, the places they go, and the activities they do on the campus. The concept of 'work and life needs to be separated clearly' (Anne, English tutor, 46 years old, in China for 2 years) was repeated many times by my participants. Third, it is economically worthwhile.

Actually, it is cheaper living off campus. I am not saving any money by living off campus but I am not spending any money. While as in the staff hotel, I thought it was very expensive for what it is, I still paid the bills on top of that, I ended up spending more money when I was living on campus. So, that is a bit of difference as well. Also for the supermarket, they are cheaper off campus and with more variety. On the days living on campus, you end up buying food from the canteen or the bar/restaurant in the staff hotel. So, it is just 'better' living off campus. (Julie, English tutor, 29 years old, in China for 1 year)

Those participants who moved out of the campus compared the amount of money they spend in both situations. The conclusion is that it is cheaper to live off campus, which means they can get a larger and nicer place off-campus with the same amount of money. On top of that, they do not need to consider the spending on commuting, because most of them strategically chose to live the residences near the campus and they always commute from home to the university by bike. Even if they chose to live far from the campus (in the central city for example), they would not spend too much money on the way, as the public transport in China is very cheap.

Fourth, it is easier to make friends.

My landlord speaks English, so we can communicate quite effectively. You can get by with very little, I found. My Chinese is terrible. I know a few words. Yes, it is easier on campus, but it is not that difficult living off campus. I actually have made more Chinese friends by living off campus. I have some English speaking local friends who can help me out if I really get stuck. (Robert, Professor, 55 years old, in China for 3 years)

The lack of language ability is a barrier for participants in making friends with local Chinese, however, it have been found that many British academics have frequent interactions with Chinese without speaking their language. This is because the economic opening-up of China has promoted thewidespread English education in the country; speak English is not that difficult for Chinese, especially for young people. On top of that, many British academics develop their sense of belonging outside the campus though self-organised leisure activities, such as music band performances in pub, pizza parties or cycling activities. These activities not only strengthen 'weak ties among colleagues' (Riemsdijk, 2014: 10), but also promote social interactions between British academics and local people. As a way of place-making, these academics develop a 'local sense of belonging on their own terms' (Riemsdijk, 2014: 10).

3.2 Chinese Academics in the UK

Hsieh (2011) found that the majority of Chinese lecturers are in need of additional support from the university, especially in terms of accommodation, because universities in China offer free accommodation to their lecturers and Ph. D students. This observation is partly true judging from information provided by my participants. However, I suggest there are a few contextual differences. First, the subject of Chinese academics' personal needs for support were generally raised during conversations with Chinese language teachers who had temporary work experience in China and other countries, or exchange academics who had newly stepped into the UK field (rather than lecturers). While other categories of Chinese academics, such as lecturers, researchers and professors, who have a proven knowledge of the local field, did not express their concern on this issue, as most of them have bought their own place in the UK. Second, the ideal of Chinese university providing free accommodation to academics is not fully the case in the present day, due to the rise of the real estate industry in China. Many academics are living in private properties in or outside the campus. Last but not least, newly arrived academics do have 'demoralised' feelings towards 'house hunting', and a large number of them did have 'frustrating' experiences of moving from one disappointing place to another:

I moved 6 times in this year, it was such a mess! One of my landlords was a Chinese chef, he was bad... as everything is included in the rent, he do not allow us turn on the heating during winter! My baby got ill a few time because of that! (Chao Fang, in her late 30s, a Chinese language teacher).

Most of my participants do not mind living outside the campus, as they can use a car or public transport to commute. But one of the key themes emerging from the study is that a Chinese style of social activity—the so-called '*chuan men*'[1] (literally 'string doors together') is missing in Chinese academic migrants' lives due the dispersion of residency:

It is very common for us to have tea at our colleague's place after dinner when I was in China, sometimes I invite them over to have lunch or dinner too. People get closer by frequent interactions. While in the UK, although we do have special activities for maintaining collegiality, we do not actually see each other very often after work, because we do not live close to each other. (Wen Zhang, 53 years old, professor in Chinese studies).

It was also revealed that the social segmentation of Chinese academics with their colleagues is more obvious out of their workplace. This is not only because of the residence decentralisation, but also due to individual interests in relation to particular social activities and their intensive focus on family life out of working hours:

My colleagues are nice, we can be really good working partners, but it does not mean that you are real friends. They often stay at home during weekends with their family. My life there is simply 'Hao Shan, Hao Shui, Hao Jimo' (Good mountain, good water, but very lonely), but it is 'Hao Zhang, Hao Luan, Hao Kuaihuo' (Very dirty, very messy, but very happy) in China (Wu Wei, 28 years old, researcher in computer science).

---

[1] Chuan Men (串门) means to pay a visit to someone's home; to drop in, but in a frequent daily basis. It is usually informal and spontaneous. It normally happens after dinner at 5—6pm, and is limited to the local neighbourhood.

This quote reveals that, for most Chinese academics, social life in the UK is rather limited compared to their experience in China. The Chinese saying Wu Wei mentioned in his interview has been circulating among Chinese migrants for a while. The former sentence is the perception of Western countries—a nice protected green environment, but can be a very lonely experience; the latter refers to Mainland China, it is quite easy to enjoy the life with feasting and different kinds of entertainment that are preferred by Chinese.

Indeed, it has been found out that not only the dissimilarities of residence distribution but also individuals' interest had become the key barriers for Chinese academics' integration with local groups of academics. Several themes have emerged in this study in relation to interaction with colleagues after work:

a) Different social places

Although, generally, the longer the migrant stayed in the UK, the more they felt comfortable in 'host' cultures (Hsieh, 2011), there are certain forms of habitus that could not be changed. Among Chinese academics in the UK, many of them have stayed in the country for a very long period. However, there are still some habits that 'both symbolise and mark the boundaries of cultures' (Gabaccia, 1998: 8) and could not be changed by time or space. As Collins (2008) suggests, migrants are making an effort to recreate a sense of familiarity by engaging with the thing they know, 're-grounding lives that have been uprooted in the process of migration' (P. 155):

Although I have lived in the UK for almost a decade, but I still eat Chinese food, speak Chinese language. Laowai's (foreigner) stuff, I know, but I do not understand. (Tang Huang, in his late 40s, professor in Chemistry).

This could be a reason to explain Chinese academic migrants' aversion to certain activities that are enjoyed by their 'western' colleagues:

For example, they love cycling, but I am not interested neither in their professional equipment nor the long distance they achieved. The weather here is normally not good. They told me I should enjoy myself under any weather condition in the UK. Really ? Should I ? They were camping outside during this weekend , and told me it was fun because their sleeping bag had been carried away by the heavy rain... well... I have nothing to say... our mind-sets are constructed differently. (Wang Chun , in her early 50s , senior researcher in Chinese Studies).

b) Different sport activities

The data of this study indicates that the integration into the local groups or exclusion with other colleagues from ' home ' is not purely determined by ethnicity but common personal interest.

My colleagues often go to gyms. I think jogging outside is much better. We should enjoy the beautiful landscapes. So , we have a team for jogging , most of the team members are my Chinese colleagues. (Wen Hui , in her 30s , lecturer).

I had a gym membership last year , but I was too busy with my work , so I rarely go there. I sometimes go there just for taking a shower , well , you know , it is not quite worth it. (Da Li , in his 40s , senior lecturer).

Riemsdijk (2014) suggests that skilled migrants in Norway often create a local sense of belonging through participating in training for sporting event with locals and colleagues, and he takes it as an example of individual place-making strategies of foreign-born professionals in Oslo. Informants in this study also indicate that participating in sporting event is an effective way of building ' social-bridges' (Ager and Strang, 2008: 170) with locals:

I like playing tennis. I usually go there everyday if the weather is good. I get to know people there. They are all Britons. Personal interest brings us together (Chongjia Wen , in his 30s , researcher).

c) Different habit of eating

We have an activity called 'Bring and share'. Everyone could bring food or snacks and share with others. But the thing is, many of my colleagues are vegetarian. This once caused an issue. I made a Chinese dish called 'Yang zhou chao fan' (Yangzhou fried rice). It is a vegetarian dish, but I did not know vegetarians cannot bear chicken essence seasoning. I am used to cooking with chicken powder and I put it in with out noticing. My colleagues are so sensitive, they know from the first second they taste it. They just spit it out in front of me... so embarrassing... Vegetarian diet is a concept I could never understand (Chao Yue, in her 40s, senior researcher).

3.3 Discussion

Here, the transnational elite refers to 'two sets of global actors: transnational businessmen and cosmopolitan professionals' (Ley, 2004: 151). Similarly, Waters (2007) finds expatriates 'appear to inhabit separate, segregated social spaces' (Waters, 2007: 494). In the case of British expatriates, social networks are often more restricted to other expatriates or western-educated Chinese nationals of the same level of income, language skills and forms of socialising, which cause a lack of interaction with local colleagues. (Willis and Yeoh, 2002). Beaverstock (2011) also stated: '... British expatriates were socially and culturally embedded within distinctive transnational social space, like expatriate clubs, which served their business, cultural and social needs' (p. 709).

Although the segregated social spaces of highly-skilled migrants has been highlighted from a classical geographical approach, the degree of dependence towards such spaces varies for different groups of migrant, even if they share the same ethnicity. It is noteworthy that the social exclusion/inclusion of migrants has complex relations to many variables, such as their profession, transnational experience, length of stay, personal interest towards local culture, language ability, and even the place they choose to live.

Correspondingly, the transnational academics, regarded as a part of elite transnational migrants, had been found to have a more complicated life-world that travels across both transnational and local spaces. This study finds the existence of scholars who tend to leave the enclosed physical and social spaces for *lao wai*❶ and expand their social networks with the locals. For instance, instead of enclaves with each other, many British academics choose to live outside their campus, in order to jump out of the so-called 'British bubble' and 'stay local'.

Bourdieu's conceptual notions, particularly habitus, have provided a fruitful line of enquiry into British and Chinese academics' attitude towards living and socialising after work with/without their colleagues. By not living in the university, British academics could enjoy the local atmosphere and enlarge their social space with Chinese and break the exclusion with the locals; while, by not living on campus, Chinese academics in the UK are found to be socially segmented with their colleagues after work in most cases. Although centralisation/decentralisation of residence could not fully determine academic migrants social inclusion/exclusion with colleagues or locals, a particular habitus that requires spatial closeness of residence (like *chuan men*) somehow affected the outcome of integration of Chinese academics with colleagues.

---

❶ '*Lao wai*' is one of several Chinese words for foreigner. It is generally a neutral term, which can refer to 'an obvious foreigner' or 'alien'. To the Chinese, the term may be used in an informal, good-humoured, or genial way.

Chapter Seven
Conclusion

By studying Chinese and British academic migrants' everyday work-life practices in a Sino-UK university joint venture, the three main empirical chapters discussed the complexity of future movement decisions, the pedagogical challenges and related solutions in transnational teaching practice, and the connections between academic practices and places on transnational university campuses. The thesis has gone beyond the national boundaries of higher education and placed the investigation in a broader frame of social, cultural and spatial analysis in order to develop a deeper understanding of academic migrants' everyday practices in a transnational era.

These three main chapters together illustrate the impact of the internationalisation of higher education on grounded academic practices, but equally grounded academic practice shapes the internationalisation of higher education. They tease out academic migrants' opportunities, difficulties, problems, misunderstandings and tensions associated with their daily work. The research develops an understanding of the ways in which transnational academics negotiate unfamiliar university rules and academic cultures embedded in the 'new' transnational academic space. These day-to-day negotiations not only help us to understand academic mobility on an individual level, but also to comprehend transnational academic space at and beyond the institutional level. The main findings suggest that the unexpected barriers in the 'new' transitional academic workplace have their own significance on academic migrants' further professional improvement and transnational mobility. They also indicate how academic migrants are not just passively adapting or integrating into the 'new' transnational professional structure, but also positively challenging and changing its boundaries.

This research takes a step forward in academic mobility studies by using grounded evidence drawn from transnational academic space to challenge the homogenising academic culture stereotypes that are bounded within national borders. It has argued for a transnational and enduring understanding of academic migrants' experience and points out that those experiences are nationally unbounded, yet locally specific. It had shed light on scholarly debates on transnational academic mobility and the internationalisation of higher education in the Sino-British context. To conclude this thesis, I will revisit the key findings revealed in the three empirical chapters and highlight issues to be explored in future studies.

1 Academic Mobility, Capital Exchange and Grounded Working Experience

The initial empirical chapter, chapter four, illuminated the power of the grounded everyday challenges of working in the 'host' university campus to alter academic mobility. It argued that the complexity of transnational academics' motivations for moving not only depend upon the capital exchange opportunities offered by national migration polices or institutional relocation plans, but are also largely influenced by their current working experience and the difficulties they are confronting in the 'host' academic workplace. By connecting the notion of transnationalism from above with grounded transnationalism and transnationalism from below, the chapter offered a fresh perspective from which to understand transnational academics' movements and motivations. It highlighted the fact that transnational mobility is not solely affected by transnational infrastructures 'from above' but also by everyday encounters and negotiations 'from below'.

In this chapter, I first discussed how recent Chinese national policy and British institutional regulations promote transnational academic mobility. Chinese academics in the UK are found to accumulate their capital in UK academia and impart their capitals through Chinese policy during their move. Meanwhile, British academics in China mainly rely upon institutional rules to realise their capital exchange. The research data reveals that transnational academic mobility is often stimulated by national policy initiatives that mobilise talent and better career opportunities provided by the academic system. For Chinese academics, the capitals gained through mobility are diverse, encompassing economic, social and symbolic capitals; while British academic migrants in China on the other hand are gaining capitals mostly in an economic sense. Moreover, I argue that capital exchange processes for Chinese academics are commonly influenced by their career stage: Early and mid-career academics are aiming for economic profits and academic opportunities, while more established professors are taking the influence of their symbolic power as a means to achieve self-realisation.

However, it needs to be noted that transnational academics do not move solely for occupational considerations and the migration process is not only bounded by opportunities from 'above' but also challenges form 'below'. The realisation of exchange through 'mobility capital' (Leung, 2012) is a short-term priority that works mostly in an economic sense, *i. e.* when the academic is in the process of 'getting the position'. Once the position is secured and the academic is actually working in the host university, other individual, sociological and political problems take precedence, which can affect their experience and future decisions about moving. In many cases, although academic migrants achieve better positions by exchanging their capital through policy, they have many problems during their actual time working in the 'host' workplace. Academics' decision making regarding moving is also largely influenced by the grounded challenges in the 'host' division of the university. For example, I found that this might be through negative social relationships with local academics or lack of local academic cultural sensitivity, *etc*.

Through my analysis of participants' grounded working experience in this chapter, I argue that capital can not only be accumulated through transnational academic mobility, but that it can also in many cases be devalued, and this can play a significant role in decisions to return to the 'home' country. The research shows that first, the possibility of capital accumulation does not automatically mean academic migrants will embrace their working life in the 'host' university; second, there can be disparities associated with 'rules of the game' in the 'home' and 'host' educational field, which hinder or prevent academic migrants' capital accumulation or devalue their capitals. I further argue that the different forms of capital accumulation can be one motive for academic mobility, but there are other factors, which can also influence their movement. I further argue that there is a need to 'ground' transnational academic migrants' motivation by focusing on the 'everyday' and the emotional aspects of these experiences as lived reality (*e. g.* Ho, 2014).

Lastly, it is important to point out some gaps that exist in immigration policy in relation to academic migrants across UK/Chinese borders. First, the findings of this research imply that the current policies, both on the Chinese and British sides, will not be sufficient to cope with the challenges posed by Chinese/British academic migrants' growing demands of long-term settlements. Therefore, UK and Chinese policy need to consider not only attracting international academics as a group but also their integration into the workplace and society as a whole. Second, the study reveals that academic migrants at different life stages have differing needs. For example, career opportunities tend to be crucial in the earlier stages of an academic's life, whereas lifestyle considerations and health concerns tend to be more important further on. So, governmental or institutional strategies could avoid taking highly-skilled migrants as a whole group by making efforts to identify a new classification of highly-skilled migration and employ relevant policies to smaller groups defined by age, occupation, location or nationality, *etc.* Last but not least, the research finds that generous salaries are important to a certain extent, but that academic migrants are not motivated to move or stay on this sole basis. Academics' motivations to stay or move are complex, and mixed with individual commitment and considerations. Policy is one but not the only driving force for their spatial mobility.

2 Transnational Teaching: Challenges, Adjustments, and Creativeness

Chapter five connected transnationalism to the teaching activities of the participants: 'The transnational classroom is a complex site of intercultural engagement, which provides both opportunities and challenges for teachers (Leask, 2015: 120). The findings demonstrate that transnational teaching can offer a range of possibilities for negotiating different pedagogies in the same academic workplace and provide opportunities for academics' pedagogical innovation which fit with the 'new' transnational academic field. It is an enriching process for academic migrants to develop their academic capability and creativity by negotiating with 'problems' that they encountered in the 'host' university campus. The chapter illustrated how, by engaging with the grounded complexities, transnational teaching practice added identical character to both the host and home academic workplace.

The chapter raised issues in relation to transnational teaching: It suggested that the geography of the local is of great importance for transnational practices.

Understanding local academic culture and developing intercultural competence is crucial for successful transnational teaching. During the teaching process overseas, academics get the chance to know the local factors that might affect their teaching efficiency, such as family expectations, relationships between teacher and students, learning habitus, *etc.* The research also found that previous transnational teaching experience could be a good foundation for teaching in a new country; it gave academic migrants enough knowledge and space for dealing with problems and conceiving their 'new' pedagogy in their current workplace. Moreover, in considering the problems academic migrants experience in their teaching practice, the IBC held workshops to discuss and identify those issues and then provide advice and guidance on pedagogical difficulties. It seems clear that developing intercultural competence is not only essential for transnational academics but also for all aspects of transnational universities.

The study reveals the essential issues in academics' offshore teaching. For British academics in China, conducting active learning has been hindered due to students' reluctance in class discussion. There are various reasons behind the issue, such as the logic of 'face saving', an onus on summative grades, family expectations, *etc.* In order to change the situation, various strategies had been designed from both the institutional and individual level of academics. Among Chinese academics in the UK, the problems were surrounded with language, self-confidence, and the foreign curriculum, *etc.* The research indicates that Chinese academics in the UK have a tendency to fit into the local academic system at their early stage of teaching, while they tend to look for their own pedagogical solutions to deal with thorny problems in class. In sum, the uneven procession of academic capital not only caused problems for academic migrants but also provided opportunities to reshape pedagogies in the transnational workplace.

The study shows that the diversity of students in transnational universities breaks national stereotypes of students' behaviour in class. By unpacking academic migrants' pedagogical experiences with students, it is not hard to find that their academic acculturation process and the impact on local educational practice were mutually constitutive. Cultural diversity can function as a double-edged sword; it can perform as a form of cultural capital that enriches teacher—student relationships and also work as a barrier to understanding local pedagogical regulations. The transnational teaching experience for academic migrants is not just a 'catalyst for intellectual development' (Bodycott and Walker, 2000), but also a contribution to local higher education institutions. The comments in this chapter also included many implications for professional development in terms of teaching, curriculum design and assessment practices. In sum, this chapter provided a snapshot of the characteristics of Chinese and British academics who teach in a transnational university and specifies detailed issues in pedagogical innovation and professional development. It also showed the impact of 'transnationalism' for the students even if they were not moving. I argued that the transnational teaching and learning space were constructed by people in its physical location.

3 Transnational Practice and University Space

As with previous chapters, by using case studies of Chinese and British academic migration to the UK and China respectively, chapter six employed a comparative lens to look at the role place plays in everyday working lives in the transnational workplace. By examining the office spaces, social spaces and residential spaces that frame academic migrants' working experiences, it became clear that the Chinese and British academics in this study treated places in the 'host' university with different attitudes, linked to their individual or group habitus. The richness that places can offer to academics' everyday offshore activities is worth exploring, as it fills a gap in current academic discourses on transnational academic migration.

I discussed the issues related to current transnational working environments in this chapter. The Sino-British branch of the university is seeking to establish a new educational model (a transnational workplace) where the host institution and British university could share good practice. However, physically, the basic facilities provided by the Chinese counterpart could not fully meet British academics' requirements and expectations. So, in order to create their sense of belonging in the new field, British academics focus more on individualised place-making in their workplace, such as decorating their office space with objects related to the UK. Or, occasionally, they chose to passively minimise office use due to the difficulty in place-making, such as the inconvenience of shipping books or dissatisfaction with shared office spaces. The main reason behind this may be related to their motivation: British academics stay in China for a short period of time, their 'staying' is for a better 'leaving'. This view is solidly supported by data in chapter four on British academic mobility.

In the UK, a different pattern was observed: Chinese academics are more proactive in their integration into the British educational field due to the long-term career expectations in the UK and personal preference of space use on the campus. Most Chinese academic migrants in this study show more positive attitudes towards their surroundings compared to British academics in China. This is partly because, initially, most of them were educated in the UK before they chose to stay. This allows them not only to be well prepared for their future academic career, but also to have enough time to pick their preferred form of HE system and working conditions. That means that if they stay, they are more or less ready to switch the old familiarity to the nuances of the new 'host' academic culture. What is particularly interesting in the case of Chinese academics in the UK is that they often take their stay in the UK as a chance to experience values such as trust and honesty, *etc.*, that they believe are hard to get in China. In this sense, they find their 'idealised workplace' in the territory of 'others' rather than China.

The study demonstrated that transnational academics' sense of belonging is closely bounded to their ways of treating the university space. For instance, in terms of place-making, Chinese academics in the UK campus like the current place to remain as it is, whereas British academics tend to want to recreate their familiar British working environment. Chinese academics' descriptions during interview are more in favour of local public infrastructure in the office rather than small objects inscribed with their national identity, as they are keener to be treated as an academic than as a Chinese in the workplace. There is something interesting going on in this case in terms of politics of national identity in the UK and China. Chinese academics often tried to hide their national identity in the workplace and let their professional ability speaks for itself, while for those British academics in China, their national identity is regarded as embedded symbolic capital which helps them to gain respect in their work practices. This tendency was seen clearly in terms of their space use on campus.

By unfolding academics' social interactions in places of the branch campus, the chapter pointed out that people in a transnational workplace could be socially divided by the differentiation of their habitus in relation to space use. For example, it is obvious that there is a clear social boundary between British academics and local administration staff on the Chinese campus. The study showed that misunderstanding related to space use between these two groups of people resulted in discontinuities between the individual habitus (Waite, 2013) and unfamiliarity with the 'rules of the game'. Here, the study echoes with Beaverstock's (2012) findings on the 'British expatriates' social club and showed that the participants were socially bounded within distinctive transitional social space on the 'host' campus, in order to serve their professional, cultural and social needs. However, it further found that the social segmentation in the transnational workplace did not just depend on academics' nationalities, as it often showed in existing literature, but also upon shared research projects, spatial proximity, or their common interests, for example. Thus, the transnational university social space is not purely divided by nation but also by the factors I have mentioned above. Correspondingly, in contrast to other studies on highly-skilled migration, which indicate that expatriates are overly dependent on their transnational social space, this research reveals that for many participants, the transnational campus is not an enclosed space or a 'comfort zone' for expatriates that separates them from the 'outside world'; they often chose to live outside the campus to get a real glimpse of the local life in China. So, this study challenges the existing academic discourse on national bounded social space, and extends it with more complex and nuanced interactions between groups of people divided by social activities, personal preference, or common interests rather than nationalities.

By examining the complexity of the connections interwoven between the 'place' and 'agents', the analyses in this chapter re-conceptualised the conjunction that exists between place and the migrant's habitus. By the same token, collective or individual practices that are tolerated or even appreciated in one academic place, say in a departmental office at a Chinese university, would be out of place in a university office in America. As such, the habitus is position-specific, age- specific, national-specific, but also place-specific. So, by connecting place with habitus, this chapter provided a vibrant and sophisticated understanding of the daily practices of academic migrants.

In this chapter, I used the examples of Chinese academics in the UK and British academics in China to expand understanding of grounded everyday experience in terms of space use. Much of the work focusing on academic mobility fails to consider the role place plays during their sojourn. I argue that transnational academics' work life and concrete materials in local places are usually linked together. Logically, a close examination of those places can help to see academic migrants' academic, cultural, social, and residential problems within transnational academic space. The main thrust of this empirical chapter was to juxtapose familiarity and unfamiliarity, transnational movement and local fixity, and transformation/preservation of certain habitus in the discussion of migrants' everyday space use on transnational campuses.

4 Final Conceptual Structure of the Thesis

In this concluding section, there is a need to systematically explain the whole conceptual structure of the thesis. Figure (7 – 1) has been adapted from

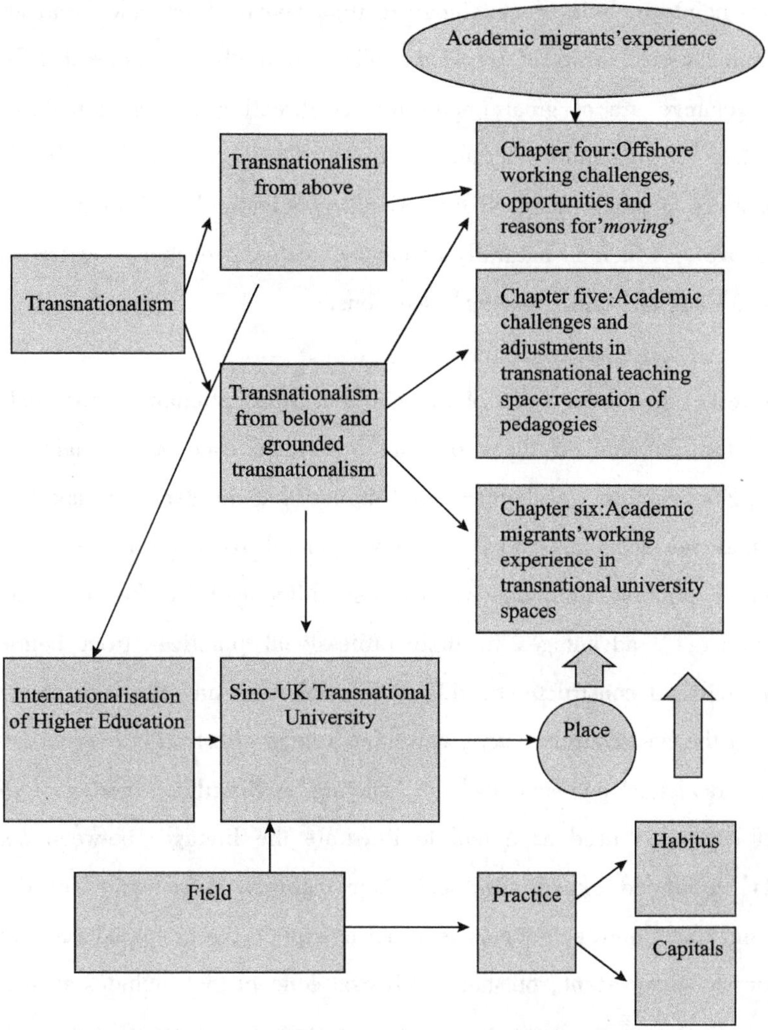

Figure 7 – 1 Final conceptual structure of the thesis

Figure 2 in Chapter 1, to show schematically how the thesis has advanced the conceptual understanding of the topic, and how new conceptual links have been made between transnationalism, the internationalisation of higher education, and Bourdieu's theory of practice in this research (See figure 7 – 1).

One of the main theoretical approaches of the study is to employ transnationalism as a framework to look at academic migrants' everyday experience. The entry points include transnationalism from above, from below and grounded transnationalism. In terms of transnationalism from above, national policy and capital exchange are of great importance in directing academic mobility (see chapter four). Academic migrants and their temporary sojourn in the host workplace are largely influenced by national policies and institutional regulations from 'above', which is naturally connected with the exchange of transnational academics' capitals and 'moving' decisions.

However, the main focus of the thesis is transnationalism from below and grounded transnationalism, concepts that penetrated each of the main empirical chapters. For example, in chapter four I argued that the decision making process of transnational academics was not only decided by opportunities/restrictions provided by policies from above, but also influenced by the reproduction of academic (dis) advantages in their professional practices from below. Local academic cultural constructions, different social rules and the lack of academic freedom of the host country, *etc.*, can have a large effect on individual academic migrants' decisions on 'moving' or 'staying'. Bourdieu's notion of different forms of capital is used as a tool to illustrate the linkages between academic migrants' grounded experiences and their mobility. However, it needs to be pointed out that Bourdieu's theory is a tool to explain the grounded experiences of academics to some extent, but not a universal concept that includes all individual situations. The moving process of academic migrants is a complex process that I found hard to explain wholly through Bourdieu. Other explanations, such as personal interest, family responsibility, unexpected opportunities *etc.*, are found also important in explaining academic mobility.

In chapter five, by linking transnational academic mobility with grounded teaching practice and classroom interactions with students, I pointed out that the offshore experience of academics did not just lie in their 'forced' assimilation to local academia, but also in their recreation of pedagogies. This allows them to 'successfully' fit into the local 'transnational' academic field, and turns the local working place into a 'pedagogy laboratory' that reflects the reality of internationalisation of higher education. The chapter is divided into two sections, the first one focused on discussing the challenges and adjustments in transnational teaching, the second mainly discussed teacher — students' relations in the classroom. As the working experience in the classroom already discussed in this chapter, the following chapter (chapter six), which deals with university spaces, intentionally excludes the classroom space. Bourdieu's theory is again used to clarify the discussion of the empirical data.

In chapter six, I connect academic migrants other working practices (other than teaching) with different spaces in the transnational university. The Sino-UK university campus, promoted by the internationalisation of higher education, is regarded as a new angle from which to understand academic migrants' offshore working experience. In this case, the ideal of Sino-UK transnational university is tied with academic mobility through the geographic notion of place and Bourdieu's theory of practice. Using habitus, place and capitals to analyse the rich data provided by participants, I argue that academic migrants' academic/social activities and university spaces mutually affect one another other. In this chapter, Bourdieu's notion of habitus and the concept of place are joined together to enrich the understanding of academic migrants' social, cultural and academic practices on the host campus.

So far, the three empirical chapters include most important aspects of academic migrants' everyday working practices. However, it needs to be pointed out that research activity is not the main focus of the study. Due to the 'trans-local' character of the research practice, it made no significant difference when academics changed their working place. So, the empirical data I gathered from the participants in relation to research activities is very limited. The empirical chapters added rich grounded resources to the current literature on transnationalism and transnational academic mobility. They allow us to gain a deeper understanding of transnational academic mobility from the greater scale of transnationalism, internationalisation of higher education, and transnational academic fields, to the more grounded practices that happen in an academic migrants' work life on an everyday basis.

5 Limitations of the Study and Suggestions for Future Study

Despite the significance of the study, it also has its own limitations. First, it only focuses on one transnational university, with means the transnational academic workplace that is specified in this study is limited to this particular institution rather than referring to the whole Sino-British transitional academic space. Knight (2015) identified three different models of internationalised university, namely 'classic' 'satellite' and 'co-founded'[1]. Based on the evidence of transnational universities' fast growing speed, it would be interesting to compare grounded experiences of migrant groups from various types of institutions, to explore how institutional structure affects migrants' everyday experience.

[1] The classic model is an internationalised university with a diversity of international partnerships, international students and staff, and multiple collaborative and intercultural activities. The satellite model includes universities that have established satellite offices in different countries of the world in the form of branch campuses, research centres, and management/project offices. The most recent generation of international universities are co-founded or co-developed by two or more partner institutions from different countries (Knight, 2015: 119-120).

Second, this study does not include reflections from those British and Chinese academic migrants who have returned to their home campus, as I have only focused on interviewing British academics in China and Chinese academics in the UK. Correspondingly, although the empirical data in this study points to Chinese academic migrants' strategies and intentions on returning to China, it does not contain a systematic investigation of those returnees' actual work life after their return. The reflections and experiences after the return and can contribute to a deeper understanding of academic mobility throughout time and space, as 'transnationalism is not solely symptomatic of globalisation, but is a theme that can be identified over generations' (Leahy, 2013: 130).

Third, this study focuses on two groups of academic migrants from China and the UK and does not include much voice from local university administrators, academics, administrative staff or students. I found in the course of this research that the variety of academic values and habitus among different groups of agents could have a profound effect upon migrants' professional practices and social relations in the transnational field. It would be significant to receive views from different groups of agents on the same issues in order to get a more accurate picture of the problems and misunderstanding that occur during the migration process.

Fourth, the thesis has focused mainly on academic migrants' work-related activities on campus. Although some life-related issues have been discussed in the study (such as residence on campus), many of the issues out of the campus life have not been fully discussed. The connection between the transnational campus and local city for example, also plays an important role in transnational academics' offshore experience and the decision-making process of their movement, as their life is not just limited on the university campus. Places, such as bars, coffee places, restaurants, camping places, *etc.*, are worth looking at in future studies. Linking academic migrants' experience in the transnational workplace and their life experience in the host city would offer a fresh angle to explore the complexity of academic mobility.

Finally, during the fieldwork the need for future work to engage with the gendered dimensions of academic life emerged. Ren and Caudie (2014) indicate that female academics face more family-related challenges than men. Many of my interviewees also expressed their feelings of being a female academic in transnational universities and their own difficulties related to gender in the transnational academic space, such as the balance between family role and transnational professional movements. The topic is worth deeper exploration in further studies.

Thus, in considering the limitation of this study, the following topics are suggested for future research directions: a comparison of academic mobility in different type of transnational institutions; an investigation on Chinese or British returnees; a liaison of different groups of academics and administrators in the discussion of transnational academic practice; and an examination of gender inequalities in transnational academic mobility.

6 Significance of the Study

Much of the work on transnational academic mobility, which largely focuses on students, fails to consider the crucial role of academics in transnational academic space. The 'transnationalism from above' (transnational capital) that is usually linked with highly-skilled migrants also clearly lacks an emphasis upon academics as a group. While transnational academics and transnational institutions have obviously increased in the last decade, acknowledgement of this particular group of people and their workplace is still limited. In this section, I develop an understanding of the extent to which this research on transnational academics contributes to transnationalism and academic mobility studies and the understanding of internationalisation of higher education.

In terms of 'transnationalism from below' and 'grounded transnationalism', this research accentuates the importance of considering the 'locality' and transnational migrants' everyday experience (in a transnational institution) in the context of global transnational capital exchange ('transnationalism from above'). More specifically, I have identified the diversity and complexity of academic migrants grounded experiences by contrasting two academic groups distinguished by their nationalities, each with their irreplaceable importance in the (Sino-British) transnational academic space. In doing so, the variety of examples in all three empirical chapters outline a host of linkages between mobility, practice, place and individuals. This contributes to a 'down to earth' understanding of highly-skilled transnational professional movement and the scholarly discourses on transnationalism from 'below' and 'above'.

In the context of internationalisation of higher education, this study looked beyond the conventional discourses around brain drain, brain gain and brain circulation, which normally consider the economic and political contributions of academic mobility for particular nations, as reviewed in the second chapter. Holding a critical view of these discourses, this study emphasises the importance of 'agency' and grounded experiences in transnational mobility studies. The vivid descriptions of academics' offshore-lived experience open up a fruitful avenue for understanding transnational migration and transnational migrants' workplaces. I argues that mobility-related experiences — be these the decision to move, the negotiation of belonging, the adjustment to the current working community, or the reflection on professional opportunities and innovation—are crucial 'ingredients' to help understand the inter-linkages between the national or institutional regulations from 'above' and the local engagements of agents from 'below'. In doing so, this study encourages transnational scholars to focus more on 'human faces' (Favell *et al.*, 2006 cited in Chen, 2015) from a variety of migration groups, in order to unlock the complexity of transnational practices.

By focusing on transnational academic mobility, this study challenges the migration assimilation and integration assumptions in traditional migration studies. This is because the 'host' academic workplace is involved with a larger proportion of international academics and more complicated institutional regulations that are affected by the local university counterpart (in the case of branch campus in China). For example, in the Sino-British branch campus, it is hard to define who is the 'host' group. Is it the Chinese administrative staff (as it is a university in China)? Or, is it the British academics (as it is a British transnational university)? Rather than agents that integrate into a solely academic workplace, the Chinese and British academics in this study are more regarded as active 'players' on a special 'transnational academic stage' that affect and in turn are affected by the internationalisation process in higher education. It stresses that the time has come to pay greater attention to the diversities within 'transnational' academic acculturation and consequently the greater professional creativeness embedded within this.

In terms of the transnational workplace, the study correspondingly underlines 'transnational academic space' as an ideal of 'flux' rather than 'fix', as it is gradually creating, growing, and being maintained by academic migrants throughout space and time. The study highlights that the boundary of the space is constantly identified, challenged and modified by national, local or individual influences. For instance, the Sino-British academic space in China had been conceived as a 'British bubble' for transnational academics to live in. It can be considered that the 'bubble' has been built since the relocation of the British university, as it was the university authorities' 'initial plan' to replicate a UK university and UK academic life in China for migrants. However, students, local administrative staff, Chinese counterparts and Chinese national policies have challenged the concept of this 'British bubble'. In this context, the particular academic space in China identified in this research adds to the discussions of 'transnational workplaces' in highly-skilled migration literature.

Moreover, this research interpreted Bourdieu's social notion of habitus from a geographical perspective. Inspired by previous studies, this research develops a spatial sense of habitus by associating academic migrants' habitus with various places on the 'host' university campuses. The notion of habitus, as a middle term between place and the body (Casey, 2001), has been used in this study to examine how transitional academics' sense of belonging is deeply entangled with place on the transnational campus. It stressed that the conception of habitus was not only closely related to time, but also place, meaning there was 'an inherent geography to habitus where a person's social disposition and the spatial location become intertwined' (Holton, 2013: 68). By examining the intricacies of academic migrants' habitus through university spaces, the study shows a more thorough engagement between locality and identity, which in turn, offers a fresh perspective with respect to migrant belongings and experiences.

In addition, this research deepens the understanding of academic mobility in three inter-woven aspects. First, methodologically, an agent-centred photograph-interview method has been adopted for this research. Academics were asked to take photographs, allowing them to visualise their working life on campus through practical action, and to have a personalised choice or interpretation of research evidence. The place-connected photos taken on campus served as a means of accessing and interpreting academic migrants' spatial practice. Second, empirically, it provides grounded analyses of Chinese/British academic migrants who work for the same international university, rather than taking all Chinese/British academics as a unitary group in the 'host' country without recognising the institutional differences. The university is also representative among the British international universities in China. Moreover, I also take differences within groups of Chinese or British academic migrants into account. Third, conceptually, as argued in Chapter two, there is a need to bring the spatial into the discussion of habitus, and I this was developed in chapter six.

In sum, the development of this thesis was prompted from my own transnational academic experience, leading me to other Chinese and British academics' experience working in a transnational university. This comparative lens enabled me to develop a dialogue between these two important groups of academic migrants from different perspectives in the Sino-UK transnational academic space that they share. This analytical dialogue encompasses the existing knowledge and current understanding of the transnational academic mobility and provides a chance to help question many 'givens' from previous literature. The main argument which holds the thesis together is the importance of using 'grounded' transnationalism to explore the spatio-temporal sense of academic migrants' everyday experiences, and the ideal of transnational academic space and places on the university campus that are not just backgrounds for those experiences, but are also mediums that influence mobility and transnational practices. In turn, the thesis breaks new ground by connecting transnationalism from 'above' with 'below', highlighting the importance of understanding academic mobility not just from the national scale, but also from local academic constructions or academic space beyond the country borders. It will be of interest to academics of transnational studies, academic mobility, and geography of education and provide grounded data for transnational university managers or policy makers. I present this thesis as one of the first literatures on Sino-UK transnational academics and look forward to further dialogue on this developing topic.

Appendix A

Dr ×/ Professor ×:

I am a second year Chinese Ph. D student in the Geography Department of Royal Holloway University of London and also a lecturer at Central South University of China. I am currently researching the processes and experiences of international academic mobility, focusing on Chinese and British academics' offshore experiences in China and the UK.

I came across with great interest your research on X and would be keen to learn more about this and your academic career. So, I am writing to ask whether you would be willing to have an interview with me about your experiences of living and working as an academic in the UK. The interview would last about one hour. I will be based on the XX campus from 01/05/2013 to 01/09/2013 and am happy to meet at a time and place which is convenient for you.

All information provided in the interview will be kept confidential and any material used in publication will be anonymised. The research has been approved through the Royal Holloway, University of London ethics procedure. It is partly funded by the University of London Research Students Fund.

I hope you will be willing to participate in this research. I am happy to provide more information if required before you make a decision. I look forward to hearing from you soon.

Yours sincerely

Tianfeng Liu

Ph. D. student

Department of Geography

Royal Holloway, University of London

Egham, Surrey TW20 0EX

Email：PWFA149@ Live. RHUL. ac. uk

Appendix B

Dear ××:

It was great to seeing you last time. Shall we meet again?

See if you are interested in this, this is a follow up interview of my research, hope you could help me with it.

As I have mentioned in our first interview, I am keen to use photograph as one of the main research methods in my study, because I am interested in knowing your working life better and would like to make sense of it visually.

Please could you take these photographs with your camera or smartphone? If you need a disposable camera however, please do not hesitate to let me know. These photographs could be of anything, from people, objects to places that mean something in relation to your working life, past or present, and which you are keen to show and discuss with me. Here are some instructions to help you further:

A. Number of photos: please do not take less than 5 or more than 30 photos in total.

B. I would be very grateful if you could take the photographs no more than 7 days after your first interview. If this is not possible, just let me know, and we can discuss.

C. It's your choice if you want to take photographs over one/a few choice days/a whole week.

D. When you are taking the photos, think about how you feel as you are taking the particular places/objects/people in day-to-day bases and what are the stories in relation to them.

E. If your photos including people in the campus environment, you need to get permission from the people who you want to take pictures of, and tell them this photo would be used for academic purpose/publications. If you want to take a photo of a place that involves lots of people, you should take the photo in distance so that the identity of those included is blurred.

F. We can rearrange a time for the follow-up interview by email or by telephone: XXXXXXXX.

During the follow-up interview, we will discuss the photos that have been taken by you. And we will talk about your experiences in relation to that particular place in each photo. At the end of the interview, you could select the images you wish to include in the research. The interview will last approximately 30 m.

Kind regards.

Tianfeng Liu
Ph. D. student
Department of Geography
Royal Holloway, University of London
Egham, Surrey TW20 0EX
Email: PWFA149@ Live. RHUL. ac. uk

Appendix C

Characteristics of the Qualitative Sample

No.	Pseudonym	Age	Gender	Discipline	Rank	length of stay
1	Xie	30s	Male	NSandE	Researcher	8
2	Du	30s	Male	NSandE	Researcher	7
3	Deng	40s	Male	NSandE	Professor	20
4	Yang	50s	Female	NSandE	Professor	25
5	Hu	30s	Male	NSandE	Researcher	3
6	Wen	30s	Male	NSandE	Researcher	8
7	Zhen	50s	Male	BandM	Professor	23
8	Zhu	60s	Male	NSandE	Professor	28
9	Wang	40s	Male	NSandE	Senior Researcher	24
10	Chen	30s	Female	NSandE	Researcher	3
11	Li	50s	Female	NSandE	Professor	19
12	Deng	30s	Male	NSandE	Researcher	2
13	Xi	30s	Female	SSandH	Lecturer	23
14	Yan	30s	Male	NSandE	Lecturer	5
15	Jun	40s	Male	NSandE	Lecturer	12
16	Hui	50s	Female	NSandE	Professor	23
17	Yi	40s	Male	BandM	Senior Lecturer	15
18	Hua	40s	Male	NSandE	Senior Lecturer	18
19	Xue	30s	Female	SSandH	Language Teacher	2
20	Wu	40s	Male	NSandE	Reader	20
21	Qi	30s	Male	NSandE	Lecturer	7

Continued

No.	Pseudonym	Age	Gender	Discipline	Rank	length of stay
22	Yu	30s	Male	BandM	Lecturer	10
23	Tan	20s	Female	BandM	Lecturer	5
24	Wei	30s	Female	SSandH	Lecturer	7
25	Dai	30s	Male	SSandH	Language Teacher	4
26	He	30s	Male	SSandH	Lecturer	5
27	Gao	40s	Male	SSandH	Language Teacher	3
28	Qiang	50s	Male	NSandE	Professor	20
29	Tuo	30s	Male	SSandH	Lecturer	2
30	Juan	30s	Male	NSandE	Senior Researcher	10
31	Rupert	50s	Male	SSandH	Senior manager	2
32	Andy	50s	Male	BandM	Manager	3
33	Claire	30s	Female	SSandH	Lecturer	1
34	Sara	20s	Female	SSandH	English tutor	2
35	Andy	40s	Male	NSandE	Senior researcher	4
36	Mike	60s	Male	NSandE	Senior manager	8
37	Dick	40s	Male	BandM	Manager	4
38	Luck	30s	Female	SSandH	Lecture	1
39	William	40s	Male	NSandE	Reader	2
40	John	40s	Male	SSandH	Professor	3
41	Lily	30s	Female	SSandH	Senior lecturer	1
42	Amy	50s	Female	SSandH	Professor	4
43	Nick	50s	Male	SSandH	Professor	6
44	Matt	50s	Male	SSandH	Senior manager	5
45	Diana	20s	Female	NSandE	Lecturer	1
46	James	50s	Male	SSandH	Professor	0. 5
47	Paul	60s	Male	SSandH	Professor	6
48	Derek	30s	Male	SSandH	Lecturer	3
49	Gary	50s	Male	NSandE	Professor	3
50	Jack	30s	Male	SSandH	English tutor	15
51	Rupert	50s	Male	BandM	Senior manager	2
52	Philippe	50s	Male	SSandH	Professor	6

Continued

No.	Pseudonym	Age	Gender	Discipline	Rank	length of stay
53	Andy	40s	Male	BandM	Senior researcher	4
54	Simon	30s	Male	BandM	Lecturer	4
55	Dickson	30s	Male	SSandH	Senior lecturer	1
56	Lisa	20s	Female	SSandH	English tutor	1
57	Lucy	50s	Female	BandM	Professor	2
58	Mark	30s	Male	SSandH	English tutor	5
59	Paul	30s	Male	SSandH	Lecturer	2
60	Jonn	30s	Male	SSandH	Senior lecturer	4

Appendix D

Interview Questions:

1. Before we start, could you introduce yourself?

Differences in administrative systems between China and the UK

2. What do you think is the most distinctive difference in terms of administrative structure in here and in China/the UK?

3. Do you have any difficulty when you communicate with the local administrators? Tell me a story if you have in relation to your experience of 'lost in translation'.

4. Please point out at least one administrative method they have adapted in here that you think it is good and you have not experienced before in your home country.

5. What do you think of your experience which effected by the local administrative system? Do you think it is a good or a bad one? Please give a few examples to illustrate what have and have not met your initial expectations.

6. What kind of service and support provided by your university, department

and Office of International Students and Scholars helpful to you? What is your suggestion for them? What areas of support do you want to see improved or made available?

Academic challenges

7. How much did you know about Chinese/British society and its academic system before you came to China/the UK? In what aspects do you think you were unprepared or less prepared?

8. What specific problems or difficulties have you encountered so far in your overseas academic experience? Do you feel that you are under internal and external pressure to do well? If yes, what do you think are the sources of such pressure?

9. Do you find it is easy to build up a good relationship with local academics or not? What is the issue that challenges you most during the communication process?

10. Do you think language ability can affect your academic progress (*e. g.* publication, lecture, access to a conference) in the host country?

11. Is your prior teaching style suitable for the new environment or you have figured out a different teaching style which have been improved to be efficient?

12. Do you think there are any differences between Chinese version of 'academic Guanxi' and British version of 'academic network'? What is the most acceptable way in here to build up academic relations? Can you get use to it?

13. Economically, do you have any difficulty in getting local funding?

The spatial configuration of the campus

14. Are there any difference between your office in here and the one in your country? Which one do you prefer? Does it have any impact on your work or communication with others?

15. Is the layout of the classroom have any impact on your pedagogical method?

16. What kind of academic activities do you participate on campus and why? Does it differ from your experience in your home country?

17. What places you usually go to at your University? Could you annotate a campus map?

18. Where do you usually meet your colleagues? Where do you usually meet your students? How does this differ from your experiences in China/Britain?

19. Do you live on campus or not? If yes, why? If not, why? Which one do you prefer? Does it have any impact on your working efficiency?

20. Imaging one of your working day, what places do you go based on timeline? What did you do in these places? How does this differ from your experiences in China/Britain? Then, get them to take photos.

Appendix E

Information Sheet and Consent Form

INFORMATION SHEET Institution: Geography Department, Royal Holloway, University of London Name of study: Transnational Academic Mobility: The Experiences of Chinese and British Academic Migrants in a Sino-UK Joint Venture University Name of Researcher: Tianfeng Liu Tel: XXXXXXXXXXX Email: PWFA149@ Live. RHUL. ac. uk Name of Supervisor: Katie Willis I am currently researching the processes and experiences of international academic mobility, focusing on British academics' offshore experiences in China. In particular I want to understand how academics negotiate different pedagogical cultures, institutional structures and the social environment of the campus. If you decide to take part, your will have an interview with me about your experiences of living and working as an academic in China. The interview would last about one hour. Participation is entirely voluntary. Participation is anonymous and confidential (only seen by myself and supervisor). Youcan decide not to answer any question if you prefer not to. Youcan withdraw at any time without giving a reason.

Your signed consent form will be stored separately from the responses you provide.
NB：You may retain this information sheet for reference and contact us with any queries.

CONSENT FORM
Name of study：Transnational Academic Mobility：The Experiences of Chinese and British Academic Migrants in a Sino-UK Joint Venture University
Name of Researcher：Tianfeng Liu
Please indicate
I have read the information sheet about this study (YES/NO)
I have had the opportunity to ask questions (YES/NO)
I have received satisfactory answers to any questions (YES/NO)
I understand that I am free to withdraw from the study at any time，without giving a reason (YES/NO)
I agree to participate in this study. (YES/NO)
Signed··························
Name··························
Date···························
NB：This Consent form will be stored separately from the responses you provide.
Please note：There should beno data collected on the consent form，as this will be stored separately from data.

Bibliography

Ackers L, Internationalisation, mobility and metrics: a new form of indirect discrimination? [J]. Minerva, 2008, 46: 411-435.

Ager A, Strang A. Understanding integration: a conceptual framework [J]. Journal of refugee studies, 2008, 21 (2): 3-37.

Aitken S. Shared lives: Interviewing couples, playing with their children [C]. Limb M and Dwyer C. Qualitative Methodologies for Geographers: Issues and Debates [M]. London: Arnold, 2001, 73-86.

Altbach P. Globalisation and the University: Myths and Realities in an Unequal World [J]. Tertiary education and management, 2004, 10 (1): 3-25.

Altbach P. Knowledge and Education as International Commodities [J]. International higher education, 2015 (a): 28.

Altbach P. Why Branch Campuses May Be Unsustainable [J]. International higher education, 2015 (b): 58.

Altbach P. Perspectives on Internationalizing Higher Education [J]. International higher education, 2015, (c): 27.

Altbach P G. Centers and peripheries in the academic profession: the special challenges of developing countries [C]. Altbach. P. G, Decline of the Guru: The Academic Profession in Developing and Middle-income Countries [M]. New York: Palgrave, 2002, 1-21.

Altbach P G, Knight J. The internationalization of higher education: motivations and realities. [J]. Journal of studies in international education, 2007, 11 (3, 4): 290-305.

Ammassari S B R. Harnessing potential of migration and return to promote development [J]. Sussex migration working paper, 2001: 6.

Anderson B, Harrison P. Taking Place: Non Representational Theories and Geography [M]. Oxford: Berg, 2009.

Anderson B, Wylie J. On geography and materiality [J]. Environment and planning A, 2009, 41 (2): 318-335.

Aneesh A. Rethinking migration: on line labour flows from India to the United States [R]. Center for comparative immigration studies, 2000.

Antonsich M. Searching for belonging—an analytical framework [J]. Geography compass, 2009 (2): 1-16.

Balme S. Entre Soi L'élite Du Pouvoir Dans La Chine Contemporaries [M]. Paris: Fayard, 2004, 3.

Barkhuizen G. Beginning to lecture at university: A complex web of socialisation patterns [J]. Higher education research and development, 2002, 21 (1): 93-109.

Barnett R, Phipps A. Academic travel: modes and directions [J]. Review of education, pedagogy, and cultural studies, 2005, 27 (1): 3-16.

Baskerville S, MacLeod F, Saunders N. A Guide to UK Higher Education and Partnerships for Overseas Universities [R]. UK Education International and Europe Unit Research Series, 2011, (9).

Basu P, Coleman S. Introduction: migrant worlds, material cultures [J]. Mobilities, 2008, 3 (3): 313-330.

Beaverstock J V. Transnational Elites in Global Cities: British highly-skilled inter-company Transferees in New York city's financial district [J]. Journal of ethnic and migration studies, 2005, 31 (2): 245-268.

Beaverstock J V. Servicing British expatriate talent in Singapore: exploring ordinary transnationalism and the role of the expatriate club [J]. Journal of ethnic and migration studies, 2011, 37 (5): 709-728.

Becher T, Trowler P R. Academic Tribes and Territories: Intellectual Inquiry and the Culture of Disciplines [M]. Buckingham: Open University Press, 2001.

Bekhradnia B, Sastry T. Migration of Academic Staff to and From the UK [M]. London: Higher Education Policy Institute, 2005.

Bennion A, Locke W. The early career paths and employment conditions of the academic profession in 17 countries [J]. European review, 2010, 18: 1-7.

Benson M. Transnational Lives in China: Expatriates in a Globalizing [M]. New York:

Palgrave Macmillan, 2015.

Benson R. Field Theory in comparative context: A new paradigm for media studies [J]. Theory and Society. 1999. 28 (3): 463-498.

Berger J. Ways of Seeing [M]. London: Penguin Books, 1972.

Berry J W. Conceptual approaches to acculturation [C]. Chun K M, Organista P B, Marín G. Acculturation: Advances in Theory, Measurement, and Applied Research [M]. Washington DC: American Psychological Association, 2002.

Besemeres M, Wierzbicka A. Translating Lives: Living with Two Languages and Cultures [M]. Brisbane: University of Queensland Press, 2007.

Bhagwati J. The brain drain [J]. International social science journal, 1976, 28: 691-729.

Bhandari R, Blumethal P. Global Student Mobility in International Institute for Education, Higher Education on the Move [M]. New York: Peter Lang, 2009: 1-15.

Biao X. A ritual economy of 'talent': China and overseas Chinese professionals [J]. Journal of ethnic and migration studies, 2011, 37 (5): 821-838.

Bigo D. Pierre bourdieu and international relations: power of practices, practices of power: pierre bourdieu and international relations [J]. International political sociology, 2011, 5 (3): 225-258.

Bissell D. Conceptualising differently mobile passengers: geographies of everyday encumbrance in the railway station [J]. Social & cultural geography, 2009, 10 (2): 173-195.

Blachford D R, Zhang B. Rethinking international migration of human capital and brain circulation: The case of Chinese—canadian academics [J]. Journal of studies in international education, 2014, 18 (3): 202-222.

Blunt A, Dowling R. Home [M]. London: Routledge. 2006.

Bodycott P, Walker A. Teaching abroad: Lessons learned about inter-cultural understanding for teachers in higher education [J]. Teaching in Higher Education, 2000, 5 (1): 79-94.

Bond K. Working with International Students: A Guide for Staff in Engineering: An Engineering Subject Centre Guide [R]. Higher Education Academy Engineering Subject Centre, 2010.

Bourdieu P. Distinction: A Social Critique of the Judgement of Taste [M]. London: Routledge and Kegan Paul, 1984.

Boyd M. Family and personal networks in international migration: recent developments and new agendas [J]. International migration review, 1989, 23 (3): 638-670.

British Council. Prime Minister's Initiative for International Education [EB/OL]. [2012-06]. http: //www British council org/learning pmi2 policy dialogues htm (accessed 21/04/12), 2008.

Brooks R, Waters J. Social networks and educational mobility globalization [J]. Societies and education, 2010, 1 (1): 43-57.

Brooks R, Waters J. International higher education and the mobility of UK students [J]. Journal of research in international education, 2009, 8 (2): 191-209.

Brown M. Using the intellectual diaspora to reverse the brain drain: some useful examples [EB/OL]. [2011-10]. http: //wwwunecaorg/eca_resouces/Conference_Reports_and_Other_Documents, accessed March 2000.

Brown M. Intellectual diaspora networks: their viability as a response to highly skilled migration [J]. Autrepart, 2002, 22: 167-178.

Brzezinski M. Migration and opportunities: a qualitative understanding of the Chinese student brain drain phenomenon [R]. Washington DC: NAFSA Working Paper, No. 41, NAFSA, USA, 1994.

Burley Allen M. Listening: the forgotten skill (a self-teaching guide) [J]. Hoboken, NJ: John Wiley & Sons, 1995.

Burrell K. Materialising the border: spaces of mobility and material culture in migration from post socialist poland [J]. Mobilities, 2008, 3 (3): 353-373.

Butz D. Autobiography, autoethnography, and intersubjectivity: analysing communication in northern Pakistan [C]. Moss P. Placing Autobiography in Geography [M]. Syracuse NY: Syracuse University Press, 2001, 149-166.

Byram M, Dervin F. Students, Staff and Academic Mobility in Higher Education [M]. Newcastle: Cambridge Scholars Publishers, 2008.

Cai H. The Chinese knowledge diaspora in the development of Chinese research universities [R]. International Conference on Diaspora for Development, 2009.

Cameron J. Focussing on the focus group [C]. Qualitative research methods in human geography [M]. Oxford: Oxford University Press, 2000, 83-102.

Cantwell B. Transnational mobility and international academic employment: gatekeeping in an academic competition arena [J]. Minerva, 2011, 49 (4): 425-445.

Castells M. L'ère De L'information, Tome I: La Société En Réseaux. (Traduit De L'anglais

Par Philippe Delamare) [M]. Paris: Fayard, 1998, 671

Castles S. International migration at the beginning of the twenty first century: global trends and issues, [J]. International social science journal, 2000, 53: 269-281.

Castles S. Migration and community formation under conditions of globalization [J]. International migration review, 2002, 36: 1143-1168.

Cattelain C, Sébastien N. Les Déclassés du Nord: une nouvelle migration chinoise en France Revue européenne des migrations internationales, vol 2, n°3 [EB/OL]. [2011-10-15] http: //remirevuesorg/index2521html (accessed 15/10/2011).

CEC Green Paper: The European Research Area: New perspectives [R]. Brussels, 2007.

Chan C K K, . Rao N. . The paradoxes revisited: the Chinese learner in changing educational contexts [J]. CERC studies in comparative education, 2010, 25 (4): 315-349.

Chang P, Zhiduan D. . The Chinese brain drain and policy options [J]. Studies in comparative international development, 1992, 27 (1): 44-60.

Chau R C M, Yu S W K. Social exclusion of Chinese people in Britain [J]. Critical social policy, 2001, 21 (1): 103-125.

Chen Q, Koyama J P. . Reconceptualising diasporic intellectual networks: mobile scholars in transnational space [J]. Globalisation, societies and education, 2013, 11 (1): 23-38.

Chen Y. . The limits of brain circulation: Chinese returnees and technological development in Beijing [J]. Pacific affairs, (2008) 81: 195-215.

Cheng X, Studies on contemporary Chinese overseas students [M]. Hong Kong: Hong Kong Social Science Publication Ltd, 2002.

Chepesiuk R. Sino American deal brings Chinese IT workers to US [J]. Asian week, 2001, (6): 8-14.

Cheung A C K, Xu Li. To return or not to return: examining the return intentions of mainland Chinese students studying at Elite Universities in the United States [J]. Studies in higher education, 2015, 40 (9): 1605-1624.

Choi H. An International Scientific Community: Asian Scholars In the United States [M]. New York, Praeger, 1995.

Chui A S, Tan C B. Old Chinese Overseas Communities and New Chinese Migrants on the Internet, The Chinese University of Hong Kong, [EB/OL]. http: //www. nia ku dk/ ISSCQ5/panels htm, (accessed 14/10/2011).

Clarke N. Detailing transnational lives of the middle: British working holiday makers in Australia [J]. Journal of ethnic and migration studies, 2005, 31 (2): 307-322.

Coe N M. Geographies of production III: making space for labour [J]. Progress in Human Geography, 2013, 37 (2): 271-284.

Cohen N. Come home, be professional? Ethnonationalism and economic rationality in Israel's return migration strategy [J]. Immigrants and minorities, 2009, 27: 1-28.

Collins D, Coleman T. Social geographies of education: looking within, and beyond, school boundaries [J]. Geography compass, 2008, 2: 281-299.

Collins F L. Of kimchi and coffee: globalisation, transnationalism and familiarity in culinary consumption [J]. Social and cultural geography, 2008, 9 (2): 151-169.

Collins F L. International students as urban agents: international education and urban transformation in Auckland, New Zealand [J]. Geoforum, 2010, 41 (6): 940-950.

Collyer M, King R. Producing transnational space: international migration and the extra-territorial reach of state power [J]. Progress in human geography, 2015, 39 (2): 185-204.

Combs J, Ziller R. Photographic self-concepts of counselees [J]. Journal of counseling psychology, 1977, 24: 452-455.

Commander S, Kangasniemi M, Winters A. The brain drain: curse or boon? [R]. NBER Working Paper, UK Cambridge, 2003.

Conradson D, Latham A. The affective possibilities of London: antipodean transnationals and the overseas experience [J]. Mobilities, 2007, 2 (2): 231-254.

Conradson D, Latham A. Transnational Urbanism: attending to everyday practices and mobilities [J]. Journal of ethnic and migration studies, 2005, 31 (2): 227-233.

Cook I. Participant observation [C]. Flowerdew R, Martin D. Methods in Human Geography [M]. Harlow: Longman, 1997.

Cortazzi M, Jin L, Zhiru W. Cultivators, Cows and computers: Chinese learners metaphors of teachers in Coverdale [C]. Jones T, Rastall P. Internationalising the university: the Chinese context [M]. Basingstoke and New York: Palgrave Macmillan, 2009, 107-129.

Cox A, Herrick T, Keating P. Accommodations: staff identity and university space [J]. Teaching in higher education, 2012, 17 (6): 697-709.

Crang M. Picturing practices: research through the tourist gaze [J]. Progress in human geography, 1997, 21: 359-373.

Crang M. Field work: making sense of group interviews [C]. Limb M, Dwyer C. Qualitative methodologies for geographers: issues and debates [M]. London: Arnold, 2001, 215-233.

Cresswell T. Place: A Short Introduction [M]. Oxford: Blackwell, 2004.

Davies G, Dwyer C. Qualitative methods: are you enchanted or are you alienated? [J]. Progress in Human Geography, 2007, 31 (2): 257-266.

De Vita G, Case P. Rethinking the internationalization agenda in UK higher education [J]. Journal of further and higher education, 2003, 27 (4): 383-398.

Dear M. Practising postmodern geography [J]. Scottish Geographical Magazine, 1995, 111: 179-181.

DeVoretz D, Parasram A. Updated 10 Mar 2010A case for a Ministry of Canadians abroad? [EB/OL]. http://www. embassymag ca/page/view/ (accessed 17/10/2011).

Dobos K. Serving two masters academics'perspectives on working at an offshore campus in Malaysia [J]. Educational review, 2011, 63 (1): 19-35.

Dodman D R. Shooting in the city: an autophotographic exploration of the urban environment in Kingston, Jamaica [J]. Area, 2003, 35 (3): 293-304.

Dowler L. Fieldwork in the trenches: participant observation in a conflict area [J]. Limb M, Dwyer C. Qualitative Methodologies for Geographers: Issues and Debates [M]. London: Arnold, 2001, 153-164.

Dreher A, Poutvaara P. Student flows and migration [R]. CE Sifo Working Paper, Konstanz, 2005.

Dunn K. Interviewing [C]. Qualitative Research Methods in Human Geography [M]. Melbourne: Oxford University Press, 2000: 50-82.

Edwards R, Usher R. Globalisation and Pedagogy [M]. London, Routledge, 2000.

Edwards V, Ran A. Building on experience: meeting the needs of Chinese students in British higher education [C]. Coverdale T, Rastall P, Basingstoke. Internationalising the University: The Chinese Context Palgrave Macmillan, 2009: 185-205.

Ehrkamp P. Placing identities: transnational practices and local attachments of Turkish immigrants in Germany [J]. Journal of ethnic and migration studies, 2005, 31 (2): 345-364.

Eldridge K, Neil C. Managing transnational education: does national culture really matter? [J]. Journal of higher education policy and management, 2009, 31 (1): 67-79.

Kuznetsov Y. Diaspora Networks and the International Migration of Skills, How Countries Can Draw on their Talent Abroad [M]. Washington: World Bank, 2006: 21-58.

England K. Interviewing elites: cautionary tales about researching women managers in Canada's banking industry [C]. Moss P. Placing Autobiography in Geography [M]. Syracuse NY: Syracuse University Press, 2001: 200-213.

Ennew C T, Fujia Y. Foreign Universities in China: a case study [J]. European journal of education, 2009, 44 (1): 21-36.

European Union Seventh research framework programme, FP7, [BE/OL]. [2007-2013]. http: //cordis europa. eu/fp7/home_en html, (accessed 21/04/12).

Fahey J, Kenway J. Thinking in a 'worldly' way: mobility, knowledge, power and geography [J]. Discourse: studies in the cultural politics of education, 2010, 31 (5): 627-640.

Fahey J, Kenway J. International academic mobility: problematic and possible paradigms [J]. Discourse: studies in the cultural politics of education, 2010, 31 (5): 563-575.

Fahey J, Kenway J. Moving ideas and mobile researchers: Australia in the global context [J]. The Australian educational researcher, 2010, 37 (4): 103-114.

Fahey J, Kenway J. The ethics of national hospitality and globally mobile researchers [C]. Apple M, Ball S, Gandin L A. International handbook of sociology of education [M]. London: Routledge, 2010: 48-57.

Farrer J. From passports to joint ventures: intermarriage between Chinese nationals and western expatriates residing in Shanghai [J]. Asian Studies Review, 2008, 32 (1): 7-29.

Fazackerley A, Worthington P. British Universities in China: the reality beyond the rhetoric [R]. Agora: The forum for culture and education, London: Agora, 2007.

Fenster T. Gender and the city: the different formations of belonging [C]. Nelson L, Seager J. A Companion to Feminist Geography [M]. Malden, MA: Blackwell, 2005: 242-257.

Findlay A M, King R, Smith F M, et al. World class? An investigation of globalization, difference and international student mobility [J]. Transactions of the Institute of British Geographers, 2012, 37: 118-131.

Findlay A M. A migration channels approach to the study of high level manpower movements: a theoretical perspective [J]. International Migration, 1990, 28: 15-23.

Findlay A M, Li F L N. Methodological issues in researching migration [J]. The Professional Geographer, 1999, 51 (1): 50-59.

Forbes D. Reading texts and writing geography' [C]. Qualitative research methods in human geography [M]. Melbourne: Oxford University Press, 2000: 122-143.

Frank A W Bourdieu. The master [J]. Canadian journal of sociology/Cahiers Canadiens de Sociologie, 2012, 37 (3): 319-330.

Frankfort Nachimas C, Nachimias D. Research Method in the Social Sciences [M). (5th Edition), London: Arnold, 1996.

Friedmann J. Place making as project? Habitus and migration in transnational cities [C]. Hillier J, Rooksby. E. Habitus: A Sense of Place [M]. Aldershot: Ashgate, 2005.

Friesen B. Designing and Conducting Your First Interview Project [M]. San Francisco Jossey-Bass, 2010.

Gabaccia D R. We Are What We Eat: Ethnic Food and the Making of Americans [M]. Cambridge: Harvard University Press, 1998.

Gao L, Watkins D A. Conceptions of teaching held by school science teachers in P R China: identification and cross-cultural comparisons [J]. International journal of science education 2002, 24: 61-79.

Gao W. Chinese New Migrants in the Context of International Migration [M]. Beijing: Zhongguo Huaqiao Chubanshe, China Overseas Chinese Press.

Garson B. Teaching abroad: A cross cultural journey [J]. Journal of education for business July/August, 2005: 322-326.

Germain A, Séguin A. Les modes d'insertion urbaine des immigrants: état de la question immigration et région: nouveaux enjeux [J]. nouvelles perspectives, 1993: 45-63.

Getty L J. False Assumptions: The Challenges and Politics of Teaching in China [J]. Teaching in Higher Education, 2011, 16 (3): 347-352.

Giles J, Park A, Wang M. The great proletarian cultural revolution, disruptions to schooling, and the returns to schooling in urban China [R]. 2008.

Giordano A, Pagano A. The Chinese policy of highly qualified human capital: A strategic factor for global competition [J]. Innovation transition studies review, 2013, 19 (3): 325-337.

Girdzijauskaite E, Radzeviciene A. International branch campus: framework and strategy [J]. Procedia social and behavioral sciences, 2014, 110: 301-308.

Gladston P. China and Other Spaces: Selected Essays by Contributors to the Research Seminar Series of the Institute of Comparative Cultural Studies at the University of Nottingham Ningbo, China 2005-2007 [M]. Nottingham: Critical, Cultural and Communications Press, 2009.

Gopal A, Zha Q. Internationalisation of higher education and global mobility [J]. Educational review, 2015, 67 (3): 386-388.

Gow, Fazackerley A. British Universities in China: the reality beyond the rhetoric [R]. Agora: The Forum for Culture and Education, 2007.

Gribble K, Ziguras C. Learning to teach offshore: pre-departure training for lecturers in transnational programs [J]. Higher education research and development, 2003. 22 (2): 205-216.

Grossman M. Diaspora knowledge flows in the global economy [R]. http: //vc bridgew. edu/management_fac/18/, 2010a.

Grossman M. Business networks, brain circulation, and the American Chinese diaspora [J]. VINE, 2010 (b), 40 (3/4): 287-300.

Gu Q. Enjoy Loneliness—Understanding Chinese Learners voices [J/OL] http: //www. hltmag. co uk/nov05/mart01 htm (accessed 01/04/2012).

Guarnizo L E, Smith M P. The locations of transnationalism [J]. Transnationalism from below, 1998, 6: 3-34.

Guerin C, Green I. Cultural Diversity and the Imagined Community of the Global Academy [J]. Asia Pacific Journal of Education, 2014, 6 (5): 1-12.

Guerrassimoff C. Le renouvellement des perspectives transnationales de la Chine, Critiques internationale [M]. vol 3, n° 32 juillet/septembre, Paris: Presses de Sciences Po, 2006: 39-52.

Gulson K, Symes C. Knowing one's place in Gulson K and Symes C (eds), Spatial theories of education [M]. London: Routledge, 2007: 1-16.

Gurney K, Adams J. Tracking UK and international researchers by an analysis of publication data [R]. Leeds: Evidence Ltd.

Hanassab S. Diversity, international students, and perceived discrimination: Implications for educators and counsellors [J]. Journal of Studies in International Education, 2006, 10 (2): 157-172.

Handal B. Global scholars as ambassadors of knowledge, in academic migration, discipline knowledge and pedagogical practice [C]. Mason C, Rawlings, Sanaei F, Springer Singapore [M]. Berlin:? Singapore, 2014: 27-38.

Harvey W. Victory can be yours in the global war for talent: Social factors and lifestyle help to attract top employees [J]. Human resource management international digest, 2013, 21 (1): 37-40.

Hasrati M. Legitimate peripheral participation and supervising Ph D students [J]. Studies in higher education, 2005, 30 (5): 557-570.

HEFCE. International student mobility, Issues Paper 2004 30 HEFCE [R]. London, 2004.

HESA. Higher Education Statistics Agency [EB/OL]. http: //www. hesa ac uk/content/ (accessed 01/04/2012), 2010.

HESA. Higher Education Statistics Agency, http: //www. hesa ac uk/content/view/1897/ 239/ (accessed 30/04/12), 2012.

Hetherington K. Spatial textures: place, touch, and praesentia [J]. Environment and planning A, 2003, 35 (11): 1933-1944.

Hitchings R. People can talk about their practices: people can talk about their practices [J]. Area, 2012, 44 (1): 61-67.

Ho E L, Madeleine E D H. Migration and everyday matters: sociality and Materiality [J]. Population, Space and Place, 2011, 17 (6): 707-713.

Ho E, Lynn Ee. Identity politics and cultural asymmetries: singaporean transmigrants fashioning cosmopolitanism [J]. Journal of Ethnic and Migration Studies, 2011, 37 (5): 729-746.

Hoffman D M. Changing academic mobility patterns and international migration: What will academic mobility mean in the 21st century? [J]. Journal of Studies in International Education, 2009, 13: 347-364.

Hofstede G. National Cultures Revisited [J]. Asia Pacific Journal of Management, 1984, (9): 22-24.

Holloway S L, Jons H. Geographies of education and learning: boundary crossings [J]. transactions of the institute of British geographers, 2012, 37 (4): 482-488.

Holt L. Embodied social capital and geographic perspectives: performing the habitus [J]. Progress in Human Geography, 2008, 32 (2): 227-246.

Holton M. Advancing student geographies: habitus, identities and (re) sensing of place [J]. University of Portsmouth, 2013.

Holton M Riley M. Student geographies：exploring the diverse geographies of students and higher education：student geographies [J]. Geography Compass，2013，(1)：61-74.

Holton M Riley M. Talking on the move：place based interviewing with undergraduate students：talking on the Move [J]. Area，2014，46 (1)：59-65.

Horton S B. Medical returns as class transformation：situating migrants medical returns within a framework of transnationalism [J]. Medical Anthropology，2013，32 (5)：417-432.

Hsieh H. Challenges facing Chinese academic staff in a UK university in terms of language，relationships and culture [J]. Teaching in higher education，2012，17 (4)：371-383.

Huang S，Yeoh B S A. Navigating the terrains of transnational education：children of Chinese study mothers in Singapore [J]. Geoforum，2011，42 (3)：394-403.

Huang W C. An empirical analysis of foreign student brain drain to the United States [J]. Economics of education review，1988，7 (2)：231-243.

Hugo G. Migration Policies to Facilitate the Recruitment of Skilled Workers in Australia，in International Mobility of the Highly Skilled [M]. Paris：OECD，2002：291-320.

Hugo G. Some emerging demographic issues on Australia's teaching academic workforce [J]. Higher Education Policy，2005，18：207-229.

Hugo G J. The new international migration in Asia：challenges for population research [J]. Asian population studies，2005，1 (1)：93-120.

Hugo G J. In and out of Australia：rethinking Indian and Chinese skilled migration to Australia [J]. Asian population studies，2008，3 (4)：267-291.

Hyndman J. The Geopolitics of Migration and Mobility [J]. Geopolitics，2012，17 (2)：243-255.

Ian G. UK-China ventures shape education landscape [J]. China daily，2012，03 (13)：16.

Iredale R. The migration of professionals：theories and typologies [J]. International migration，2001，39：7-24.

Iredale R，Bilik N，Wang S，Guo F，et al. Contemporary Minority Migration，Education and Ethnicity in China [M]. Cheltenham，Edward Elgar，2001.

Jary D. Parker M. The McUniversity：organisation，management and academic subjectivity [J]. Organisation，1995，2 (2)：319-338.

Jawitz J. New academics negotiating communities of practice：Learning to swim with the big fish [J]. Teaching in Higher Education，2007，12 (2)：185-197.

Jensen O B, Sheller M, Wind S. Together and apart: affective ambiences and negotiation in families everyday life and mobility [J]. Mobilities, 2015, 10 (3): 363-382.

Jiang X, Napoli R D, Borg M, et al. Becoming and being an academic: the perspectives of Chinese staff in two research intensive UK universities [J]. Studies in Higher Education, 2010, 35 (2): 155-170.

Jin L X, Cortazzi M. Changing practices in Chinese cultures of learning Language [J]. Culture, and Curriculum, 2006, 19 (1): 5-20.

Johnston R, Trlin A, Henderson A, et al. Sustaining and creating migration Chains among skilled immigrant groups: Chinese, Indians and South Africans in New Zealand [J]. Journal of ethnic and migration studies, 2006, 32 (7): 1227-1250.

Jons H. Brain Circulation and transnational knowledge networks: studying long term effects of Academic mobility to germany, 1954-2000 [J]. Global networks, 2009, 9 (3): 315-338.

Julia L R. Transitions into research careers in Switzerland [J]. Education and training, 2002, 44 (4/5): 186-198.

Kangasniemi M, Mas M, Robinson C, et al. The Economic Impact of Migration: Productivity Analysis for Spain and the UK [J]. Journal of Productivity Analysis, 2012, 38 (3): 333-343.

Kapur D. McHale J. Sojourns and software: internationally mobile human capital and high-tech industry development in India, Ireland, and Israel [J]. Underdogs to tigers: The rise and growth of the software industry in some emerging economies, 2005: 236-274.

Kearns R. Being there: research through observing and participating [C]. Hay I. Qualitative research methods in human geography [M]. Melbourne: Oxford University Press, 2000: 103-121.

Keay J, May H, O Mahony J. Improving learning and teaching in transnational education: can communities of practice help? [J] Journal of education for teaching, 2014, 40 (3): 251-266.

Kelly P, Lusis T. . Migration and the Transnational Habitus: Evidence from Canada and the Philippines [J]. Environment and Planning A, 2006, 38 (5): 831-847.

Kenway J, Fahey J. Globalizing the research imagination [M]. London: Routledge, 2008.

Kenway J, Fahey J. International academic mobility: problematic and possible paradigms [J]. Discourse: studies in the cultural politics of education, 2010, 31 (5): 563-575.

Kenway J, Fahey J. Getting emotional about brain mobility [J]. Emotion, space and society, 2011, 4 (3): 187-194.

Kenway J J, Fahey A. Transgressive global research imagination [J]. Thesis Eleven, 2009, 96 (1): 109-127.

Kenway J, Bullen E, Fahey J. Haunting the knowledge economy international library of sociology [M]. London. Routledge, 2006.

Khadria B. Shifting Paradigms of Globalization: The Twenty First Century Transition Towards Generics in Skilled Migration from India [J]. International Migration, 2001, 39: 45-69.

Kim A, Hollingworth S. Sticky subjects or cosmopolitan creatives? social class, place and urban young people's aspirations for work in the knowledge economy [J]. Urban Studies, 2013, 50 (3): 499-517.

Kim T. Internationalisation of higher education in South Korea: reality, rhetoric, and disparity in academic culture and Identities [J]. Australian journal of education, 2005, 49 (1): 89-103.

Kim T. Shifting patterns of transnational academic mobility: A comparative and historical approach [J]. Comparative Education, 2009, 45 (3): 387-403.

Kim T. Transnational academic mobility, internationalization and interculturality in higher education [J]. Intercultural Education, 2009, 20 (5): 395-405.

Kim T. Transnational academic mobility, knowledge, and identity capital [J]. Discourse: Studies in the Cultural Politics of Education, 2010, 31 (5): 456-477.

Kim T. Internationalisation of higher education and global mobility [J]. Comparative education, 2014, 50 (4): 507-509.

Kim T, Locke W. Transnational academic mobility and the academic profession [R]. Centre for Higher Education Research and Information, London: The Open University, 2010.

King R. Translocal geographies: spaces, places and connections [J]. Journal of Ethnic and Migration Studies, 2013, 39 (3): 521-522.

King R, Ruiz Gelices E. International student migration and the European year abroad [J]. International Journal of Population Geography, 2003, 9: 229-252.

King R, Parvati Raghuram. International Student Migration: Mapping the Field and New Research Agendas: Mapping the Field and New Research Agenda in ISM [J]. Population, Space and Place, 2013, 19 (2): 127-137.

Kinnell M. The Learning Experiences of Overseas Students [M]. Milton Keynes, Open

University Press, 1990.

Knight J. International universities misunderstandings and emerging models? [J]. Journal of studies in international education, 2015, 19 (2): 107-121.

Kobayashi A. Negotiating the personal and the political in critical qualitative research [J]. Limb M, Dwyer C. Qualitative methodologies for geographers: issues and debates [M]. London: Arnold, 2001: 55-70.

Koch R, Latham A. On the hard work of domesticating a public space [J]. Urban studies, 2013, 50 (1): 6-21.

Koehn P H, Rosenau J N. Transnational competence in an emergent epoch [J]. International studies perspectives, 2002, 3 (2): 105-127.

Kofman E. The invisibility of skilled female migrants and gender relations in studies of skilled migration in Europe [J]. International Journal of Population Geography, 2000, 6: 45-59.

Koser K Salt J. The geography of highly skilled international migration [J]. International Journal of Population Geography, 1997, 3: 285-303.

Kostogriz, Alex, Eleanor Peeler. Professional identity and pedagogical space: negotiating difference in teacher workplaces [J]. Teaching Education, 2007, 18 (2): 107-122.

Kuptsch C. Students and talent flow the case of Europe [C]. Kuptsch. C, Pang. E. Competing for Global Talent ILO [M]. Geneva, 2006: 33-62.

Kvale S. Interviews: An Introduction to Qualitative Research Interviewing Sage [M]. London.

Lamont M. How Has Bourdieu Been Good to Think With? The Case of the United States: How Has Bourdieu Been Good to Think With? [J]. Sociological Forum, 2012, 27 (1): 228-237.

Larner W. Globalising knowledge networks: Universities, diaspora strategies, and academic intermediaries [J]. Geoforum, 2015, 59: 197-205.

Latham A. Research, performance, and doing human geography: some reflections on the diary-photograph, diary interview method [J]. Environment and planning A, 2003, 35 (11): 1993-2017.

Laurier E, Whyte A. Buckner K. An ethnography of a neighbourhood café: informality, table arrangements and background noise [J]. Journal of mundane behaviour, 2001, 2 (2): 195-232.

Le Bail H, Wei S. Le retour des cerveaux en Chine：quel impact socio politique ? Centre Asie IFRI [R]. Asie Visions, 2008,

Leahy S. Translocal geographies：spaces, places, connections [J]. Social and cultural geography, 2013, 14 (1)：129-130.

Lee C F, Amjadi M. The role of materiality：knowing through objects in work practice [J]. European management journal, 2014, 32 (5)：723-734.

Lee T M L. Intercultural teaching in higher education [J]. Intercultural Education, 2005, 16 (3)：201-215.

Lee W O. Academic Migration and Reshaping of Pedagogy and Epistemology：An Insider-Outsider Perspective, in Academic Migration, Discipline Knowledge and Pedagogical Practice, . [M]. Springer Singapore, Singapore, 2014, 161-175.

Leemann R J. Gender inequalities in transnational academic mobility and the ideal type of academic entrepreneur [J]. Discourse：studies in the cultural politics of education, 2010, 31 (5)：605-625.

Leo C Francis, Seunghee Pak. Language and skilled migration：the outcomes of overseas language study for south Korean students in New Zealand [J]. Asian population studies, 2008, 4 (3)：347-362.

Lepori B, Seeber M, Bonaccorsi A. Competition for talent country and organizational level effects in the internationalization of European higher education institutions [J]. Research policy, 2015, 44 (3)：789-802.

Leung M. Collecting intellectual mileage：a study of transnational academic mobility of Chinese scholars [R]. Paper presented at DIME workshop globalization and the changing geographies of production and innovation, Utrecht, 2009：5-7.

Leung M. Of Corridors and Chains：Translocal developmental impacts of academic mobility between China and Germany [J]. International Development Planning Review, 2011, 33 (4)：475-489.

Leung M. Geographical mobility and capital accumulation among Chinese scholars：Geographical mobility and capital accumulation among Chinese scholars [J]. Transactions of the institute of British geographers, 2013, 38 (2)：311-324.

Leung M. Unraveling the skilled mobility for sustainable development mantra：An analysis of China—EU academic mobility [J]. Sustainability, 2013, 5 (6)：2644-2663.

Leung M. Talk to her, she is also Chinese：a reflection on the spatial temporal reach of co-ethnicity in migration research [R]. In Forum Qualitative Sozialforschung/Forum: Qualitative Social Research, 2015, 16.

Leung M, Waters L J. British degrees made in Hong Kong: an enquiry into the role of space and place in transnational education [J]. Asia pacific education review, 2013, 14 (1): 43-53.

Lévy P. L'intelligence collective Pour une anthropologie du cyberespace [M]. Paris: La Découverte, 1994: 243

Lewis V. Embedding Marketing in International Campus Development: Lessons from UK Universities [J]. Perspectives: policy and practice in higher education, 2015: 1-8.

Ley D. Millionaire Migrants: Transpacific Life Lines [M]. Chichester: Wiley Blackwell, 2010.

Ley D, Kobayashi A. Back to Hong Kong: return migration or transnational sojourn [J]. Return migration of the next generations: 21st century transnational mobility, 2009: 119-138.

Li F N, Findlay A M, Jowett A J. Skeldon migrating to learn and learning to migrate: A study of the experiences and intentions of international student migrants [J]. International Journal of Population Geography, 1996, 2: 51-67.

Li H, Joel Andreas. Rise of the Red Engineers: The Cultural Revolution and the Origins of China's New Class [M]. California Stanford University Press Stanford, 2010.

Li P. Immigration from China to Canada in the age of globalization: Issues of brain gain and brain loss [J]. Pacific Affairs, 2008, 81: 217-339.

Li X, Joanne R, Yan Y, et al. Knowledge sharing in China UK higher education alliances [J]. International business review, 2014, 23 (2): 343-355.

Lin C S A. Study on development of Hakka radio stations in Taiwan: adopting perspectives of bourdieu field theory and capital theory [R]. http: //thesis lib ncu edu tw/ETD db/ETD search/view_etd? URN=967305014. , 2011.

Lin W. Beyond flexible citizenship: towards a study of many Chinese transnationalisms [J]. Geoforum, 2012, 43 (1): 137-146.

Liu J. Examining massification policies and their consequences for equality in Chinese higher education: A cultural perspective [J]. Higher education, 2012, 64 (5): 647-660.

Liu L. Mobility, community and identity: Chinese student/professional migration to the United States since 1978 and transnational citizenship [R]. USA: The faculty of the graduate school, The University of Minnesota, 2009.

Liu X F. A case study of the labour market status of Chinese immigrants, Metropolitan Toronto. international migration intergovernmental committee for European migration [R]. Geneva: Research group for European migration problems, 1997, 34: 583-608.

Liu X F. Refugee flow or brain? The humanitarian policy and post Tiananmen Mainland Chinese immigration to Canada [J]. International Journal of Population Geography, vol. 3, UK: Chichester/ West Sussex: Wiley, 1997: 15-29.

Longhurst R. Semi structured interviews and focus groups [C]. Clifford N J, Valentine G, Key methods in geography [M]. London: Sage, 2003: 117-132.

Low C C. Defending national identity and national interests: the limits of citizenship transnationalism in Germany and China [J]. Journal of international migration and integration 2015: 16 (3): 717-741.

Lowell L, Gerova S G. Diasporas and economic development: state of knowledge, Institute for the Study of International Migration, [R]. Washington: Georgetown University, 2004.

Lui H, Old linkages, new networks: the globalization of overseas Chinese voluntary associations and its implications [J]. The China Quarterly, 1998, 155: 582-609.

Lui H. New migrants and the revival of overseas Chinese nationalism [J]. Journal of contemporary China, 2005, 43 (14): 291-316.

Luxon T, Peelo M. Academic sojourners, teaching and internationalization: the experience of non UK staff in a British university [J]. Teaching in higher education, 2009, 14: 649-659.

Lynn E, Ho Ee. An emotional economy of migration driving mainland Chinese transnational Sojourning across migration regimes [J]. 2012.

Ma Mung E. Dispersal as resource [J]. Diaspora, 2004, 13: 211-225.

Mack N, Woodsong C, MacQueen K. Qualitative Research Methods: A Data Collector's Field Guide, [R]., 2005.

Mahroum S. Highly skilled globetrotters: mapping the international migration of human capital [J]. R&D Management, 2000, 30 (1): 23-31.

Marginson S. Van Der Wande M. Globalisation and higher education [R]. Education working group paper 8, Paris: OECD, 2007.

Martin J L. What is field theory? [J]. American journal of sociology, 2003, 109 (1):

1-49.

Martin P. Policies for admitting highly skilled workers into the United States, In international mobility of the highly skilled [M]. Paris: OECD, 2002: 271-289.

Mason C, Rawlings Sanaei F. Introduction: where is the narrative around academic migration? [C]. Academic Migration, Discipline Knowledge and Pedagogical Practice [M]. Singapore: Springer Singapore, 2014: 161-175.

Mavroudi E, Warren A. Highly skilled migration and the negotiation of immigration policy: non EEA postgraduate students and academic staff at English universities [J]. Geoforum, 2013, 44 (2): 61-70.

McBurnie G. International branch campuses: Australian case studies [J]. International higher education, 2015: 29.

McClure J W. International graduates cross cultural adjustment: experiences, coping strategies, and suggested programmatic responses [J]. Teaching in higher education, 2007, 12 (2): 199-217.

McGregor J. Spatiality and the place of the material in schools [J]. Pedagogy, culture and society, 2004, 12 (3): 347-372.

McIlwaine C. Constructing transnational social spaces among Latin American Migrants in Europe: perspectives from the UK [J]. Cambridge Journal of Regions, Economy and Society, 2012, 5 (2): 289-304.

McMurty J. Education and the market model [J]. Journal of philosophy of education, 1991, 25 (2): 209-218.

Merle A, Sztanke M. Tudiants chinois Qui sont les élites de demain? [J]. Paris: Autrement, 2006: 109

Meyer J, Wattiaux J. Diaspora knowledge networks: Vanishing doubts and increasing evidence [J]. International journal on multicultural societies, 2006, 8 (1): 4-24.

Meyer J B. Network approach versus brain drain: lessons from the diaspora [J]. International migration, 2001, 39 (5): 91-110.

Meyer J P, Brown M. . Scientific diasporas: a new approach to the brain drain [R]. World Conference on Science, Budapest: UNESCO ICSU, 1999.

MOE. Ministry of Education of the People's Republic of China [EB/OL]. http: //www moe edu. cn/publicfiles/business/htmlfiles/moe/moe _ 2792/index html, (Accessed 15/06/2012).

Moi T. Appropriating bourdieu: feminist theory and pierre bourdieu's sociology of culture [J]. New literary history, 1991, 22 (4): 1017.

Moore R. Capital [M]. Pierre Bourdieu: Key Concepts, 2008.

Moss P. Placing Autobiography in Geography [M]. Syracuse NY, Syracuse University Press, 2001.

Munk M D, Krarup T M. Cultural Capital Theory Revisited: Explanations of Educational Reproduction and Beyond [R]. 2011.

Murphy Lejeune E. Student Mobility and Narrative in Europe [M]. London, Routledge, 2002.

Nankervis A R. Building for the future? Government and industry responses to the challenges of talent management in China following the GFC [J]. Asia Pacific Business Review, 2013, 19 (2): 186-199.

New York Times, US slips in attracting the world's best students [R]. 2004, 12: 21.

Newman W L. Social Research Methods: Qualitative and Quantitative Approaches [M]. Boston: Allyn and Bacon, 2003.

Noble G. It is home but it is not home: habitus, field and the migrant [J]. Journal of Sociology, 2013, 49 (2, 3): 341-356.

Noble J, Davies P. Cultural capital as an explanation of variation in participation in higher education [J]. British Journal of Sociology of Education, 2009, 30: 591-605.

Nonis S, Swift C O. An examination of the relationship between academic dishonesty and workplace dishonesty: a multi-campus investigation [J]. Journal of Education for Business, 2001, 77 (2): 69-77.

Nukaga M. Planning for a successful return home: transnational habitus and education strategies among Japanese expatriate mothers in Los Angeles [J]. International Sociology, 2013, 28 (1): 66-83.

Nuttall J, Edwards S. Teacher education research and the role of place [J]. Asia Pacific Journal of Teacher Education, 2014, 42 (2): 103-104.

Nyiri P. Expatriating is patriotic? The discourse on new migrants in The People's Republic of China and identity construction among recent migrants from the PRC [J]. Journal of Ethnic and Migration Studies, 2001, 27 (4): 635-653.

Oldenburg R. The Great Good Place: Cafés, Coffee Shops, Bookstores, Bars, Hair Salons, and Other Hangouts at the Heart of a Community Marlowe and Company [M]. New York:

Marlowe & Company, 1999.

Oliver C K O. Reilly A. Bourdieusian analysis of class and migration: habitus and the Individualizing Process [J]. Sociology, 2010, 44 (1): 49-66.

Olson L C, Kroeger K R. Global competency and intercultural sensitivity [J]. Journal of studies in international education, 2001, 5 (2): 116-137.

Ong A. Flexible citizenship [M]. Durham NC. Duke UP, 1999.

Orlikowski W J. Sociomaterial practices: exploring technology at work [J]. Organization studies, 2007, 28 (9): 1435-1448.

Ostrower F. The arts as cultural capital among elites [J]. Art and aesthetics: the social organization of art and aesthetics, 2009, 3: 35.

Ouyang H. Understanding the Chinese learners' community of practice: an insider outsider's view report on responding to the needs of the Chinese learner in higher education: internationalizing the University, 2nd Biennial International Conference [R]. University of Portsmouth, 2006.

Papatsiba V. Making higher education more European through student mobility? [J]. Comparative education, 2006, 42: 93-111.

Parker D. Reflections on research performance measures and the rise of Asia [J]. International higher education, 1994. 59.

Pennycuick D. Great Britain, and department for international development school effectiveness in developing countries: a summary of the research evidence [R]. London. Dept for International Development, 1998.

Pherali T J. Academic mobility, language, and cultural capital: the experience of transnational academics in British higher education institutions [J]. Journal of studies in international education, 2012, 16 (4): 313-333.

Pieke F N. Immigrant China [J]. Modern China, 2012, 38 (1): 40-77.

Pinder D. Arts of urban exploration [J]. Cultural geographies, 2005, 12: 383-411.

Pio E, Essers C. Professional migrant women decentring otherness: A transnational perspective: professional migrant women decentring otherness [J]. British journal of management, 2014, 25 (2): 252-265.

Ploger J. Becker A. Social networks and local incorporation—grounding high skilled migrants in two German cities [J]. Journal of ethnic and migration studies, 2015, 41 (10): 1517-1535.

Pluss C. Chinese migrants in New York：explaining inequalities with transnational positions and capital conversions in transnational spaces [J]. International sociology，2013，28 (1)：12-28.

Poole D，Ewan C. Academics as part time marketers in university offshore programs：an exploratory study [J]. Journal of higher education policy and management，2010，32 (2)：149-158.

Poole D，Ewan C. Academics as part time marketers in university offshore programs：an exploratory study [J]. Journal of higher education policy and management，2010，32：149-158.

Povrzanovic F M. Diversity and similarity beyond ethnicity：migrants' material practices [M]. Sens Public，2010.

Qian N. Chinese Students Encounter [M]. Hong Kong：America University Press，2002.

Raghuram P. Which migration? Which development? Unsettling the edifice of migration and development [J]. Population，Space and Place，2009，15：103-117.

Raghuram P. Theorising the spaces of student migration：theorising the spaces of student migration [J]. Population，space and place，2013，19 (2)：138-154.

Razzaque M A. Traversing the Academic Terrain Across the Continents：A Reflective Account of My Journey and Transformation，in Academic Migration，Discipline Knowledge and Pedagogical Practice，[M]. Singapore：Springer，161-175.

Reay D. It's all becoming a habitus：beyond the habitual use of habitus in educational research [J]. British Journal of Sociology of Education，2004，25 (4)：431-444.

Reay D，Crozier G，Clayton J. Fitting In or Standing Out：working class students in UK higher education [J]. British Educational Research Journal，2010，36：18-26.

Remoe S O. Building the European research area：Socio-economic research in practice [M]. New York：Peter Lang，115-175.

Ren X，Caudle D. Walking the tightrope between work and Non-work life：strategies employed by British and Chinese academics and their implications [J]. Studies in higher education，2014，14：1-20.

Riemsdijk V M. International migration and local emplacement：everyday place making practices of skilled migrants in Oslo，Norway [J]. Environment and Planning a，2014，46 (4)：963-979.

Ritzer G. The Blackwell Companion to Major Contemporary Social Theorists Blackwell

Companions to Sociology [M]. Malden: Blackwell, 2007.

Robertson S L. Critical response to special section: international academic mobility [J]. Discourse: Studies in the Cultural Politics of Education, 2010, 31 (5): 641-647.

Robinson R. Actually, existing cosmopolitanisms [C]. Cheah P. Robbins B. Cosmopolites: Thinking and Feeling Beyond the Nation [M]. Minneapolis: University of Minnesota Press, 1998.

Robson S, Turner Y. Teaching is a co-learning experience: academics reflecting on learning and teaching in an internationalized faculty [J]. Teaching in higher education, 2007, 12 (1): 41-54.

Rosales V M. The domestic work of consumption: materiality, migration and home making [J]. Etnogrάfica Revista do Centro em Rede de Investigao em Antropologia, 2010, 14 (3): 507-525.

Rose G. Using photographs as illustrations in human geography [J]. Journal of geography in higher education, 2008, 32 (1): 151-160.

Rosenau J N. Turbulence in World Politics: A Theory of Change and Continuity [M]. NJ: Princeton University Press, 1990.

Rubin H J, Rubin I S. Qualitative Interviewing: The Art of Hearing Data [M]. Thousand Oaks, CA. Sage, 2004.

Rudestam, K & Newton, R. Surviving your dissertation: a comprehensive guide to content and process [M]. Newbury Park, CA. Sage, 1992.

Ryan L, Mulholland J. Trading places: French highly skilled migrants negotiating mobility and emplacement in London [J]. Journal of ethnic and migration studies, 2014, 40 (4): 584-600.

Salt, J International Movements of the Highly Skilled [M]. Paris, OECD, 1997.

Saltmarsh S, Swirski T. Pawns and prawns: international academics observations on their transition to working in an Australian University [J]. Journal of higher education policy and management, 2010, 32 (3): 291-301.

Santoro M. From Bourdieu to cultural sociology [J]. Cultural sociology, 2011, 5 (1): 3-23.

Sawir E. Embarking Upon a New Academic culture: Implications for Identity and Educational Practice, Academic Migration, Discipline Knowledge and Pedagogical Practice [M]. Singapore: Springer, 2014: 131-142.

Sawir E. Embarking Upon a New Academic Culture: Implications for Identity and Educational Practice, in Academic Migration, Discipline Knowledge and Pedagogical Practice [M]. Singapore: Springer Singapore, 2014: 161-175.

Saxenian A. From brain drain to brain circulation: transnational communities and regional upgrading in India and China [J]. Studies in international comparative development, 2005, 40: 35-61.

Saxenian A. Silicon Valley's new immigrant entrepreneurs [R]. paper presented at the conference on The International Migration of the Highly Skilled, USA, University of California, San Diego, 2000.

Saxenian A. Transnational communities and the evolution of global production networks: the cases of Taiwan, China and India [J]. Industry and Innovation, 2002, 9 (3): 183-202.

Saxenian A. The new argonauts regional advantage in a Global Economy [M]. Cambridge: Harvard University Press, 2006.

Séguin B, Singer P A, Abdallah S. Scientific diasporas [J]. Science, 2006, 312: 1603

Sercu L. Assessing intercultural competence: A framework for systematic test development in foreign language education and beyond [J]. Intercultural Education, 2004, 15 (1): 73-89.

Shams F, Huisman J. The role of institutional dual embeddedness in the strategic local adaptation of international branch campuses: evidence from Malaysia and Singapore [J]. Studies in Higher Education, 2014, 9 (10): 1-16.

Shaw J, Moore P, Gandhidasan S. . Educational Acculturation and Educational Integrity: Outcomes of an Intervention Subject for International Postgraduate Public Health Students [J]. Journal of Academic Language and Learning, 2007, 1: 55-67.

Shen H. Progress of the Academic Profession in Mainland China in The Changing Academic Profession in the International, Comparative, and Quantitative Perspectives (Report of the International Conference on the Changing Academic Profession Project] [R]. RIHE, Hiroshima University, 2008.

Shen W. China in the Global Migration Order—historical Perspectives and New Trends [J]. Asia Europe Journal, 2010, 8 (1): 25-43.

Simpson P. So, as you can see...: some reflections on the utility of video methodologies in the study of embodied practices [J]. Area, 2011, 43: 343-352.

Singer P, Gregg T. How ethical is Australia? An examination of Australia's record as a global citizen [M]. Melbourne, Black Inc, 2004.

Smeby J C. Trondal J. Globalisation or Europeanisation? International Contact among University Staff [J]. Higher Education, 2005. 49 (4): 449-466.

Smith F M. Doing qualitative research: From interpretation to action [J]. Limb M, Dwyer C. Qualitative methodologies for geographers: Issues and debates [M]. London: Arnold, 2001: 23-40.

Smith F M. Working in different cultures in Clifford [C]. Valentine G, Key Methods in Geography [M]. London: Sage, 2003: 179-193.

Solimano A. Globalizing talent and human capital: implications for developing countries [R]. Santiago: UN, 2002.

Solimano A. The International Mobility of Talent [M]. Oxford Oxford University Press, 2008.

Spinney J. Cycling the City: Movement, Meaning and Method [J]. Geography Compass, 2009, 3: 817-835.

Stenning A, Champion T, Conway C, et al. Assessing the local and regional impacts of international migration [R]. New Horizons Report to DCLG Newcastle: CURDS, 2006.

Strauss A, Corbin J. Basics of Qualitative Research: Techniques and Procedures for Developing Grounded Theory [M]. London: Sage, 1998.

Swales J M. Research Genres: Explorations and Applications [M]. Cambridge, Cambridge University Press, 2004.

Szerszynski B, Urry J. Cultures of Cosmopolitanism [J]. The Sociological review, 2002, 50 (4): 461-481.

Tapper T, Palfreyman D. Understanding Mass Education London [M]. Londen: Routledge, 2004.

Taylor J E, Arango J, Hugo G, et al. International Migration and National Development [J]. Population index, 1996, 62: 181-212.

Teichler U. The changing debate on internationalization of higher education [J]. Higher Education, 2004, 48: 2-26

Therien J P, Beyond the north south divide: the two tales of world poverty [J]. Third World Quarterly, 1999, 20 (4): 723-742.

Thrift N. Non-representational theory: space, politics, affect [M]. London: Routledge, 2007.

Trahar S. Teaching and learning：The international higher education landscape，Subject Centre for Education［M］. Bristol：ESCalate，2007.

Trahar S. Changing landscapes，shifting identities in higher education：narratives of academics in the UK［J］. Research in Education，2011，86（1）：46-60.

Trahar S，Hyland F. Experiences and perceptions of internationalisation in higher education in the UK［J］. Higher education research and development，2011，30（5）：623-633.

Tremblay R，Hardwick S，ONeill J. academic migration at the Canada-US border［J］. American review of Canadian studies，2014，44（1）：118-134.

Trowler P R. Academics Responding to Change：New Higher Education Frameworks and Academic Cultures［M］. Buckingham，Open University Press/SRHE，1997.

Tsang E W K. Adjustment of mainland Chinese academics and students to Singapore［J］. International Journal of Intercultural Relations，2001，25：347-372.

Tsolidis G. Schooling，Gender and Diaspora Being Feminist and Being Different［M］. Open University，Buckingham，2001.

Tuan Y. Place：an experiential perspective［J］. Geographical Review，1975，65（2）：151.

UCEA. Recruitment and Retention of staff in higher education 2008 Melbourne Universities and Colleges Employers Association［R］. 2008.

Universities UK Talent wars：The international market for academic staff. London Universities UK，2007.

Urry J. Mobilities Polity［M］. Cambridge，2007.

Valentine G. People like us：negotiating sameness and difference in the research process［C］. Flowerdew R，Martin D. Methods in Human Geography［M］. Essex：Longman：2002：116-126.

Varghese N. Globalization of higher education and cross border student mobility［R］. Paris：International Institute for Education Planning，2008.

Vertovec S. Conceiving and researching transnationalism［J］. Ethnic and Racial Studies，1999：22（2）：447-462.

Vertovec S. Transnational Networks and Skilled Labour Migration［R］. Transnational Communities Programme Working Paper，WRTC，02-02，2002.

Voela A. The Enjoyment of space：the university campus in students narratives and photography［J］. Pedagogy，Culture & Society，2014，22（1）：61-78.

Waite S. Knowing your place in the world: How Place and Culture Support and Obstruct Educational Aims [J]. Cambridge Journal of Education, 2013, 43 (4): 413-433.

Walker P. The globalisation of higher education and the sojourner academic: insights into challenges experienced by newly appointed international academic staff in a UK University [J]. Journal of research in international education, 2015, 14 (1): 61-74.

Walker R. Finding a silent voice for the researcher: using photographs in evaluation and research [C]. Schratz M. Qualitative Voices in Educational Research [M]. London: Falmer, 1993: 74-92.

Walsh K. It got very debauched, very Dubai! heterosexual intimacy amongst single british expatriates [J]. Social & Cultural Geography, 2007, 8 (4): 507-533.

Wang L. Higher education governance and university autonomy in China, globalisation [J]. Societies and education, 2010, 8 (4): 477-495.

Warner J, Talbot D, Bennison G. The cafe as affective community space: re-conceptualizing care and emotional labour in everyday life [J]. Critical Social Policy, 2013, 33 (2): 305-324.

Warren A, Mavroudi E. Managing surveillance? The impact of biometric residence permits on UK migrants [J]. Journal of ethnic and migration studies, 2011, 37 (9): 1495-1511.

Warwick P. The international business of higher education-a managerial perspective on the internationalisation of UK universities [J]. The international journal of management education, 2014, 12 (2): 91-103.

Waters J L. Transnational family strategies and education in the contemporary Chinese diaspora [J]. Global Networks, (2005) 5: 359-378.

Waters J. Flexible citizens: Transnational and citizenship amongst economic migrants in Vancouver [J]. Canadian Geographer, 2003, 47: 219-234.

Waters J, Leung M. Immobile transnationalisms? Young people and their in situ experiences of 'International' education in Hong Kong [J]. Urban Studies, 2013, 50 (3): 606-620.

Waters J L. Geographies of cultural capital: education, international migration and family strategies between Hong Kong and Canada [J]. Transactions of the Institute of British Geographers, 2006, 31 (2): 179-192.

Waters J L. Geographies of international education: mobilities and the reproduction of social (dis) advantage: geographies of international education [J]. Geography Compass, 2012, 6 (3): 23-36.

Waters J, Maggi L. A colourful university life? Transnational higher education and the spatial dimensions of institutional social capital in Hong Kong: transnational higher education in Hong Kong [J]. Population, Space and Place, 2013, 19 (2): 155-167.

Watkins D, Biggs J. The paradox of the Chinese learner and beyond. teaching the Chinese learner: Psychological and pedagogical perspectives, comparative education research centre/Australian council for educational research [R]. Hong Kong/Melbourne, 2001: 3-23.

Weda Z, Lemmer E. Managing status: a grounded theory of teacher migration from Zimbabwe to South Africa [J]. Mediterranean journal of social sciences, 2014, 1 (5): 13-29.

Welch A. Higher Education Between the Dragon and the Tiger Cubs: China ASEAN Relations in Higher Education in the GATS Era [C]. Jarvis D, Welch A. The Dragon and the Tiger Cubs: ASEAN Industries and the Challenge from China [M]. London, 2008.

Welch A, Hao J. Global Argonauts: Returnees and Diaspora as Sources of Innovation in China and Israel [J]. Globalisation, Societies and Education, 2015, 24 (6): 1-26.

Welch A, Yang R. The Chinese knowledge diaspora and the international knowledge network: Australian and Canadian Universities compared: A case study of the University of Toronto [R]. Australian Research Council Discovery Project, 2009.

Welch A R, Zhen Z. The rise of the Chinese knowledge diaspora: possibilities, problems and prospects for South and North, realising the Global University [R]. London: World Universities Network Forum, 2007.

Welch A, Zhen Z. Higher education and global talent flows: brain drain, overseas Chinese intellectuals, and diasporic knowledge networks [J]. Higher education policy, 2008, 21: 519-537.

Welch A R, Zhen Z. The Chinese Knowledge Diaspora, Communication Networks Among Overseas Chinese Intellectuals in Epstein D, Boden R, Deem R, Rizvi F, and Wright S eds [M]. World Yearbook of Education, 2008: 338-354.

Welch A R. Nation State, Diaspora and Comparative Education: The Place of Place in Comparative Education, In Changing Educational Landscapes [M]. Netherlands Dordrecht: Springer, 2010: 285-308. .

Welikala T, Watkins C. Improving Intercultural Learning Experiences in Higher Education: Responding to Cultural Scripts for Learning [R]. London: Institute of Education, 2008.

Wertz F, Charmaz K, McMullen L, et al. Five Ways of Doing Qualitative Research [M].

New York: Guilford Press, 2011.

Wescott C. Harnessing knowledge exchange among overseas professionals [J]. International Public Management Review, 2006, 7: 30-67.

Wilkins S, Huisman J. The international branch campus as transnational strategy in higher education [J]. Higher Education, 2012, 64 (5): 627-645.

Wilkins S, Balakrishnan M S, Huisman J. Student choice in higher education: motivations for choosing to study at an international branch campus [J]. Journal of studies in international education, 2012, 16 (5): 413-433.

Williams A, Balaz M. International Migration and Knowledge [M]. London: Routledge, 2009.

Willis K. Brenda S A Y. Gender and transnational household strategies: Singaporean migration to China [J]. Regional Studies, 2000, 34 (3): 253-264.

Willis K, Yeoh B. Gendering transnational communities: a comparison of Singaporean and British migrants in China [J]. Geoforum, 2002, 33 (4): 553-565.

Wood N, Duffy M, Smith S J. The art of doing (geographies of) music [J]. Environment and Planning D: Society and Space, in press, 2007.

Woolley R, Turpin T, Marceau J et al. Mobility matters: research training and network building in science [J]. Comparative technology transfer and society, 2009, 6 (3): 159-184.

Wu X. Economic transition, school expansion and educational inequality in China, 1990-2000 [J]. Research in Social Stratification and Mobility, 2010, 28 (1): 91-108.

Wyse D, Nikolajeva M, Charlton E, et al. Place related identity, texts, and transcultural meanings [J]. British educational research journal, 2012, 38 (6): 1019-1039.

Xiang B. Structuration of Indian Information Technology Professionals [J]. Migration to Australia: an ethnographic study, international migration, 2001, 39: 73-88.

Yang R. Globalization and higher education [J]. International review of higher education, 2003, 49: 269-291.

Yang R. The Chinese professoriate in comparative perspective: self-perceptions, academic life, gender differences and internal differentiation, Welch A R. The Professors: Profile of a Profession [M]. Dordrecht: Springer, 2005: 179-192.

Yang R, Welch A R. Globalisation, transnational academic mobility and the Chinese knowledge diaspora: an Australian case study [J]. Discourse: studies in the cultural politics of education, 2010, 31 (5): 593-607.

Yang R. Globalisation and higher education development: a critical analysis [J]. International review of education, 2003, 49 (3-4): 269-291.

Yeh K H, Yi C C, Tsao W C, et al. Filial piety in contemporary Chinese societies: a comparative study of Taiwan, Hong Kong, and China [J]. International Sociology, 2013, 28 (3): 277-296.

Yeh M. International theory and the transnational critic: China in the age of multiculturalism [J]. Boundary, 1998, 225 (3): 193.

Yeoh B, Willis K. Singaporeans in China: transnational women Elites and the negotiation of gendered identities [J]. Geoforum, 2005, (b) 36 (2): 211-222.

Yeoh B, Ramdas K. Gender, migration, mobility and transnationalism, gender [J]. Place and Culture, 2014, 21 (10): 1197-1213.

Yeoh B, Willis K. Singaporean and British transmigrants in China and the cultural politics of contact zones [J]. Journal of ethnic and migration studies, 31 (2): 269-285.

Yi L. Auditing Chinese higher education? The perspectives of returnee scholars in an elite university [J]. International journal of educational development, 2011, 31 (5): 505-514.

Young L, Barrett H. Adapting visual methods: action research with Kampala street children [J]. Area, 2001: 141-52.

Yu L L, Wei J W. High Skill Migration and Chinese Taipei's Industrial Development, [R]. Paris: In International Mobility of the Highly Skilled, OECD, 2002: 253-269.

Yuan Y. Acquiring, positioning and connecting: the materiality of television and the politics of mobility in a Chinese rural migrant community [J]. Media, culture & society, 2014, 36 (3): 336-350.

Zane N, Mak W. Major approaches to the measurement of acculturation among ethnic minority populations: A content analysis and an alternative empirical strategy [C]. Chun K M. Acculturation: advances in theory, measurement, and applied research [M]. Washington: American Psychological Association, 2002.

Zhang G. Migration of Chinese highly skilled to Europe: Trend and perspective [J]. International Migration, 2003, 41 (3): 73-97.

Zhang G, Li W. International Mobility of China's Resources in Science and Technology and Its Impact, In International Mobility of the Highly Skilled [M]. Paris: OECD, 2002, 189-200.

Zhang X, Liu W. Harvard Girl Liu Yiting [M]. Beijing: Writers, 2000.

Zhao R. Factors promoting or hindering the academic adjustment of Chinese visiting scholars in an American University [D], Teachers College, Columbia University, 2008.

Zhuang L, Tang A X. Sino UK transnational education in China: rhetoric versus reality [J]. Journal of technology management in China, 2012, 7 (2): 218-234.

Ziller R, Lewis D. Orientations: Self, social and environmental percepts through auto-photography [J]. Personality and Social Psychology Bulletin, 1981, 7: 338-343.

Zou P. Chinese Cultural Heritage: Influences on University Learning and Teaching, in Academic Migration, Discipline Knowledge and Pedagogical Practice [M]. Singapore: Springer Singapore, 2014, 161-175.

Zweig D, Chen C. China's brain drain to the United States: views of overseas Chinese students and scholars in the 1990s [R]. China Research Monograph, Institute of East Asian Studies, University of California, 1995.

Zweig D, Chen C, Rosen S. Globalization and Transnational Human Capital: Overseas and Returnee Scholars to China [J]. The China Quarterly, 2004, 179: 735-757.

Zweig D, Fung C S, Han D. Redefining the brain drain China's "diaspora option" [J]. Science Technology Society, 2008, 13: 1-33.